EXPLORATIONS

By the same author

*

DRAMA AND SOCIETY IN THE AGE OF JONSON
SHAKESPEARE'S POLITICS
SHAKESPEARE: THE HISTORIES
AN APPROACH TO HAMLET
SOME SHAKESPEAREAN THEMES

With Northrop Frye and others

*

MYTH AND SYMBOL: CRITICAL APPROACHES
AND APPLICATIONS

EXPLORATIONS

ESSAYS IN CRITICISM
MAINLY ON THE LITERATURE OF
THE SEVENTEENTH CENTURY

by

L. C. KNIGHTS

GREENWOOD PRESS, PUBLISHERS
WESTPORT, CONNECTICUT

PR
433
K5
1975

Library of Congress Cataloging in Publication Data

Knights, Lionel Charles, 1906-
Explorations.

    Reprint of the 1964 ed. published by New York
University Press, New York.
    Includes bibliographical references.
    1. English literature--Early modern, 1500-1700--
History and criticism--Addresses, essays, lectures.
I. Title.
PR433.K5 1975   820'.9'003   75-32459
ISBN 0-8371-8548-3

To

MY WIFE

CONTENTS

PREFACE

THE ONLY UNITY that can be claimed for this small collection of essays—all of which have already appeared in print during the last ten years or so—is the unity of a point of view. The idea that informs them is that "good reading" is the beginning—even if it is not, as one critic has said, the whole secret—of good judgment; that literary criticism is a form of disciplined exploration—exploration, in the first place, of words in a certain arrangement; and that the main function of criticism is to prompt other readers to fresh insights, based on fresh disciplined explorations of their own. This idea is so simple that one would hesitate to pronounce it so pontifically were it not for the fact that it is one of those ideas that need constantly to be retrieved from the status of platitude and realized afresh, in all their implications, as living truths. At the present time especially it seems necessary to remind ourselves that works of literature, once they have left their authors' hands, are only kept alive by being *possessed* by individuals as intimate parts of their own living experience; and that they are only so possessed when they are re-created by each reader from the action and interaction of the minute particulars of which they are composed.[1] The only merit I should care to claim for these essays is that they do attempt to keep in the forefront of attention the primary impact of the works they discuss, so that if the reader disagrees with any particular judgment he is at least invited to formulate his disagreement in terms of the primary impact on *him*—not in terms of general notions and abstract ideas. Which is far from denying that I hope some of my conclusions

[1] In a recent essay by I. A. Richards I find an admirable definition of the *creative* activity that reading a good poem (or play or novel) is. Commenting on some lines from Donne's *An Anatomy of the World,* he writes: "In the Donne, I suggest, there is a prodigious activity between the words as we read them. Following, exploring, realizing, *becoming* that activity is, I suggest, the essential thing in reading the poem. Understanding it is not a preparation for reading the poem. It is itself the poem. And it is a constructive, hazardous, free creative process, a process of conception through which a new being is growing in the mind." ("The Interaction of Words," in *The Language of Poetry,* edited by Allen Tate.) Dr. Richards is also the critic referred to in the second sentence above (*Practical Criticism,* p. 305).

9

will be found apt by others. But—and this applies to all forms of criticism—it is the redirection of attention to the works themselves that matters.

There is another aspect of the present book on which I should like to comment briefly here. In a book published some years ago called *Drama and Society in the Age of Jonson* I suggested that the relations of literature and "society"—a topic then, as now, much in the air—could only be profitably discussed in relation to particular works written in a particular place and period. I also promised a fuller account than I could give there of the culture that most interested me—namely that of the Elizabethan and early Stuart period—in relation to the everyday environment. For various reasons I have so far been unable to keep this promise, and if I carry out my plan it will certainly be along lines rather different from those envisaged then. Meanwhile—and this is the point of an otherwise irrelevant piece of autobiography—some of the essays in this volume may suggest the kind of approach that I consider most likely to be fruitful in investigating the relations between literature and the complicated set of circumstances that, at any time, make up its social and cultural "background." It is an approach that *starts from* literary criticism, and it might take for a motto Matthew Arnold's remark that "the great safeguard is never to let oneself become abstract, always to retain an intimate and lively consciousness of the truth of what one is saying, and, the moment that fails us, to be sure that something is wrong." Not, of course, that "pure" literary criticism will take us the whole way: the discipline of criticism needs to be complemented by other disciplines; but unless an investigation of this kind is informed and guided by literary sensitiveness, by the tact or personal feeling for specific values that springs from literary criticism as I have tried to define it, the result is likely to be nothing more than a fresh set of abstractions of a kind common enough. The essays presented here on George Herbert, on Bacon, and on Restoration Comedy (if I may point to some examples) are primarily attempts at elucidation and interpretation of the authors concerned, but I hope the reader will find in them some substantial grounds for the views expressed in this paragraph. The last essay in the book discusses, from the point of view of a

PREFACE

university teacher, some possible correlations between "criticism" and "history," with a view to that wider and deeper understanding of the sources of cultural health, for lack of which so many present-day discussions of the prospects of civilization seem unreal.

One disadvantage of reprinting articles written over a period of years is that some of them are bound to carry, for the author at least, a more or less strong scent of the past. If I were writing *How Many Children Had Lady Macbeth?* to-day I should make far more allowance for the extraordinary variety of Shakespeare's tragedies (a variety of course within the larger unity of the plays when taken together); and I should not, I hope, write as though there were only one "right" approach to each and all of them. I reprint the essay substantially as written, however, partly because it still seems to me to say some things worth saying, partly because it may have some subsidiary interest as a period-piece—the literary period in question being that in which a new valuation of Shakespeare's greatness was in process. Throughout the first half of the essay I detect a slight headiness springing from the exhilaration of attacking what was still the orthodox academic view of Shakespeare. The second half shows clearly an extensive indebtedness to the early work of Mr. Wilson Knight. Time has confirmed the impression I registered then (in a note omitted from the present reprint), that "a preoccupation with imagery and symbols, unless minutely controlled by a sensitive intelligence directed upon the text, can lead to abstractions almost as dangerous as does a preoccupation with 'character.'" But a recognition of the limitations of Mr. Knight's highly personal method should not be allowed to obscure the genuine original insight contained, in good measure, in *The Wheel of Fire* and *The Imperial Theme*. The only part of the present book where radical revision might seem called for is my account of *The Beast in the Jungle* at the end of the essay on Henry James. Since I cannot omit this without sacrificing the rest of the essay, and since this in turn still seems to me to expose some strands of "the figure in the carpet" of James's work as a whole, these two or three pages are included

11

PREFACE

with the rest. They may at least serve to commend the story to the attention of those who are interested in the subconscious factors lurking behind some of the work of that great writer.

Acknowledgments for permission to reprint are made as follows: for Number 1 (based on a paper read to the Shakespeare Association), Mr. Gordon Fraser, the Minority Press (Heffer), Cambridge; for Number 4 (ii), originally a review in the *Criterion*, Mr. T. S. Eliot; for Numbers 9, 10 and 11, reprinted from *The Southern Review*, the Louisiana State University Press; and for the remainder, my co-editors of *Scrutiny*.

L. C. KNIGHTS

MANCHESTER UNIVERSITY,
January 1945

EXPLORATIONS

Chapter One

HOW MANY CHILDREN HAD
LADY MACBETH?

PART I

I

FOR SOME YEARS there have been signs of a re-orientation of Shakespeare criticism. The books that I have in mind have little in common with the majority of those that have been written on Shakespeare, but they are likely to have a decisive influence upon criticism in the future. The present, therefore, is a favourable time in which to take stock of the traditional methods, and to inquire why so few of the many books that have been written are relevant to our study of Shakespeare as a poet. The inquiry involves an examination of certain critical presuppositions, and of these the most fruitful of irrelevancies is the assumption that Shakespeare was pre-eminently a great "creator of characters." So extensive was his knowledge of the human heart (so runs the popular opinion) that he was able to project himself into the minds of an infinite variety of men and women and present them "real as life" before us. Of course, he was a great poet as well, but the poetry is an added grace which gives to the atmosphere of the plays a touch of "magic" and which provides us with the thrill of single memorable lines and lyric passages.

This assumption that it is the main business of a writer—other than the lyric poet—to create characters is not, of course, confined to criticism of Shakespeare, it long ago invaded criticism of the novel. "Character creation," says Mr. Logan Pearsall Smith, "is regarded as the very essence of English fiction, the *sine qua non* of novel writing." And in a recent book of extracts from Scott, Mr. Hugh Walpole writes:

> The test of a character in any novel is that it should have existed before the book that reveals it to us began and should continue after the book is closed. . . . These are our friends for life—but it is the

penalty of the more subconscious school of modern fiction that, when the book is closed, all that we have in our hands is a boot-button, a fragment of tulle, or a cocktail shaker. We have dived, it seems, so very deep and come to the surface again with so little in our grasp. . . . But [he continues] however gay, malicious, brilliant and amusing they [modern novels] may be, this hard business of creating a world for us, a world filled with people in whom we may believe, whom we may know better than we know our friends, is the gift of the very few.[1]

It should be obvious that a criterion for the novel by which we should have to condemn *Wuthering Heights, Heart of Darkness, Ulysses, To the Lighthouse* and the bulk of the work of D. H. Lawrence does not need to be very seriously considered.

There is no need to search for examples in the field of Shakespeare criticism. In the latest book on Shakespeare that has come to hand, we read: "His creations are not *ideas* but *characters*— real men and women, fellow humans with ourselves. We can follow their feelings and thoughts like those of our most intimate acquaintances." [2] The case is even better illustrated by Ellen Terry's recently published *Lectures on Shakespeare*. To her the characters are all flesh and blood and she exercises her ingenuity on such questions as whether Portia or Bellario thought of the famous quibble, and whether it was justified.[3] And how did the Boy in *Henry V* learn to speak French? "Robin's French is quite fluent. Did he learn to speak the lingo from Prince Hal, or from Falstaff in London, or did he pick it up during his few weeks in France with the army?" [4] Ellen Terry of course does not represent critical Authority; the point is not that she could write as she did, but that the book was popular. Most of the reviewers were enthusiastic. The *Times Literary Supplement* said that the book showed "the insight of a genius," and the reviewer in the *Times,* speaking of her treatment of Falstaff's page, declared, "To Ellen Terry, Robin was as alive and as real as could be; and we feel as if she had given us a new little friend to laugh with and be sorry for."

And if we wish for higher authority we have only to turn to the

[1] *The Waverley Pageant,* pp. 38-40.
[2] Ranjee G. Shahani, *Shakespeare Through Eastern Eyes,* p. 177.
[3] *Four Lectures on Shakespeare,* pp. 119-120.
[4] *Op. cit.,* p. 49.

HOW MANY CHILDREN HAD LADY MACBETH?

book by Mr. Logan Pearsall Smith, *On Reading Shakespeare*. Mr. Smith demands respect as the author of *Words and Idioms*, in which he showed the kind of interest in language needed for the critical approach to Shakespeare. But there is nothing of that interest in the present essay. Here Shakespeare is praised because he provides "the illusion of reality," because he puts "living people" upon the stage, because he creates characters who are "independent of the work in which they appear . . . and when the curtain falls they go on living in our imaginations and remain as real to us as our familiar friends."—"Those inhabitants of the world of poetry who, in our imagination, lead their immortal lives apart." [1]

The most illustrious example is, of course, Dr. Bradley's *Shakespearean Tragedy*. The book is too well known to require much descriptive comment, but it should be observed that the Notes, in which the detective interest supersedes the critical, form a logical corollary to the main portions of the book. In the Lectures on *Macbeth* we learn that Macbeth was "exceedingly ambitious. He must have been so by temper. The tendency must have been greatly strengthened by his marriage." But "it is difficult to be sure of his customary demeanour." And Dr. Bradley seems surprised that "This bold ambitious man of action has, within certain limits, the imagination of a poet." These minor points are symptomatic. It is assumed throughout the book that the most profitable discussion of Shakespeare's tragedies is in terms of the characters of which they are composed.—"The centre of the tragedy may be said with equal truth to lie in action issuing from character, or in character issuing in action. . . . What we feel strongly, as a tragedy advances to its close, is that the calamities and catastrophe follow inevitably from the deeds of men, and that the main source of these deeds is character. The dictum that, with Shakespeare, 'character is destiny' is no doubt an exaggeration . . . but it is the exaggeration of a vital truth." It is this which leads Dr. Bradley to ask us to imagine Posthumus in the place of Othello, Othello in the place of Posthumus, and to con-

---

[1] Mr. Smith reminds us that, "There are other elements too in this draught of Shakespeare's brewing—in the potent wine that came to fill at last the great jewelled cup of words he fashioned, to drink from which is one of the most wonderful experiences life affords."

jecture upon Hamlet's whereabouts at the time of his father's death.

The influence of the assumption is pervasive. Not only are all the books of Shakespeare criticism (with a very few exceptions) based upon it, it invades scholarship (the notes to the indispensable Arden edition may be called in evidence), and in school children are taught to think they have "appreciated" the poet if they are able to talk about the characters—aided no doubt by the neat summaries provided by Mr. Verity which they learn so assiduously before examinations.

In the mass of Shakespeare criticism there is not a hint that "character"—like "plot," "rhythm," "construction" and all our other critical counters—is merely an abstraction from the total response in the mind of the reader or spectator, brought into being by written or spoken words; that the critic therefore—however far he may ultimately range—begins with the words of which a play is composed. This applies equally to the novel or any other form of art that uses language as its medium. "A Note on Fiction" by Mr. C. H. Rickword in *The Calendar of Modern Letters* expresses the point admirably with regard to the novel: "The form of a novel only exists as a balance of response on the part of the reader. Hence schematic plot is a construction of the reader's that corresponds to an aspect of the response and stands in merely diagrammatic relation to the source. Only as precipitates from the memory are plot or character tangible; yet only in solution have either any emotive valency." [1]

A Shakespeare play is a dramatic poem. It uses action, gesture, formal grouping and symbols, and it relies upon the general conventions governing Elizabethan plays. But, we cannot too often remind ourselves, its end is to communicate a rich and controlled experience by means of words—words used in a way to which, without some training, we are no longer accustomed to respond. To stress in the conventional way character or plot or

[1] *The Calendar*, October 1926. In an earlier review, Mr. Rickword wrote: "Mere degree of illusion provides no adequate test: novelists who can do nothing else are able to perform the trick with ease, since 'nothing is easier than to create for oneself the idea of a human being, a figure and a character, from glimpses and anecdotes.'" (*The Calendar*, July 1926; reprinted in *Towards "Standards of Criticism,"* Wishart.)

any of the other abstractions that can be made is to impoverish the total response. "It is in the total situation rather than in the wrigglings of individual emotion that the tragedy lies." [1] "We should not look for perfect verisimilitude to life," says Mr. Wilson Knight, "but rather see each play as an expanded metaphor, by means of which the original vision has been projected into forms roughly correspondent with actuality, conforming thereto with greater or less exactitude according to the demands of its nature. . . . The persons, ultimately, are not human at all, but purely symbols of a poetic vision." [2]

It would be easy to demonstrate that this approach is essential even when dealing with plays like *Hamlet* or *Macbeth* which can be made to yield something very impressive in the way of "character." And it is the only approach which will enable us to say anything at all relevant about plays like *Measure for Measure* or *Troilus and Cressida* which have consistently baffled the critics. And apart from Shakespeare, what are we to say of *Tamburlaine, Edward II, The Revenger's Tragedy* or *The Changeling* if we do not treat them primarily as poems?

Read with attention, the plays themselves supply the clue of how they should be read. But those who prefer another kind of evidence have only to consider the contemporary factors that conditioned the making of an Elizabethan play, namely the native tradition of English drama descending from the morality plays, the construction of the playhouse and the conventions depending, in part, upon that construction, and the tastes and expectations of the audience. I have not space to deal with any of these in detail. Schücking has shown how large a part was played in the Elizabethan drama by "primitive technique," but the full force of the morality tradition remains to be investigated. It is, I think, impossible to appreciate *Troilus and Cressida* on the one hand, or the plays of Middleton (and even of Ben Jonson) on the other, without an understanding of the "morality" elements that they contain. As for the second factor, the physical peculiarities of the stage and Elizabethan dramatic conventions, I can only refer to Miss Bradbrook's *Elizabethan Stage Conditions*. We can make a

[1] M. C. Bradbrook, *Elizabethan Stage Conditions*, p. 102.
[2] G. Wilson Knight, *The Wheel of Fire*, p. 16.

hasty summary by saying that each of these factors determined that Elizabethan drama should be non-realistic, conditioned by conventions that helped to govern the total response obtained by means of the language of each play. A consideration of Shakespeare's use of language demands a consideration of the reading and listening habits of his audience. Contrary to the accepted view that the majority of these were crude and unlettered, caring only for fighting and foolery, bombast and bawdry, but able to *stand* a great deal of poetry, I think there is evidence (other than the plays themselves) that very many of them had an educated interest in words, a passionate concern for the possibilities of language and the subtleties of poetry. At all events they were trained, by pamphlets, by sermons and by common conversation to listen or to read with an athleticism which we, in the era of the *Daily Mail* and the Best Seller, have consciously to acquire or do our best to acquire. And all of them shared the speech idiom that is the basis of Shakespeare's poetry.[1]

II

We are faced with this conclusion: the only profitable approach to Shakespeare is a consideration of his plays as dramatic poems, of his use of language to obtain a total complex emotional response. Yet the bulk of Shakespeare criticism is concerned with his characters, his heroines, his love of Nature or his "philosophy" —with everything, in short, except with the words on the page, which it is the main business of the critic to examine. I wish to consider as briefly as possible how this paradoxical state of affairs arose. To examine the historical development of the kind of criticism that is mainly concerned with "character" is to strengthen the case against it.

A start must be made towards the end of the seventeenth century, and it is tempting to begin with Thomas Rymer. If Rymer is representative his remarks on *Othello* [2] show how completely the Elizabethan tradition had been lost. Of one of the storm

[1] I have presented some of the evidence in an essay on "Education and the Drama in the Age of Shakespeare," *The Criterion*, July 1932.
[2] In *A Short View of Tragedy* (1693).

speeches (II, i), important both as symbol and ironic commentary, he says, "Once in a man's life, he might be content at *Bedlam* to hear such a rapture. In a Play one should speak like a man of business." He had no conception of the function of rhetoric on the Elizabethan stage; of Othello's speech

> O now, for ever
> Farewell, the Tranquill minde; farewell Content;

he says, "These lines are recited here, not for any thing Poetical in them, besides the sound, that pleases." Combining a demand for realistic verisimilitude with an acceptance of the neo-classic canons he has no difficulty in ridiculing the play:

> The moral, sure, of this Fable is very instructive.
> First, This may be a caution to all Maidens of Quality how, without their Parents consent, they run away with Blackamoors.
> Secondly, This may be a warning to all good Wives that they look well to their Linnen.
> Thirdly, This may be a lesson to Husbands that before their Jealousie be Tragical the proofs may be Mathematical.

And so on to the triumphant conclusion:

> What can remain with the Audience to carry home with them from this sort of Poetry for their use and edification? how can it work, unless (instead of settling the mind and purging our passions) to delude our senses, disorder our thoughts, addle our brain, pervert our affections, hair our imaginations, corrupt our appetite, and fill our head with vanity, confusion, *Tintamarre*, and Jingle-jangle, beyond what all the Parish Clarks of *London* with their *Old Testament* farces and interludes, in *Richard* the second's time, could ever pretend to? . . . The tragical part is plainly none other than a Bloody Farce, without salt or savour.[1]

But perhaps Rymer is not sufficiently representative for his work to be called as evidence. He had a following which included such critics as Gildon and Dennis, and even Pope was in-

---

[1] I cannot understand Mr. Eliot's remark that he has "never seen a cogent refutation of Thomas Rymer's objections to *Othello*" (*Selected Essays*, p. 141). A narrow sensibility, a misunderstanding of the nature of dramatic conventions, and the command of a few debating tricks (e.g. the description of the play in terms of the external plot, which would make any tragedy look ridiculous) are sufficient to account for his objections. A point by point refutation is possible but hardly necessary.

EXPLORATIONS

fluenced by him, but he was censured by Dryden, Addison and Rowe, amongst others, and the rules he stood for never gained anything like a complete ascendancy in the criticism of the eighteenth century. For evidence of the kind that we require we must turn to Dryden, who was not only "a representative man" but also an enthusiastic admirer of Shakespeare, and if he was not "the father of English criticism," he was at least a critic whose opinions must be reckoned with. When Rymer says of the Temptation scene in *Othello,* "Here we see a known Language does wofully encumber and clog the operation, as either forc'd, or heavy, or trifling, or incoherent, or improper, or most what improbable," it is permissible to disregard him; but when we find that Dryden makes similar remarks of other plays of Shakespeare, it is obvious not only that ways of thought and feeling have changed sufficiently since the Elizabethan period to demand a different idiom, but that the Shakespearean idiom is, for the time being, out of the reach of criticism. In the Preface to his version of *Troilus and Cressida* (1679) Dryden says: "Yet it must be allowed to the present age, that the tongue in general is so much refined since Shakespeare's time that many of his words, and more of his phrases, are scarce intelligible. And of those which we understand, some are ungrammatical, others coarse; and his whole style is so pestered with figurative expressions, that it is as affected as it is obscure." And of *Troilus and Cressida*: "I undertook to remove that heap of rubbish under which many excellent thoughts lay wholly buried . . . I need not say that I have refined the language, which before was obsolete." [1]

Not only the idiom but the Elizabethan conventions were now inaccessible. In the *Defence of the Epilogue* (1672) Dryden takes exception to *The Winter's Tale, Love's Labour's Lost* and *Measure for Measure,* "which were either grounded on impossibilities, or at least so meanly written, that the comedy neither moved your

[1] Later he remarks: "I will not say of so great a poet that he distinguished not the blown puffy style from true sublimity; but I may venture to maintain that the fury of his fancy often transported him beyond the bounds of judgment, either in coining of new words and phrases, or racking words which were in use into the violence of a catachresis. It is not that I would explode the use of metaphors from passion, for Longinus thinks 'em necessary to raise it: but to use 'em at every word, to say nothing without a metaphor, a simile, an image, or description, is, I doubt, to smell a little too strongly of the buskin."—The force of Elizabethan language springs from its metaphorical life.

mirth, nor the serious part your concernment." And he proceeds to criticize Fletcher in the true spirit of William Archer.

The implications of Dryden's remarks became the commonplaces of criticism for the succeeding generations. It was permissible to speak of Shakespeare's "Deference paid to the reigning Barbarism" (Theobald), and "The vicious taste of the age" (Hanmer), and to write, "The Audience was generally composed of the meaner sort of people" (Pope), and "The publick was gross and dark. . . . Those to whom our author's labours were exhibited had more skill in pomps or processions than in poetical language" (Johnson). In his *Preface* (1747) Warburton writes:

> The Poet's hard and unnatural construction . . . was the effect of mistaken Art and Design. The Public Taste was in its Infancy; and delighted (as it always does during that state) in the high and turgid; which leads the writer to disguise a vulgar expression with hard and forced constructions, whereby the sentence frequently becomes cloudy and dark . . . an obscurity that ariseth, not from the licentious use of a single Term, but from the unnatural arrangement of a whole sentence. . . . Not but in his best works (he continues), we must allow, he is often so natural and flowing, so pure and correct, that he is even a model for style and language.

Of all the eighteenth-century critics only Johnson (an exception we have often to make) at times transcended the limitations of conventional Shakespeare criticism. He censures Hanmer, who in his edition of Shakespeare "is solicitous to reduce to grammer what he could not be sure that his author intended to be grammatical," and he writes admirably of "a style which never becomes obsolete. . . . This style is probably to be sought in the common intercourse of life, among those who speak only to be understood, without ambition of elegance." But he stops short at that. This "conversation above grossness and below refinement, where propriety resides" is where Shakespeare "seems to have gathered his *comick* dialogue." But it is in Shakespeare's tragedies that his style is most vividly idiomatic and full bodied, and Johnson was capable of writing, "His comedy pleases by the thoughts and language, and his tragedy for the greater part by incident and action." Johnson's great virtues as a critic did not include an understanding of Shakespeare's idiom. For him, "The style of Shakespeare was in itself ungrammatical, perplexed and obscure," and many passages remained "obscured by obsolete phraseology, or by the writer's unskilfulness and affectation." We remember also how he could "scarcely check his risibility" at the "blanket of the dark" passage in *Macbeth*.

It should not be necessary to insist that I do not wish to deny the achievements of the Augustan age in poetry and criticism. But an age of which the commonplaces of criticism were that "Well placing of words, for the sweetness of pronunciation, was not known till Mr. Waller introduced it," [1] and that Pope's *Homer* "tuned the English tongue"; [2] an age which produced the *Essay on Criticism* and the *Satires of Dr. Donne Versified,* and which consistently neglected the Metaphysical poets and the minor Elizabethans, such an age was incapable of fully understanding Shakespeare's use of words. Since the total response to a Shakespeare play can only be obtained by an exact and sensitive study of the quality of the verse, of the rhythm and imagery, of the controlled associations of the words and their emotional and intellectual force, in short by an exact and sensitive study of Shakespeare's handling of language, it is hardly reasonable to expect very much relevant criticism of Shakespeare in the eighteenth century. What can be expected is criticism at one remove from the plays, that is, of every aspect that can be extracted from a play and studied in comparative isolation; of this kind of criticism an examination of "characters" is the most obvious example.

A significant passage occurs in Shaftesbury's *Advice to an Author,* published in 1710:

> Our old dramatick Poet, Shakespeare, may witness for our good Ear and manly Relish. Notwithstanding his natural Rudeness, his unpolish'd style, his antiquated Phrase and Wit, his want of Method and Coherence, and his Deficiency in almost all the Graces and Ornaments of this kind of Writings; yet by the Justness of his *Moral,* the Aptness of many of his *Descriptions,* and the plain and natural Turn of several of his *Characters,* he pleases his Audience, and often gains their Ear, without a single Bribe from Luxury or Vice.

[1] Dryden, *Defence of the Epilogue.*
[2] Johnson, *Life of Pope.*

HOW MANY CHILDREN HAD LADY MACBETH?

We see here the beginning of that process of splitting up the indivisible unity of a Shakespeare play into various elements abstracted from the whole. If a play of Shakespeare's could not be appreciated as a whole, it was still possible to admire and to discuss his moral sentiments, his humour, his poetic descriptions and the life-likeness of his characters. Thus, Warburton mentions, ". . . the Author's Beauties . . . whether in Style, Thought, Sentiment, Character, or Composition."

The intensive study of Shakespeare's characters was not fully developed until the second half of the eighteenth century. Dryden had remarked that "No man ever drew so many characters, or generally distinguished 'em from one another, excepting only Jonson," and Pope observed, "His *Characters* are so much Nature herself, that 'tis a sort of injury to call them by so distant a name as copies of her. . . . Every single character in Shakespeare is as much an Individual as those in Life itself; it is as impossible to find any two alike"; and Theobald echoed him in a lyrical passage,—"If we look into his Characters, and how they are furnished and proportion'd to the Employment he cuts out for them, how are we taken up with the Mastery of his Portraits! What draughts of Nature! What variety of Originals, and how differing each from the other!" [1] But in the second half of the century character study became one of the main objects of Shakespeare criticism. This is sufficiently indicated by the following titles: *A Philosophical Analysis and Illustration of some of Shakespeare's Remarkable Characters* (Richardson, 1774), *An Essay on the Character of Hamlet* (Pilon, 1777), *Essays on Shakespeare's Dramatic Characters* (Richardson, 1784), *Remarks on some of the Characters of Shakespeare* (Whately, 1785), *Shakespeare's Imitation of Female Characters* (Richardson, 1789), and so on.

Of the essays of this kind, the most famous is Maurice Morgann's *Essay on the Dramatic Character of Sir John Falstaff* (1777). The pivot of Morgann's method is to be found in one of his footnotes:

> The reader must be sensible of something in the composition of *Shakespeare's* characters, which renders them essentially different

[1] Pope adds: "Had all the speeches been printed without the very names of the Persons, I believe one might have apply'd them with certainty to every speaker."

from those drawn by other writers. The characters of every Drama must indeed be grouped, but in the groupes of other poets the parts which are not seen do not in fact exist. But there is a certain roundness and integrity in the forms of *Shakespeare,* which give them an independence as well as a relation, insomuch that we often meet with passages which, tho' perfectly felt, cannot be sufficiently explained in words, without unfolding the whole character of the speaker. . . . The reader will not now be surprised if I affirm that those characters in Shakespeare, which are seen only in part, are yet capable of being unfolded and understood in the whole; every part being in fact relative, and inferring all the rest. It is true that the point of action or sentiment, which we are most concerned in, is always held out for our special notice. But who does not perceive that there is a peculiarity about it, which conveys a relish of the whole? And very frequently, when no particular point presses, he boldly makes a character act and speak from those parts of the composition which are *inferred* only, and not distinctly shown. This produces a wonderful effect; it seems to carry us beyond the poet to nature itself, and gives an integrity and truth to facts and character, which they could not otherwise obtain. And this is in reality that art in *Shakespeare* which, being withdrawn from our notice, we more emphatically call *nature.* A felt propriety and truth from causes unseen, I take to be the highest point of Poetic composition. If the characters of *Shakespeare* are thus *whole,* and as it were original, whilst those of almost all other writers are mere imitation, *it may to be fit to consider them rather as Historic than Dramatic beings; and, when occasion requires, to account for their conduct from the* WHOLE *of character, from general principles, from latent motives, and from policies not avowed.*[1]

It is strange how narrowly Morgann misses the mark. He recognized what can be called the full-bodied quality of Shakespeare's work—it came to him as a feeling of "roundness and integrity." But instead of realizing that this quality sprang from Shakespeare's use of words, words which have "a network of tentacular roots, reaching down to the deepest terrors and desires," he referred it to the characters' "independence" of the work in which they appeared, and directed his exploration to "latent motives and policies not avowed." Falstaff's birth, his early life, his association with John of Gaunt, his possible position as head

---

[1] These last italics are mine.

of his family, his military service and his pension are all examined in order to determine the grand question, "Is Falstaff a constitutional coward?" [1]

In the Essay, of course, "Falstaff is the word only. Shakespeare is the theme," and several admirable things are said incidentally. But more than any other man, it seems to me, Morgann has deflected Shakespeare criticism from the proper objects of attention by his preposterous references to those aspects of a "character" that Shakespeare did not wish to show. He made explicit the assumption on which the other eighteenth-century critics based their work, and that assumption has been pervasive until our own time. In 1904 Dr. Bradley said of Morgann's essay, "There is no better piece of Shakespeare criticism in the world." [2]

I have already suggested the main reason for the eighteenth-century approach to Shakespeare via the characters, namely an inability to appreciate the Elizabethan idiom and a consequent inability to discuss Shakespeare's plays as poetry. And of course the Elizabethan dramatic tradition was lost, and the eighteenth-century critics in general were ignorant of the stage for which Shakespeare wrote.[3] But other factors should also be considered; for instance, the neo-classic insistence upon the moral function of art (before you can judge a person in a play he must have more or less human "motives"), and the variations of meaning covered by the term "nature" from the time of Pope to the time of Wordsworth. Literary psychologizing also played a part; Kames and William Richardson [4] both found Shakespeare's persons useful illustrations of psychological theories, and Samuel Richardson fostered an interest in introspective analysis, so that Macbeth's soliloquies were assumed to have something in common with the introspections of Clarissa. Finally (and Richardson serves to remind us) "the sentimental age set in early in the eighteenth century." If we consider any of the Character writers of the seven-

---

[1] I have discussed Falstaff's dramatic function—the way in which he helps to define Shakespeare's total attitude towards the matter in hand—in *Determinations*, edited by F. R. Leavis (Chatto and Windus).

[2] *The Scottish Historical Review*, Vol. I, p. 291.

[3] "Shakespeare's plays were to be acted in a paltry tavern, to an unlettered audience, just emerging from barbarity."—Mrs. Montagu, *Essay on the Writings and Genius of Shakespeare* (Fifth Edition, 1785), p. 13.

[4] See Note, see page 52.

teenth century, Earle, Overbury or Hall, we find that they preserve a distance from their subjects which the eighteenth-century
creators of characters do not. The early Characters have a frame
round them, whereas the Vicar of Wakefield, Beau Tibbs, and
even Sir Roger de Coverley make a more direct appeal to human
sympathy and emotion. The "human" appeal ("These are our
friends for life . . ."), which has made the fortune of Best Sellers,
is an intrusion which vitiated, and can only vitiate, Shakespeare
criticism.

One form of the charge against eighteenth-century Shakespeare
criticism is that it made the approach too easy. In Pope's edition,
"Some of the most shining passages are distinguish'd by commas
in the margin," and Warburton also marked what he considered
particularly beautiful passages. From this it was but a step to
collect such passages into anthologies. The numerous editions
of the collections of *Beauties* show how popular this method of
reading Shakespeare had become by the end of the century. This
is an obvious method of simplification, but it is only part of the
process whereby various partial (and therefore distorted) responses
were substituted for the full complex response demanded by a
Shakespeare play—a process that was fatal to criticism.[1]

There is no need, even if it were possible, to discuss nineteenth-
century Shakespeare criticism in detail, partly because it is more
familiar, partly because—as Mr. Nichol Smith and Mr. Babcock
have helped us to realize—the foundations of modern Shakespeare
criticism were laid in the eighteenth century. In the nineteenth
century the word "poetry" changed its significance, but preconceptions about "the poetic" derived from reading Keats (or
Tennyson) did not increase understanding of seventeenth-century
poetry. And everything combined to foster that kind of interest in
Shakespeare that is represented at certain levels by Mrs. Jame-
son's *Shakespeare's Heroines* and Mary Cowden Clarke's *Girlhood
of Shakespeare's Heroines*. In so far as the word "romantic" has
other than an emotive use, it serves to distinguish individualist

[1] For the collections of Shakespeare's *Beauties* see R. W. Babcock, *The Genesis
of Shakespeare Idolatry*, pp. 115-118. The most famous of these anthologies, William
Dodd's *Beauties of Shakespeare*, first published in 1752, not only went through
many editions in the eighteenth century, but was frequently reprinted in the
nineteenth.

qualities as opposed to the social qualities covered by "classical." One of the main results of the Romantic Revival was the stressing of "personality" in fiction. At the same time, the growth of the popular novel, from Sir Walter Scott and Charlotte Brontë to our own Best Sellers, encouraged an emotional identification of the reader with hero or heroine (we all "have a smack of Hamlet" nowadays).[1] And towards the end of the century the influence of Ibsen was responsible for fresh distortions which can best be studied in Archer's *The Old Drama and the New*.

In Shakespeare criticism from Hazlitt to Dowden we find the same kind of irrelevance. Hazlitt says of Lady Macbeth:

> She is a great bad woman, whom we hate, but whom we fear more than we hate.

And of the Witches:

> They are hags of mischief, obscene panders to iniquity, malicious from their impotence of enjoyment, enamoured of destruction, because they are themselves unreal, abortive, half-existences—who become sublime from their exemption from all human sympathies and contempt for all human affairs, as Lady Macbeth does by the force of passion! Her fault seems to have been an excess of that strong principle of self-interest and family aggrandisement, not amenable to the common feelings of compassion and justice, which is so marked a feature in barbarous nations and times.

What has this to do with Shakespeare? And what the lyric outburst that Dowden quotes approvingly in his chapter on *Romeo and Juliet*?

> Who does not recall those lovely summer nights, in which the forces of nature seem eager for development, and constrained to remain in drowsy languor? . . . The nightingale sings in the depths of the woods. The flower-cups are half-closed.

And so on.

Wherever we look we find the same reluctance to master the words of the play, the same readiness to abstract a character and

---

[1] See the letters to popular novelists quoted on p. 58 of Q. D. Leavis's *Fiction and the Reading Public*: "Your characters are so human that they live with me as friends," etc.

treat him (because he is more manageable that way) as a human being. When Gervinus says that the play *Hamlet* "transports us to a rude and wild period from which Hamlet's whole nature recoils, and to which he falls a sacrifice because by habit, character and education he is alienated from it, and like the boundary stone of a changing civilization touches a world of finer feeling," he exhibits the common fault. In this instance Hamlet is wrenched from his setting and violently imported into the society described by Saxo Grammaticus. Criticism is not all so crass as Sir Herbert Tree's remark that "We must interpret Macbeth, before and at the crisis, by his just and equitable character as a king that history gives him." [1] But there are enough modern instances to show that the advice that Hartley Coleridge gave in *Blackwood's* needed no arguing. "Let us," he said, "for a moment, put Shakespeare out of the question, and consider Hamlet as a real person, a recently deceased acquaintance." [2]

The habit of regarding Shakespeare's persons as "friends for life," or, maybe, "deceased acquaintances," is responsible for most of the vagaries that serve as Shakespeare criticism. It accounts for the artificial simplifications of the editors ("In a play one should speak like a man of business"). It accounts for the "double time" theory for *Othello*. It accounts for Dr. Bradley's Notes and for the criticism in Ward's *History of the English Drama*. It is responsible for all the irrelevant moral and realistic canons that have been applied to Shakespeare's plays, for the sentimentalizing of his heroes (Coleridge and Goethe on Hamlet) and his heroines. And the loss is incalculable. Losing sight of the *whole* dramatic pattern of each play, we inhibit the development of that full complex response that makes our experience of a Shakespeare play so very much more than an appreciation of "character"— that is, usually, of somebody else's "character." That more complete, more intimate possession can only be obtained by treating Shakespeare primarily as a poet.

[1] *Illustrated London News*, September 9, 1911.
[2] *Blackwood's Magazine*, Vol. XXIV (1828), p. 585.

PART II

I

SINCE EVERYONE who has written about Shakespeare probably imagines that he has "treated him primarily as a poet," some explanation is called for. How should we read Shakespeare?

We start with so many lines of verse on a printed page which we read as we should read any other poem. We have to elucidate the meaning (using Dr. Richards's fourfold definition [1]) and to unravel ambiguities; we have to estimate the kind and quality of the imagery and determine the precise degree of evocation of particular figures; we have to allow full weight to each word, exploring its "tentacular roots," and to determine how it controls and is controlled by the rhythmic movement of the passage in which it occurs. In short, we have to decide exactly why the lines "are so and not otherwise."

As we read other factors come into play. The lines have a cumulative effect. "Plot," aspects of "character," recurrent "themes" and "symbols"—all "precipitates from the memory"— help to determine our reaction at a given point. There is a constant reference backwards and forwards. But the work of detailed analysis continues to the last line of the last act. If the razor-edge of sensibility is blunted at any point we cannot claim to have read what Shakespeare wrote, however often our eyes may have travelled over the page. A play of Shakespeare's is a precise particular experience, a poem—and precision and particularity are exactly what is lacking in the greater part of Shakespeare criticism, criticism that deals with *Hamlet* or *Othello* in terms of abstractions that have nothing to do with the unique arrangement of words that constitutes these plays.

Obviously what is wanted to reinforce the case against the traditional methods is a detailed examination of a particular play. Unfortunately anything approaching a complete analysis is precluded by the scope of the present essay. The following remarks on one play, *Macbeth,* are, therefore, not offered as a final criti-

[1] *Practical Criticism*, pp. 181-188.

31

cism of the play; they merely point to factors that criticism must take into account if it is to have any degree of relevance, and emphasize the kind of effect that is necessarily overlooked when we discuss a Shakespeare play in terms of characters "copied from life," or of "Shakespeare's knowledge of the human heart."

Even here there is a further reservation to be made. In all elucidation there is an element of crudity and distortion. "The true generalization," Mr. Eliot reminds us, "is not something superposed upon an accumulation of perceptions; the perceptions do not, in a really appreciative mind, accumulate as a mass, but form themselves as a structure; and criticism is the statement in language of this structure; it is a development of sensibility." [1] Of course, the only *full* statement in language of this structure is in the exact words of the poem concerned; but what the critic can do is to aid "the return to the work of art with improved perception and intensified, because more conscious, enjoyment." He can help others to "force the subject to expose itself," he cannot fully expose it in his own criticism. And in so far as he paraphrases or "explains the meaning" he must distort. The main difference between good and bad critics is that the good critic points to something that is actually contained in the work of art, whereas the bad critic points away from the work in question; he introduces extraneous elements into his appreciation—smudges the canvas with his own paint. With this reservation I should like to call the following pages an essay in elucidation.

II

Macbeth is a statement of evil. I use the word "statement" (unsatisfactory as it is) in order to stress those qualities that are "non-dramatic," if drama is defined according to the canons of William Archer or Dr. Bradley. It also happens to be poetry, which means that the apprehension of the whole can only be obtained from a lively attention to the parts, whether they have an immediate bearing on the main action or "illustrate charac-

---

[1] *The Sacred Wood* (Second Edition, 1928), p. 15. See also p. 11, *op. cit.*, and *Selected Essays*, p. 205.

ter," or not. Two main themes, which can only be separated for the purpose of analysis, are blended in the play—the themes of the reversal of values and of unnatural disorder. And closely related to each is a third theme, that of the deceitful appearance, and consequent doubt, uncertainty and confusion. All this is obscured by false assumptions about the category "drama"; *Macbeth* has greater affinity with *The Waste Land* than with *The Doll's House*.[1]

Each theme is stated in the first act. The first scene, every word of which will bear the closest scrutiny, strikes one dominant chord:

> Faire is foule, and foule is faire,
> Hover through the fogge and filthie ayre.

It is worth remarking that "Hurley-burley" implies more than "the tumult of sedition or insurrection." Both it and "when the Battaile's lost, and wonne" suggest the kind of metaphysical pitch-and-toss that is about to be played with good and evil. At the same time we hear the undertone of uncertainty: the scene opens with a question, and the second line suggests a region where the elements are disintegrated as they never are in nature; thunder and lightning are disjoined, and offered as alternatives. We should notice also that the scene expresses the same movement as the play as a whole: the general crystallizes into the immediate particular ("Where the place?"—"Upon the Heath."—"There to meet with Macbeth.") and then dissolves again into the general presentment of hideous gloom. All is done with the greatest speed, economy and precision.

The second scene is full of images of confusion. It is a general principle in the work of Shakespeare and many of his contemporaries that when A is made to describe X, a minor character

---

[1] See the Arden Edition, p. xxii: "The scenes (Act IV, scenes ii and iii) seem to have been composed with evident effort, as if Shakespeare felt the necessity of stretching out his material to the ordinary length of a five-act tragedy, and found lack of *dramatic* material, which was certainly wanting in his authority, Holinshed. Hence his introduction in Act V of the famous 'sleep-walking scene' . . . and the magnificently *irrelevant* soliloquies of the great protagonist himself." The italics are mine. There is something wrong with a conception of "the dramatic" that leads a critic to speak of Macbeth's final soliloquies as "irrelevant" even though "magnificent." I deal with the dramatic function of Act IV, scene ii, and Act IV, scene iii, below.

or event, the description is not merely immediately applicable to X, it helps to determine the way in which our whole response shall develop. This is rather crudely recognized when we say that certain lines "create the atmosphere" of the play. Shakespeare's power is seen in the way in which details of this kind develop, check, or provide a commentary upon the main interests that he has aroused.[1] In the present scene the description

> —Doubtfull it stood,
> As two spent Swimmers, that doe cling together,
> And choake their Art—

applies not only to the battle but to the ambiguity of Macbeth's future fortunes. The impression conveyed is not only one of violence but of unnatural violence ("to bathe in reeking wounds") and of a kind of nightmare gigantism—

> Where the Norweyan Banners flowt the Skie,
> And fanne our people cold.

(These lines alone should be sufficient answer to those who doubt the authenticity of the scene.) When Duncan says, "What he hath lost, Noble *Macbeth* hath wonne," we hear the echo,

> So from that Spring, whence comfort seem'd to come,
> Discomfort swells,

—and this is not the only time the Captain's words can be applied in the course of the play. Nor is it fantastic to suppose that in the account of Macdonwald Shakespeare consciously provided a parallel with the Macbeth of the later acts when "The multiplying Villanies of Nature swarme upon him." After all, everybody has noticed the later parallel between Macbeth and Cawdor ("He was a Gentleman, on whom I built an absolute Trust").

A poem works by calling into play, directing and integrating certain interests. If we really accept the suggestion, which then

---

[1] Cf. Coleridge, *Lectures on Shakespeare, etc.* (Bohn Edition), p. 406: "Massinger is like a Flemish painter, in whose delineations objects appear as they do in nature, have the same force and truth, and produce the same effect upon the spectator. But Shakespeare is beyond this;—he always by metaphors and figures involves in the thing considered a universe of past and possible experiences."

becomes revolutionary, that *Macbeth* is a poem, it is clear that the impulses aroused in Act I, scenes i and ii, are part of the whole response, even if they are not all immediately relevant to the fortunes of the protagonist. If these scenes are "the botching work of an interpolator," he botched to pretty good effect.

In Act I, scene iii, confusion is succeeded by uncertainty. The Witches

> looke not like th' Inhabitants o' th' Earth,
> And yet are on't.

Banquo asks Macbeth,

> Why doe you start, and seeme to feare
> Things that doe sound so faire?

He addresses the Witches,

> You should be women,
> And yet your Beards forbid me to interprete
> That you are so. . . .
> . . . i'th' name of truth
> Are ye fantasticall, or that indeed
> Which outwardly ye shew?

When they vanish, "what seem'd corporall" melts "as breath into the Winde." The whole force of the uncertainty of the scene is gathered into Macbeth's soliloquy,

> This supernaturall solliciting
> Cannot be ill; cannot be good . . .

which with its sickening see-saw rhythm completes the impression of "a phantasma, or a hideous dream." [1] Macbeth's echoing of the Witches' "Faire is foule" has often been commented upon.

---

[1] The parallel with *Julius Caesar*, Act II, scene i, 63-69, is worth notice:

> Between the acting of a dreadfull thing,
> And the first motion, all the Interim is
> Like a Phantasma, or a hideous Dreame . . .

Macbeth speaks of "the Interim," and his "single state of Man" echoes Brutus'

> The state of man,
> Like to a little Kingdome, suffers then
> The nature of an Insurrection.

The rhythm of Macbeth's speech is repeated in Lady Macbeth's

> What thou would'st highly,
> That would'st thou holily, etc.

EXPLORATIONS

In contrast to the preceding scenes, Act I, scene iv, suggests the natural order which is shortly to be violated. It stresses: natural relationships—"children," "servants," "sons" and "kinsmen"; honourable bonds and the political order—"liege," "thanes," "service," "duty," "loyalty," "throne," "state" and "honour"; and the human "love" is linked to the natural order of organic growth by images of husbandry. Duncan says to Macbeth,

> I have begun to plant thee, and will labour
> To make thee full of growing.

When he holds Banquo to his heart Banquo replies,

> There if I grow,
> The Harvest is your owne.

Duncan's last speech is worth particular notice,

> . . . in his commendations, I am fed:
> It is a Banquet to me.

At this point something should be said of what is meant by "the natural order." In *Macbeth* this comprehends both "wild nature"—birds, beasts and reptiles—and humankind since "humane statute purg'd the gentle Weale." The specifically human aspect is related to the concept of propriety and degree,—

> communities,
> Degrees in Schooles and Brother-hoods in Cities,
> Peacefull Commerce from dividable shores,
> The primogenitive, and due of byrth,
> Prerogative of Age, Crownes, Scepters, Lawrels.

In short, it represents society in harmony with nature, bound by love and friendship, and ordered by law and duty. It is one of the main axes of reference by which we take our emotional bearings in the play.

In the light of this the scene of Duncan's entry into the castle gains in significance. The critics have often remarked on the irony. What is not so frequently observed is that the key words of the scene are "loved," "wooingly," "bed," "procreant Cradle," "breed, and haunt," all images of love and procreation, supernaturally sanctioned, for the associations of "temple-haunting" colour the whole of the speeches of Banquo and Duncan.[1] We do violence to the play when we ignore Shakespeare's insistence upon the "holy supernatural" as opposed to the "supernaturall solliciting" of the Witches. I shall return to this point. Meanwhile it is pertinent to remember that Duncan himself is "The Lords anoynted Temple" (Act II, scene iii, 70).[2]

The murder is explicitly presented as unnatural. After the greeting of Ross and Angus, Macbeth's heart knocks at his ribs "against the use of Nature." Lady Macbeth fears his "humane kindnesse"; she wishes herself "unsexed," that she may be troubled by "no compunctious visitings of Nature," and invokes the "murth'ring Ministers" who "wait on Natures Mischiefe." The murder is committed when

> Nature seemes dead, and wicked Dreames abuse
> The Curtain'd sleepe,

and it is accompanied by portents "unnaturall, even like the deed that's done." The sun remains obscured, and Duncan's horses "Turn'd wilde in nature." Besides these explicit references to the unnatural we notice the violence of the imagery—

> I have given Sucke, and know
> How tender 'tis to love the Babe that milkes me,
> I would, while it was smyling in my Face,
> Have pluckt my Nipple from his Bonelesse Gummes,
> And dasht the Braines out. . . .

Not only are the feelings presented unnatural in this sense, they are also strange—peculiar compounds which cannot be classified by any of the usual labels—"fear," "disgust," etc. Macbeth's words towards the end of Act II, scene i, serve to illustrate this:

> Thou sowre [sure] and firme-set Earth
> Heare not my steps, which way they walke, for feare
> Thy very stones prate of my where-about,

[1] See F. R. Leavis, *How to Teach Reading* (now reprinted as an appendix to *Education and the University*), for a more detailed analysis of these lines.
[2] Later, Macduff says to Malcolm:
> Thy Royall Father
> Was a most Sainted King.
> (Act IV, scene iii, 108.)

And take the present horror from the time,
Which now sutes with it.

The first three lines imply a recognition of the enormity of the crime; Macbeth asks that the earth ("sure and firme-set" contrasted with the disembodied "Murder" which "moves like a Ghost") shall not hear his steps, for if it does so the very stones will speak and betray him—thereby breaking the silence and so lessening the horror. "Take" combines two constructions. On the one hand, "for fear they take the present horror from the time" expresses attraction, identification with the appropriate setting of his crime. But "take" is also an imperative, expressing anguish and repulsion. "Which now sutes with it" implies an acceptance of the horror, willing or reluctant according to the two meanings of the previous line. The unusual sliding construction (unusual in ordinary verse, there are other examples in Shakespeare, and in Donne) expresses the unusual emotion which is only crudely analysed if we call it a mixture of repulsion and attraction fusing into "horror."

"Confusion now hath made his Master-peece," and in the lull that follows the discovery of the murder, Ross and an Old Man, as chorus, echo the theme of unnatural disorder. The scene (and the act) ends with a "sentence" by the Old Man:

Gods benyson go with you, and with those
That would make good of bad, and Friends of Foes.

This, deliberately pronounced, has an odd ambiguous effect. The immediate reference is to Ross, who intends to make the best of a dubious business by accepting Macbeth as king. But Macduff also is destined to "make good of bad" by destroying the evil. And an overtone of meaning takes our thoughts to Macbeth, whose attempt to make good of bad by restoring the natural order is the theme of the next movement; the tragedy lies in his inevitable failure.

A key is found in Macbeth's words spoken to the men hired to murder Banquo (Act III, scene i, 91-100). When Dr. Bradley is discussing the possibility that *Macbeth* has been abridged he remarks ("very aptly" according to the Arden editor), "surely, anyone who wanted to cut the play down would have operated, say, on Macbeth's talk with Banquo's murderers, or on Act III, scene vi, or on the very long dialogue of Malcolm and Macduff, instead of reducing the most exciting part of the drama." [1] No, the speech to the murderers is not very "exciting"—but its function should be obvious to anyone who is not blinded by Dr. Bradley's preconceptions about "drama." By accepted canons it is an irrelevance; actually it stands as a symbol of the order that Macbeth wishes to restore. In the catalogue,

> Hounds, and Greyhounds, Mungrels, Spaniels, Curres,
> Showghes, Water-Rugs, and Demy-Wolves

are merely "dogs," but Macbeth names each one individually; and

> the valued file
> Distinguishes the swift, the slow, the subtle,
> The House-keeper, the Hunter, every one
> According to the gift, which bounteous Nature
> Hath in him clos'd.

It is an image of order, each one in his degree. At the beginning of the scene, we remember, Macbeth had arranged "a feast," "a solemn supper," at which "society" should be "welcome." And when alone he suggests the ancient harmonies by rejecting in idea the symbols of their contraries—"a fruitlesse Crowne," "a barren Scepter," and an "unlineall" succession. But this new "health" is "sickly" whilst Banquo lives, and can only be made "perfect" by his death. In an attempt to re-create an order based on murder, disorder makes fresh inroads. This is made explicit in the next scene (Act III, scene ii). Here the snake, usually represented as the most venomous of creatures, stands for the natural order which Macbeth has "scotched" but which will "close, and be her selfe." [2]

---

[1] *Shakespearan Tragedy*, p. 469. *Macbeth*, Arden Edition, pp. xxi-xxii. I discuss the importance of Act III, scene vi, and of the Malcolm-Macduff dialogue later.

[2] The murder of Banquo, like the murder of Duncan, is presented as a violation of natural continuity and natural order. Macbeth will "cancell and teare to pieces that great Bond" which keeps him pale. "Bond" has a more than general significance. The line is clearly associated with Lady Macbeth's "But in them, Natures Coppie's not eterne," and the full force of the words is only brought out if we remember that when Shakespeare wrote them, copyholders formed numerically

EXPLORATIONS

At this point in the play there is a characteristic confusion. At the end of Act III, scene ii, Macbeth says, "Things bad begun, make strong themselves by ill," that is, all that he can do is to ensure his physical security by a second crime, although earlier (Act III, scene i, 106-107) he had aimed at complete "health" by the death of Banquo and Fleance, and later he says that the murder of Fleance would have made him

perfect,
Whole as the Marble, founded as the Rocke.

(Act III, scene iv, 21-22).

The truth is only gradually disentangled from this illusion.

The situation is magnificently presented in the banquet scene. Here speech, action and symbolism combine. The stage direction *"Banquet prepar'd"* is the first pointer. In Shakespeare, as Mr. Wilson Knight has remarked, banquets are almost invariably symbols of rejoicing, friendship and concord. Significantly, the nobles sit in due order.

> *Macbeth.* You know your owne degrees, sit downe:
> At first and last, the hearty welcome.

> *Lords.* Thankes to your Majesty.

> *Macbeth.* Our selfe will mingle with Society,
> And play the humble Host:
> Our Hostesse keepes her State, but in best time
> We will require her welcome.

> *Lady Macbeth.* Pronounce it for me Sir, to all our Friends,
> For my heart speakes, they are welcome.

Enter first Murderer.

There is no need for comment. In a sense the scene marks the climax of the play. One avenue has been explored; "Society,"

---

the largest land-holding class in England whose appeal was always to "immemorial antiquity" and "times beyond the memory of man." The Macbeth-Banquo opposition is emphasized when we learn that Banquo's line will "stretch out to the cracke of Doome" (Act IV, scene i, 117). Macbeth is cut off from the natural sequence, "He has no children" (Act IV, scene iii, 217), he is a "Monster (Act V, scene vii, 54). Macbeth's isolation is fully brought out in the last Act.

HOW MANY CHILDREN HAD LADY MACBETH?

"Host," "Hostess," "Friends" and "Welcome" repeat a theme which henceforward is heard only faintly until it is taken up in the final orchestration, when it appears as "Honor, Love, Obedience, Troopes of Friends." With the disappearance of the ghost, Macbeth may be "a man againe," but he has, irretrievably,

> displac'd the mirth,
> Broke the good meeting, with most admir'd disorder.

The end of the scene is in direct contrast to its beginning.

> Stand not upon the order of your going,
> But go at once

echoes ironically, "You know your owne degrees, sit downe."

Before we attempt to disentangle the varied threads of the last Act, two more scenes call for particular comment. The first is the scene in Macduff's castle. Almost without exception the critics have stressed the pathos of young Macduff, his "innocent prattle," his likeness to Arthur, and so on—reactions appropriate to the work of Sir James Barrie which obscure the complex dramatic function of the scene.[1] In the first place, it echoes in different keys the theme of the false appearance, of doubt and confusion. At its opening we are perplexed with questions:—Is Macduff a traitor? If so, to whom, to Macbeth or to his wife? Was his flight due to wisdom or to fear? Ross says,

> But cruell are the times, when we are Traitors
> And do not know our selves: when we hold Rumor
> From what we feare, yet know not what we feare.

Lady Macduff says of her son,

> Father'd he is,
> And yet hee's Father-lesse.[2]

[1] Dr. Bradley says of this and the following scene: "They have a technical value in helping to give the last stage of the action the form of a conflict between Macbeth and Macduff. But their chief function is of another kind. It is to touch the heart with a sense of beauty and pathos, to open the springs of love and of tears."—*Shakespearean Tragedy*, p. 391, see also p. 394.

[2] Compare the equivocation about Macduff's birth.

She teases him with riddles, and he replies with questions.

Secondly, the scene shows the spreading evil. As Fletcher has pointed out, Macduff and his wife are "representatives of the interests of loyalty and domestic affection." [1] There is much more in the death of young Macduff than "pathos"; the violation of the natural order is completed by the murder. But there is even more than this. That the tide is about to turn against Macbeth is suggested both by the rhythm and imagery of Ross's speech:

> But cruell are the times, when we are Traitors
> And do not know our selves: when we hold Rumor
> From what we feare, yet know not what we feare,
> But floate upon a wilde and violent Sea
> Each way, and move—— [2]

The comma after "way," the complete break after "move," give the rhythm of a tide, pausing at the turn. And when Lady Macduff answers the Murderer's question, "Where is your husband?"

> I hope in no place so unsanctified,
> Where such as thou may'st find him

we recall the associations set up in Act III, scene vi, a scene of choric commentary upon Macduff's flight to England, to the "pious Edward," "the Holy King."

Although the play moves swiftly, it does not move with a simple directness. Its complex subtleties include cross-currents, the ebb and flow of opposed thoughts and emotions. The scene in Macduff's castle, made up of doubts, riddles, paradoxes and uncertainties, ends with an affirmation, "Thou ly'st thou shagge-ear'd Villaine." But this is immediately followed, not by the downfall of Macbeth, but by a long scene which takes up once more the theme of mistrust, disorder and evil.

The conversation between Macduff and Malcolm has never been adequately explained. We have already seen Dr. Bradley's

---

[1] Quoted by Furness, p. 218. The whole passage from Fletcher is worth attention.

[2] The substitution of a dash for the full stop after "move" is the only alteration that seems necessary in the Folio text. The other emendations of various editors ruin both the rhythm and the idiom. Ross is in a hurry and breaks off; he begins the next line, "Shall not be long," omitting "I" or "it"—which some editors needlessly restore. In the Folio a colon is used to indicate the breaking off of a sentence in Act V, scene iii, 20.

opinion of it. The Clarendon editors say, "The poet no doubt felt this scene was needed to supplement the meagre parts assigned to Malcolm and Macduff." If this were all, it might be omitted. Actually the Malcolm-Macduff dialogue has at least three functions. Obviously Macduff's audience with Malcolm and the final determination to invade Scotland help on the story, but this is of subordinate importance. It is clear also that Malcolm's suspicion and the long testing of Macduff emphasize the mistrust that has spread from the central evil of the play.[1] But the main purpose of the scene is obscured unless we realize its function as choric commentary. In alternating speeches the evil that Macbeth has caused is explicitly stated, without extenuation. And it is stated impersonally.

> Each new Morne,
> New Widdowes howle, new Orphans cry, new sorowes
> Strike heaven on the face, that it resounds
> As if it felt with Scotland, and yell'd out
> Like Syllable of Dolour.

> Our Country sinkes beneath the yoake,
> It weepes, it bleeds, and each new day a gash
> Is added to her wounds.

> Not in the Legions
> Of horrid Hell, can come a Divell more damn'd
> In evils, to top *Macbeth*.

> I grant him Bloody,
> Luxurious, Avaricious, False, Deceitfull,
> Sodaine, Malicious, smacking of every sinne
> That has a name.

With this approach we see the relevance of Malcolm's self-accusation. He has ceased to be a person. His lines repeat and magnify the evils that have already been attributed to Macbeth, acting as a mirror wherein the ills of Scotland are reflected. And

---

[1] As an example of the slight strands that are gathered into the pattern of the play consider the function of the third Murderer in Act III, scene iii. It seems that Macbeth has sent him "to make security doubly sure." Only after some doubt do the first two decide that the third "needs not their mistrust."

the statement of evil is strengthened by contrast with the opposite virtues, "As Justice, Verity, Temp'rance, Stablenesse."

There is no other way in which the scene can be read. And if dramatic fitness is not sufficient warrant for this approach, we can refer to the pointers that Shakespeare has provided. Macbeth is "luxurious" and "avaricious," and the first sins mentioned by Malcolm in an expanded statement are lust and avarice. When he declares,

> Nay, had I powre, I should
> Poure the sweet Milke of Concord, into Hell,
> Uprore the universall peace, confound
> All unity on earth,

we remember that this is what Macbeth has done.[1] Indeed Macduff is made to answer,

> These Evils thou repeat'st upon thy selfe,
> Hath banish'd me from Scotland.[2]

Up to this point at least the impersonal function of the speaker is predominant. And even when Malcolm, once more a person in a play, announces his innocence, it is impossible not to hear the impersonal overtone:

> For even now
> I put my selfe to thy Direction, and
> Unspeake mine owne detraction. Heere Abjure
> The taints, and blames I laide upon my selfe,
> For strangers to my Nature.

He speaks for Scotland, and for the forces of order. The "scotch'd Snake" will "close, and be her selfe."

There are only two alternatives; either Shakespeare was a bad dramatist, or his critics have been badly misled by mistaking the *dramatis personae* for real persons in this scene. Unless of course the ubiquitous Interpolator has been at work upon it.

---

[1] For a more specific reference see Act IV, scene i, 50-61,—
> Though the treasure
> Of Natures Germaine tumble altogether,
> Even till destruction sicken . . .

[2] "Hath" is third person plural. See Abbott, *Shakespearian Grammar*, §334. I admit the lines are ambiguous but they certainly bear the interpretation I have given them. Indeed most editors print, "upon thyself Have banished . . ."

HOW MANY CHILDREN HAD LADY MACBETH?

I have called *Macbeth* a statement of evil; but it is a statement not of a philosophy but of ordered emotion. This ordering is of course a continuous process (hence the importance of the scrupulous analysis of each line), it is not merely something that happens in the last act corresponding to the dénouement or unravelling of the plot. All the same the interests aroused are heightened in the last act before they are finally "placed," and we are given a vantage point from which the whole course of the drama may be surveyed in retrospect. There is no formula that will describe this final effect. It is no use saying that we are "quietened," "purged" or "exalted" at the end of *Macbeth* or of any other tragedy. It is no use taking one step nearer the play and saying we are purged, etc., because we see the downfall of a wicked man or because we realize the justice of Macbeth's doom whilst retaining enough sympathy for him or admiration of his potential qualities to be filled with a sense of "waste." It is no use discussing the effect in abstract terms at all; we can only discuss it in terms of the poet's concrete realization of certain emotions and attitudes.

At this point it is necessary to return to what I have already said about the importance of images of grace and of the holy supernatural in the play. For the last hundred years or so the critics have not only sentimentalized Macbeth—ignoring the completeness with which Shakespeare shows his final identification with evil—but they have slurred the passages in which the positive good is presented by means of religious symbols. In Act III the banquet scene is immediately [1] followed by a scene in which Lennox and another Lord (both completely impersonal) discuss the situation; the last half of their dialogue is of particular importance. The verse has none of the power of, say, Macbeth's soliloquies, but it would be a mistake to call it undistinguished; it is serenely harmonious, and its tranquillity contrasts with the

---

[1] If we omit Act III, scene v, where for once the editors' "spurious" may be allowed to stand. I thought at first that Shakespeare intended to portray the Witches at this point as rather shoddy creatures, thereby intensifying the general irony. Certainly the rhythm of Hecate's speech is banal—but so is the obvious rhythm of *Sweeney Agonistes*, and it does provide a contrast with the harmony of the verse in the next scene. Certainly also Shakespeare did not intend to portray the Witches as in any way "dignified" ("Dignified, impressive, sexless beings, ministers of fate and the supernatural powers . . . existing in the elemental poetry of wind and storm"—*Macbeth*, Arden Edition, p. xlii). But the verse is too crude to serve even this purpose.

turbulence of the scenes that immediately precede it and follow it, as its images of grace contrast with their "toile and trouble." Macduff has fled to "the pious Edward," "the Holy King," who has received Malcolm "with such grace." Lennox prays for the aid of "some holy Angell,"

> that a swift blessing
> May soone returne to this our suffering Country,
> Under a hand accurs'd.

And the "other Lord" answers, "Ile send my Prayers with him." Many of the phrases are general and abstract—"grace," "the malevolence of Fortune," "his high respect"—but one passage has an individual particularity that gives it prominence:

> That by the helpe of these (with him above
> To ratifie the Worke) we may againe
> Give to our Tables meate, sleepe to our Nights:
> Free from our Feasts, and Banquets bloody knives;
> Do faithful Homage, and receive free Honors,
> All which we pine for now.

Food and sleep, society and the political order are here, as before, represented as supernaturally sanctioned. I have suggested that this passage is recalled for a moment in Lady Macduff's answer to the Murderer (Act IV, scene ii, 80), and it is certainly this theme which is taken up when the Doctor enters after the Malcolm-Macduff dialogue in Act IV, scene iii; the reference to the King's Evil may be a compliment to King James, but it is not merely that. We have only to remember that the unseen Edward stands for the powers that are to prove "the Med'cine of the sickly Weale" of Scotland to see the double meaning in

> there are a crew of wretched Soules
> That stay his Cure. . . .

Their disease "is called the Evill." The "myraculous worke," the "holy Prayers," "the healing Benediction," Edward's "vertue," the "sundry Blessings . . . that speake him full of Grace" are reminders not only of the evil against which Malcolm is seeking support, but of the positive qualities against which the evil and disorder

must be measured. Scattered notes ("Gracious England," "Chris-
tendome," "heaven," "gentle Heavens") remind us of the theme
until the end of the scene, when we know that Macbeth (the
"Hell-Kite," "this Fiend of Scotland")

> Is ripe for shaking, and the Powers above
> Put on their Instruments.

The words quoted are not mere formalities; they have a positive
function, and help to determine the way in which we shall respond to the final scenes.

The description of the King's Evil (Act IV, scene iii, 141-159)
has a particular relevance; it is directly connected with the disease
metaphors of the last Act; [1] and these are strengthened by combining within themselves the ideas of disorder and of the unnatural which run throughout the play. Lady Macbeth's sleep-
walking is a "slumbry agitation," and "a great perturbation in
Nature." Some say Macbeth is "mad." We hear of his "distemper'd cause," and of his "pester'd senses" which

> recoyle and start,
> When all that is within him, do's condemne
> It selfe, for being there.

In the play general impressions are pointed by reference to the
individual and particular (cf. Act IV, scene iii, where "the general
cause" is given precision by the "Fee-griefe due to some single
breast"); whilst at the same time particular impressions are reflected and magnified. Not only Macbeth and his wife but the
whole land is sick. Caithness says,

> Meet we the Med'cine of the sickly Weale,
> And with him poure we in our Countries purge,
> Each drop of us.

And Lennox replies,

---

[1] The original audience would be helped to make the connexion if, as is likely,
the Doctor of Act IV, scene iii, and the Doctor of Act V were played by the same
actor, probably without any change of dress. We are not meant to think of two
Doctors in the play (Dr. A of Harley Street and Dr. B of Edinburgh) but simply,
in each case, of "a Doctor."

> Or so much as it needes,
> To dew the Soveraigne Flower, and drowne the Weeds
> (Act V, scene ii, 27-30)

—an admirable example, by the way, of the kind of fusion already referred to, since we have not only the weed-flower opposition, but a continuation of the medical metaphor in "Soveraigne," which means both "royal" and "powerfully remedial." [1] And the images of health and disease are clearly related to moral good and evil. The Doctor says of Lady Macbeth,

> More needs she the Divine, than the Physitian:
> God, God forgive us all.

Macbeth asks him,

> Can'st thou not Minister to a minde diseas'd,
> Plucke from the Memory a rooted Sorrow,
> Raze out the written troubles of the Braine,
> And with some sweet Oblivious Antidote
> Cleanse the stufft bosome, of that perillous stuffe
> Which weighes upon the heart?

There is terrible irony in his reply to the Doctor's "Therein the Patient must minister to himselfe": "Throw Physicke to the Dogs, Ile none of it."

We have already noticed the association of the ideas of disease and of the unnatural in these final scenes—

> unnatural deeds
> Do breed unnatural troubles,

and there is propriety in Macbeth's highly charged metaphor,

> My way of life
> Is falne into the Seare, the yellow Leafe.

---

[1] Macbeth himself says:
> If thou could'st Doctor, cast
> The Water of my Land, finde her Disease,
> And purge it to a sound and pristine Health,
> I would applaud thee to the very Eccho.

And he continues:
> What Rubarb, Senna, or what Purgative drugge
> Would scowre these English hence?
> (Act V, scene iii, 50-56)

The characteristic reversal (the English forces being represented as an impurity which has to be "scoured") need not surprise us since Macbeth is the speaker.

But the unnatural has now another part to play, in the peculiar "reversal" that takes place at the end of *Macbeth*. Hitherto the agent of the unnatural has been Macbeth. Now it is Malcolm who commands Birnam Wood to move, it is "the good Macduff" who reveals his unnatural birth, and the opponents of Macbeth whose "deere causes" would "excite the mortified man." Hitherto Macbeth has been the deceiver, "mocking the time with fairest show"; now Malcolm orders,

> Let every Souldier hew him downe a Bough,
> And bear't before him, thereby shall we shadow
> The numbers of our Hoast, and make discovery
> **Erre in report of us.**

Our first reaction is to make some such remark as "Nature becomes unnatural in order to rid itself of Macbeth." But this is clearly inadequate; we have to translate it and define our impressions in terms of our response to the play at this point. By associating with the opponents of evil the ideas of deceit and of the unnatural, previously associated solely with Macbeth and the embodiments of evil, Shakespeare emphasizes the disorder and at the same time frees our minds from the burden of the horror. After all, the movement of Birnam Wood and Macduff's unnatural birth have a simple enough explanation.

There is a parallel here with the disorder of the last Act. It begins with Lady Macbeth sleep-walking—a "slumbry agitation" —and the remaining scenes are concerned with marches, stratagems, fighting, suicide, and death in battle. If we merely read the play we are liable to overlook the importance of the sights and sounds which are obvious on the stage. The frequent stage directions should be observed—*Drum and Colours, Enter Malcolm . . . and Soldiers Marching, A Cry within of Women*—and there are continuous directions for *Alarums, Flourishes,* and fighting. Macduff orders,

> Make all our Trumpets speak, give them all breath,
> Those clamorous Harbingers of Blood, and Death,

and he traces Macbeth by the noise of fighting:

> That way the noise is: Tyrant shew thy face.
>   . . . There thou should'st be,
> By this great clatter, one of greatest note
> Seemes bruited.

There are other suggestions of disorder throughout the Act. Macbeth

> cannot buckle his distemper'd cause
> Within the belt of Rule.

He orders, "Come, put mine Armour on," and almost in the same breath, "Pull't off I say." His "Royal Preparation" is a noisy confusion. He wishes "th' estate o' th' world were now undon," though the tone is changed now since he bade the Witches answer him,

> Though bladed Corne be lodg'd and Trees blown downe,
> Though Castles topple on their Warders heads:
> Though Pallaces, and Pyramids do slope
> Their heads to their Foundations.

But all this disorder has now a positive tendency, towards the good which Macbeth had attempted to destroy, and which he names as "Honor, Love, Obedience, Troopes of Friends." At the beginning of the battle Malcolm says,

> Cosins, I hope the dayes are neere at hand
> That Chambers will be safe,

and Menteith answers, "We doubt it nothing." Siward takes up the theme of certainty as opposed to doubt:

> Thoughts speculative, their unsure hopes relate,
> But certaine issue, stroakes must arbitrate,
> Towards which, advance the warre.

And doubt and illusion are finally dispelled:

> Now neere enough:
> Your leavy Skreenes throw downe,
> And shew like those you are.

By now there should be no danger of our misinterpreting the greatest of Macbeth's final speeches.

> To morrow, and to morrow, and to morrow,
> Creepes in this petty pace from day to day,
> To the last syllable of Recorded time.
> And all our yesterdays, have lighted Fooles
> The way to dusty death. Out, out, breefe Candle.
> Life's but a walking Shadow, a poore Player,
> That struts and frets his houre upon the Stage,
> And then is heard no more. It is a Tale
> Told by an Ideot, full of sound and fury
> Signifying nothing.

The theme of the false appearance is revived—with a difference. It is not only that Macbeth sees life as deceitful, but the poetry is so fine that we are almost bullied into accepting an essential ambiguity in the final statement of the play, as though Shakespeare were expressing his own "philosophy" in the lines. But the lines are "placed" by the tendency of the last Act [1] (order emerging from disorder, truth emerging from behind deceit), culminating in the recognition of the Witches' equivocation ("And be these Jugling Fiends no more believ'd . . ."), the death of Macbeth, and the last words of Siward, Macduff and Malcolm (Act V, scene vii, 64-105).

This tendency has behind it the whole weight of the positive values which Shakespeare has already established, and which are evoked in Macbeth's speech—

> My way of life
> Is falne into the Seare, the yellow Leafe,
> And that which should accompany Old-Age,
> As Honor, Love, Obedience, Troopes of Friends,
> I must not looke to have: but in their stead,
> Curses, not lowd but deepe, Mouth-honor, breath
> Which the poore heart would faine deny, and dare not.

Dr. Bradley claims, on the strength of this and the "To morrow, and to morrow" speech, that Macbeth's "ruin is never complete. To the end he never totally loses our sympathy. . . . In the very depths a gleam of his native love of goodness, and with it a tinge of tragic grandeur, rests upon him." But to concentrate attention

---

[1] Contrast the effect of the last words of Mr. Kurtz in *Heart of Darkness*.

thus on the *personal* implications of these lines is to obscure the fact that they have an even more important function as the keystone of the system of values that gives emotional coherence to the play. Certainly those values are likely to remain obscured if we concentrate our attention upon "the two great terrible figures, who dwarf all the remaining characters of the drama," if we ignore the "unexciting" or "undramatic" scenes, or if conventional "sympathy for the hero" is allowed to distort the pattern of the whole.

I must repeat that I have no illusions about the adequacy of these remarks as criticism; they are merely pointers. But if we follow them our criticism at least will not be deflected, by too great a stress upon "personality," into inquiries into "latent motives and policies not avowed," or into pseudo-critical investigations that are only slightly parodied by the title of this essay.

NOTE (See p. 27)

William Richardson illustrates so well the main tendencies of later eighteenth-century criticism that a few quotations seem permissible. (The page references are to the fifth edition, 1797, of the *Essays on Some of Shakespeare's Dramatic Characters* which incorporated his Essays "On Shakespeare's Imitation of Female Characters" and "On the Faults of Shakespeare"):

" 'The operations of the mind,' as has been well observed by an anonymous writer . . . 'are more complex than those of the body: its motions are progressive: its transitions abrupt and instantaneous: its attitude uncertain and momentary. . . . It would therefore be of great importance to philosophical scrutiny, if the position of the mind, in any given circumstances, could be fixed till it was deliberately surveyed: if the causes which alter its feelings and operations could be accurately shewn, and their effects ascertained with precision.' To accomplish these ends, the dramatic writers, and particularly Shakespeare, may be of the greatest use. An attempt has accordingly been made . . . to employ the light which he affords us in illustrating some curious and interesting views of human nature.

"In Macbeth, misled by an overgrown and gradually perverted passion, 'we trace the progress of that corruption, by which the virtues of the mind are made to contribute to the completion of its depravity' [He is quoting Burke]. In Hamlet we have a striking representation of the pain, of the dejection, and contention of spirit, produced in a person, not only of exquisite, but of moral, and correct sensibility, by the conviction of extreme enormity of conduct in those whom he loves, or wishes to love. . . . King Lear illustrates, that mere sensibility, uninfluenced by a sense of propriety, leads men to an extravagant expression both of social and unsocial feelings," and so on (pp. 395-397).

"In the faithful display of character, he has not hitherto been surpassed. . . . If we consider the sentiments and actions, attributed by the poet to his various characters, as so many facts; if we observe their agreement or disagreement, their aim or their origin; and if we class them according to their common qualities . . . we shall ascertain with some accuracy, the truth of the representation. . . . Thus the moralist becomes a critic: and the two sciences of ethics and criticism appear to be intimately and very naturally connected" (pp. 398-399).

The essay on the Character of Macbeth ends: "Thus, by considering the rise and progress of a ruling passion, and the fatal consequences of its indulgence, we have shown how a beneficent mind may become inhuman: and how those who are naturally of an amiable temper, if they suffer themselves to be corrupted, will become more ferocious and more unhappy than men of a constitution originally hard and unfeeling. The formation of our characters depends considerably upon ourselves; for we may improve or vitiate every principle we receive from nature" (p. 68). Shakespeare indeed "furnishes excellent illustrations of many passions and affections, and of many singular combinations of passion, affection and ability" (p. 397).

Mrs. Montagu places character delineation among "the chief purposes of theatrical representation" (*An Essay on the Writings and Genius of Shakespeare,* fifth edition, 1785, pp. 19-20), and speaks of Shakespeare's "invariable attention to consistency of character."

On "The Appreciation of Characters" and "The Psychologizing of Shakespeare" in the later eighteenth century, see Chapters XI and XII of R. W. Babcock's *The Genesis of Shakespeare Idolatry, 1766-1799,* from which I extract some further illuminating quotations:

"We always behold the portrait of living nature [in Shakespeare] and find ourselves surrounded with our fellows"—*The Lady's Magazine,* 1784.

"Shakespeare's characters have that appearance of reality which always has the effect of actual life."—William Jackson, *Thirty Letters,* 1782.

". . . the historical dramas of Shakespeare. The wonder-working power of the poet's pen is there most eminently displayed. . . . His characters . . . are such genuine copies from life, that we must suppose the originals acted and spoke in the manner he represents them."—Richard Hole ["T.O."] in the Exeter Society *Essays,* 1796.

Shakespeare's characters "are masterly copies from nature; differing each from the other, and animated as the originals though correct to a scrupulous precision."—T. Whately, *Remarks on Some of the Characters of Shakespeare,* 1785.

I should like to acknowledge my indebtedness to Mr. Babcock's extremely thorough piece of research.

Chapter Two

SHAKESPEARE'S SONNETS

I

THAT THERE IS so little genuine criticism in the terrifying number of books and essays on Shakespeare's Sonnets can only be partly accounted for by the superior attractiveness of gossip. A more radical explanation is to be found in certain widespread, more or less unconscious assumptions. In the first place, although consciously we may not believe that the Sonnets—even the first hundred and twenty-six—form a continuous and ordered collection, we tend to assume that the collection is more homogeneous than in fact it is, and we tend, therefore, to make rather sweeping generalizations about "The Sonnets" as a whole.[1] A second assumption was made amusingly explicit in the words that John Benson, the publisher of the 1640 edition—who had an eye on changing taste—addressed to the Reader: "In your perusall you shall finde them SEREN, cleere and eligantly plaine, such gentle straines as shall recreate and not perplex your braine, no intricate or cloudy stuffe to puzzell intellect, but perfect eloquence." Many of the Sonnets were written about the time of *A Midsummer Night's Dream* and *Romeo and Juliet;* the verse is therefore essentially unlike the verse of *King Lear*—it is incapable of subtleties; the meaning is on the surface. No doubt this is an exaggeration, but the effects of an assumption not very dissimilar to this can be seen in such essays as keep decently clear of William Hughes the sea cook, and the rest, and that attempt to approach the Sonnets directly, as poetry. George Wyndham, for example, in his essay on "The Poems of Shakespeare" does not entirely confine himself to pointing out the more picturesque aspects of imagery and the melodic effect of certain lines; but his criticism encourages the belief not only that such things have an

[1] The tendency is encouraged by the fact that the Sonnets are printed in a numbered sequence, without titles. And remembering the part played by verbal habit in directing thought, we may consider the effect of the mere repetition of the phrase, "The Sonnets."

intrinsic importance, but that visual imagery, "the music of vowel and consonant" and so on, have much the same function in the Sonnets as they have, say, in Spenser's stanzas on the Bower of Bliss. "Apart from all else, it is the sheer beauty of diction in Shakespeare's Sonnets which has endeared them to poets." Maybe (though they were endeared to Keats and Coleridge for other reasons, and Spenser, we remember, is the Poets' Poet); but the sentence illustrates the kind of limitation that the second assumption imposes: criticism is confined to a surface approach; it remains inappropriately and unnecessarily naïve. It is unfortunate that most readers are familiar with the Sonnets only in modern editions in which, as Laura Riding and Robert Graves pointed out, "the perversely stupid reorganizing of lines and regrouping of ideas"—all in the interests of "clarity"—is achieved by the simple expedient of altering the original punctuation.[1] In the Arden Edition the majority of deviations of this kind are not even recorded in the textual notes. The assumption is thus imposed and perpetuated by the common text.

If we can rid ourselves of these two presuppositions we shall have gone some way towards a revaluation of the Sonnets. "Shakespeare's Sonnets" is a miscellaneous collection of poems, written at different times, for different purposes, and with very different degrees of poetic intensity. (Gildon's edition had the appropriate title, *Poems on Several Occasion*.) The first necessity of criticism is to assess each poem independently, on its merits as poetry, and not to assume too easily that we are dealing with an ordered sequence. The second necessity is to know what kind of *development* to look for—which is a different matter.

I may as well say here that I believe all the Sonnets to be comparatively early in date—roughly from 1592 to 1597 or 1598; none of them is likely to have been written after the second part of *King Henry IV*.[2] We have no means of knowing how they

[1] See their analysis of Sonnet 129 in *A Survey of Modernist Poetry*, pp. 63-81. No one need suppose that, in complaining of wanton "emendations," I am claiming complete infallibility for the Quarto, of which, by the way, there is an admirable facsimile edition published by Noel Douglas at 5s.

[2] "The mortal moon hath her eclipse endur'd" (107)—the only "external reference" of any difficulty—is more likely to refer to the ending of the Queen's climacterical year (1596) than to her death—as Dr. G. B. Harrison has pointed out.

came to be published by Thorpe in 1609 (J. M. Robertson made some attractive guesses), but the evidence suggests that the publication was unauthorized by Shakespeare, that the poems therefore had not been revised for publication, and that the arrangement adopted in the Quarto, except for the grouping of certain Sonnets that obviously go together, has no particular validity; although the printed sequence seems to represent a rough approximation to the time order in which they were composed. The possibility that some of the Sonnets—like *A Lover's Complaint*, which was published with them—are not by Shakespeare is not likely to be disputed on *a priori* grounds by those who are familiar with the habits of contemporary publishers and the fortunes of authors' manuscripts in the sixteenth and seventeenth centuries. (The fate of the MS. of *Astrophel and Stella* is a common instance.) One can point to such things as the seventeenth-century poetical miscellanies with their haphazard assignment of authorship; and Cowley's Preface to the 1656 edition of his Poems begins with some interesting remarks in this connexion. But since there is no room for argument of this kind I assume a high degree of authenticity.

II

I do not of course propose to employ my slender resources in the long-standing Southampton-Pembroke controversy and its subtle ramifications; but the popular view that the Sonnets are in some way "autobiographical" demands some notice. The eloquent chapters in which Frank Harris melts out Shakespeare's personal history from the poetic alloy ("The Sonnets give us the story, the whole terrible, sinful, magical story of Shakespeare's passion") are merely an exotic development of a kind of writing that is common among more eminent critics. "No capable poet," says Dr. Bradley, "much less a Shakespeare, intending to produce a merely 'dramatic' series of poems, would dream of inventing *a story like that of the Sonnets,* or, even if he did, of treating it as they treat it." [1] Now the first point that I wish to make against the common forms of biographical excursion (leaving aside for

[1] I have italicized the phrase that forces the dilemma: *either* autobiographical *or* "merely dramatic" and conventional.

the moment more important considerations) is that the foundations on which they are built have not, to say the least, been the
subject of any very discriminating attention. Those who are unwilling to accept the particular validity of Mr. Eliot's remark
that "the more perfect the artist, the more completely separate in
him will be the man who suffers and the mind which creates; the
more perfectly will the mind digest and transmute the passions
which are its material," backed though it is by the authority of
Coleridge (compare *Biographia Literaria,* XV, 2), have only to
turn to the Sonnets of supposedly highest biographical significance and consider them as examples of personal poetry: that is,
as expressions by a powerful mind of reactions to a situation in
which the man himself is deeply concerned.

Sonnets 33 to 42 are headed by Sir Israel Gollancz "Love's
First Disillusioning," the various sub-titles ending with "Forgiveness." Sonnet 42 runs:

> That thou hast her it is not all my griefe,
> And yet it may be said I lov'd her deerely,
> That she hath thee is of my wayling cheefe,
> A losse in love that touches me more neerely.

Since the obvious is sometimes necessary, we may say that if
Shakespeare had suffered the experience indicated by a prose
paraphrase (for some of the biographical school the Sonnets might
as well have been in prose) it would have affected him very differ-
ently from *this*. The banal movement, the loose texture of the
verse, the vague gestures that stand for emotion, are sufficient
index that his interests are not very deeply involved. (Contrast
the run and ring of the verse, even in minor sonnets, when Shakespeare is absorbed by his subject—"Devouring time blunt thou
the Lyons pawes . . .") His sole interest is in the display of wit,
the working out of the syllogism:

> Loving offendors thus I will excuse yee,
> Thou doost love her, because thou knowst I love her,
> And for my sake even so doth she abuse me,
> Suffering my friend for my sake to approove her,
>
> .   .   .   .   .
>
> But here's the joy, my friend and I are one,
> Sweete flattery, then she loves but me alone.

This, I admit, is a particularly glaring example, though it has its parallels amongst the False Friend and Faithless Mistress sonnets of "Group B" (Numbers 127-152) to which the notes commonly refer us at this point, and the complete insipidity of one "autobiographical" sonnet is enough to cause some honest doubt. Sonnets 78 to 86, dealing with the rival poets, are superior as poetry, but here also it is plain that Shakespeare derived a good deal of pleasure from the neatness of the argument:

> I grant (sweet love) thy lovely argument
> Deserves the travaile of a worthier pen,
> Yet what of thee thy Poet doth invent,
> He robs thee of, and payes it thee againe.

Wyndham remarked that these nine sonnets are "playful throughout, suggesting no tragedy"—though "playful" hardly does them justice. They are rather fine examples of an unusual mode of compliment and complaint, at once courtly and ironic. Those who picture Shakespeare as completely enthralled by his love for a particular friend or patron, and therefore deeply wounded by neglect, can hardly have noticed the tone of critical, and sometimes amused, detachment adopted towards himself ("Cleane starved for a looke"), the rival ("He of tall building and of goodly pride"), and the recipient of his verses ("You to your beautious blessings adde a curse, Being fond on praise, which makes your praises worse").

Of course I do not mean to imply that Shakespeare had never felt love or friendship or exasperation, or that his personal experiences had no effect on his poetry. One can hardly say of the Sonnets, as Johnson said of Cowley's *Mistress*, that "the compositions are such as might have been written for penance by a hermit, or for hire by a philosophical rhymer who had only heard of another sex." I am merely insisting that those who are attracted by biographical speculation should be quite sure of what Shakespeare is doing, of the direction and quality of his interests, before they make a flat translation into terms of actual life: that is, even the biographers must be literary critics. Some of the most interesting and successful sonnets may well have had their context in a personal relationship; but whenever we analyze their interest (further illustration at this point would involve a good deal of repetition later) we find that it lies, not in the general theme or situation, which is all that is relevant to a biographical interpretation, but in various accretions of thought and feeling, in "those frequent witty or profound reflexions, which the poet's ever active mind has deduced from, or connected with, the imagery and the incidents," in the exploration of a mood or discrimination of emotion. If this is so, the attempt to isolate the original stimulus (which in any case *may* have been an imagined situation—"Emotions which the poet has never experienced will serve his turn as well as those familiar to him") is not only hazardous, it is irrelevant. After all, even if Shakespeare had assured us that the Sonnets were written under the stress of a friendship broken and restored and an intrigue with Mary Fitton, the only importance they could have for us would be as poetry, as something *made out of* experience.

With this criterion of importance we can see in proper perspective a second argument—commonly offered as the only alternative to the biographical theory—that the sonnets are exercises on conventional themes, embellished with conventional ornaments. The argument has a place in criticism, and we should be grateful to Sir Sidney Lee for his exhaustive collection of parallels. When we read

> Not marble, nor the guilded monument,
> Of Princes shall out-live this powrefull rime

it is perhaps as well that we should know that the lines have an ancestry reaching back at least as far as Horace; it is as well that we should be familiar with the theme of mutability and the various forms of diluted Platonism that were common when Shakespeare wrote. But a convention is a general thought, a general attitude, or a general mode of presentation, and a discussion of Shakespeare's Sonnets in terms of the "typical" Elizabethan sonnet sequence tells us no more about them than an account of the Revenge Play tells us about *Hamlet*.

III

The most profitable approach to the Sonnets is, it seems to me, to consider them in relation to the development of Shakespeare's blank verse. There are certain obvious difficulties: the Sonnets take their start from something that can, for convenience, be called the Spenserian mode, whereas the influence of Spenser on the early plays is both slighter and more indirect; and the dramatic verse naturally contains a good many elements that are not to be found in any of the sonnets. But it is only by making what may seem an unnecessarily roundabout approach—even then at the risk of over-simplification—that one can hope to shift the stress to those aspects of the Sonnets that it is most profitable to explore.

No account of the development of Shakespeare's blank verse in general terms can be very satisfactory. A comparison will help to point my few necessary generalizations. Richard II's lament at Pomfret is a fairly typical example of the early set speeches:

> And here have I the daintiness of ear
> To check time broke in a disorder'd string;
> But for the concord of my state and time
> Had not an ear to hear my true time broke.
> I wasted time, and now doth time waste me;
> For now hath time made me his numbering clock:
> My thoughts are minutes; and with sighs they jar
> Their watches on unto mine eyes, the outward watch,
> Whereto my finger, like a dial's point,
> Is pointing still, in cleansing them from tears.
> Now sir, the sound that tells what hour it is
> Are clamorous groans, which strike upon my heart,
> Which is the bell: so sighs and tears and groans
> Show minutes, times, and hours: but my time
> Runs posting on in Bolingbroke's proud joy,
> While I stand fooling here, his Jack o' the clock.

The only line that could possibly be mistaken for an extract from a later play is the last, in which the concentrated bitterness ("Jack o' the clock" has a wide range of relevant associations, and the tone introduces a significant variation in the rhythm) serves to emphasize the previous diffuseness. It is not merely that the imagery is elaborated out of all proportion to any complexity of thought or feeling, the emotion is suspended whilst the conceit is developed, as it were, in its own right. Similarly the sound and movement of the verse, the alliteration, repetition and assonance, seem to exist as objects of attention in themselves rather than as the medium of a compulsive force working from within. Such emotion as is communicated is both vague and remote.

Set beside this the well-known speech of Ulysses:

> Time hath, my lord, a wallet at his back,
> Wherein he puts alms for oblivion,
> A great-siz'd monster of ingratitudes:
> Those scraps are good deeds past; which are devour'd
> As fast as they are made, forgot as soon
> As done: perseverance, dear my lord,
> Keeps honour bright: to have done is to hang
> Quite out of fashion, like a rusty mail
> In monumental mockery. Take the instant way;
> For honour travels in a strait so narrow
> Where one but goes abreast: keep then the path;
> For emulation hath a thousand sons
> That one by one pursue: if you give way,
> Or hedge aside from the direct forthright,
> Like to an enter'd tide they all rush by
> And leave you hindmost.

The verse of course is much more free, and the underlying speech movement gives a far greater range of rhythmic subtlety. The sound is more closely linked with—is, in fact, an intimate part of—the meaning. The imagery changes more swiftly. But these factors are only important as contributing to a major development: the main difference lies in the greater immediacy and concreteness of the verse. In reading the second passage more of the mind is involved, and it is involved in more ways. It does not contemplate a general emotion, it *lives* a particular experience. Crudely, the reader is not told that there is a constant need for action, he experiences a particular urgency.

This account could be substantiated in detail, but for my purpose it may be sufficient to point to a few of the means by which the reader is influenced in this way. Oblivion, at first a kind of negative presence, becomes (via "monster") an active, devouring force, following hard on the heels of time. ("Forgot," balancing "devoured," keeps the image in a proper degree of subordination.) The perseverance that keeps honour bright introduces a sense of effort, as in polishing metal, and (after a particularly effective jibe at inactivity) the effort is felt as motion. Moreover, "Take the instant way" and "keep then the path," involving muscular tension, suggest the strain of keeping foremost. In the next two lines the roar and clatter of emulation's thousand sons are audible, and immediately we feel the pressure of pursuit ("hedge aside" is no dead metaphor) and—in the movement of the verse, as though a dam had broken—the overwhelming tide of pursuers. The short and exhausted line, "And leave you hindmost," is the lull after the wave has passed.

This line of development, continued in the plays of complete maturity, is central. Primarily it is a matter of technique—the words have a higher potency, they release and control a far more complex response than in the earlier plays—but it is much more than that. The kind of immediacy that I have indicated allows the greatest subtlety in particular presentment (The thing "which shackles accidents, and bolts up change" is *not* the same as "The deed which puts an end to human vicissitude"), whilst "the quick flow and the rapid change of the images," as Coleridge noted, require a "perpetual activity of attention on the part of the reader," generate, we may say, a form of activity in which thought and feeling are fused in a new mode of apprehension. That is, the technical development implies—is dependent on—the development and unification of sensibility. It is this kind of development (in advance of the dramatic verse of the same period in some respects and obviously behind it in others) that we find in the Sonnets, and that makes it imperative that discussion should start from considerations of technique.

Those aspects of technique that can to some extent be isolated as showing "the first and most obvious excellence . . . the sense of musical delight" have been well illustrated by George Wyndham, but his belief that "Eloquent Discourse" is "the staple of the Sonnets and their highest excellence" precludes the more important approach.

After 1579 the most pervasive influence on Elizabethan lyric poetry was that of Spenser. *Astrophel and Stella* may have been the immediate cause of the numerous sonnet cycles, but it was from Spenser that the sonneteers derived many of their common characteristics—the slow movement and melody, the use of imagery predominantly visual and decorative, the romantic glamour, the tendency towards a gently elegiac note. In the Spenserian mode no object is sharply forced upon the consciousness.

> Of mortall life the leafe, the bud, the floure,
> Ne more doth flourish after first decay,
> That earst was sought to decke both bed and bowre,
> Of manie a Ladie, and many a Paramoure:
> Gather therefore the Rose, whilest yet is prime . . .

As music this is perfect and one is forced to admire; but one is only mildly affected by the vision of the passage of time, and even the injunction to pluck the rose has no urgency. Now there is in Shakespeare's Sonnets a quality that, at a first reading, seems very near to this: Sonnets 98 and 102, for example, are successful as fairly direct developments of the Spenserian mode. But if we turn to Sonnet 35 we see the conjunction of that mode with something entirely new.

> No more bee greev'd at that which thou hast done,
> Roses have thornes, and silver fountaines mud,
> Cloudes and eclipses staine both Moone and Sunne,
> And loathsome canker lives in sweetest bud.
> All men make faults, and even I in this,
> Authorizing thy trespas with compare,
> My selfe corrupting salving thy amisse,
> Excusing thy sins more then thy sins are:
> For to thy sensuall fault I bring in sence,
> Thy adverse party is thy Advocate,
> And gainst my selfe a lawfull plea commence,
> Such civill war is in my love and hate,
> That I an accessary needs must be,
> To that sweet theefe which sourely robs from me.

The first four lines we may say, both in movement and imagery, are typically Spenserian and straightforward. The fifth line begins by continuing the excuses, "All men make faults," but with an abrupt change of rhythm Shakespeare turns the generalization against himself: "All men make faults, and even I in this," i.e. in wasting my time finding romantic parallels for your sins, as though intellectual analogies ("sence") were relevant to your sensual fault. The painful complexity of feeling (Shakespeare is at the same time tender towards the sinner and infuriated by his own tenderness) is evident in the seventh line, which means both "I corrupt myself when I find excuses for you" (or "when I comfort myself in this way") and "I'm afraid I myself make you worse by excusing your faults"; and although there is a fresh change of tone towards the end (the twelfth line is virtually a sigh as he gives up hope of resolving the conflict), the equivocal "needs must" and the sweet-sour opposition show the continued civil war of the emotions.

Some such comment as this was unavoidable, but it is upon the simplest and most obvious of technical devices that I wish to direct attention. In the first quatrain the play upon the letters *s* and *l* is mainly musical and decorative, but with the change of tone and direction the alliterative *s* becomes a hiss of half-impotent venom:

> All men make faults, and even I in this,
> Authorizing thy trespas with compare,
> My selfe corrupting salving thy amisse,
> Excusing thy sins more then thy sins are:
> For to thy sensuall fault I bring in sence . . .

The scorn is moderated here, but it is still heard in the slightly rasping note of the last line,

> To that sweet theefe which sourely robs from me.

From the fifth line, then, the alliteration is functional: by playing off against the comparative regularity of the rhythm it expresses an important part of the meaning, and helps to carry the experience alive into the mind of the reader. With Spenser or Tennyson in mind we should say that both alliteration and assonance were primarily musical devices, as indeed they are in many of the Sonnets:

> Noe longer mourne for me when I am dead,
> Than you shall heare the surly sullen bell
> Give warning to the world that I am fled
> From this vile world with vildest wormes to dwell.

Here, for example, the sound, if not independent of the meaning, usurps a kind of attention that is incompatible with a full and sharp awareness. But that which links the Sonnets, in this respect, with the later plays is the use of assonance and alliteration to secure a heightened awareness, an increase of life and power:

> Your love and pity doth the impression fill,
> Which vulgar scandall stampt upon my brow.

> Cheared and checkt even by the self-same skie.

> All this the world well knowes yet none knowes well.

> So shall I taste
> At first the very worst of fortune's might.

> And made myselfe a motley to the view.

In reading the last line the nose wrinkles in disgust, and we hear the rattle of the fool,—but I hope the reader will be inclined to look up the examples in their context (112, 15, 129, 90, and 110 respectively).

A slight shift of attention brings into focus a second aspect of development connected with the first. If we open any of the great plays almost at random we find effects comparable in kind to this, from *Lear*:

> Crown'd with rank fumiter and furrow-weeds,
> With hor-docks, hemlocks, nettles, cuckoo-flowers,
> Darnel, and all the idle weeds that grow
> In our sustaining corn.

The rank and bristling profusion of the weeds is there, in the clogged movement of the first two lines, whilst the unimpeded sweep of the verse that follows contributes powerfully to the image of never-failing fertility. In many of the Sonnets we can see Shakespeare working towards this use of his medium, learning to use a subtly varied play of the speech rhythm and movement against the formal pattern of the verse:

> Ah yet doth beauty like a Dyall hand,
> Steale from his figure, and no pace perceiv'd.

> And on just proofe surmise, accumilate.

> Then hate me when thou wilt, if ever, now,
> Now while the world is bent my deeds to crosse . . .

> That it could so preposterouslie be stain'd . . .

In the steady movement of the first extract, in the slightly impeded progress of the second,[1] in the impetuous movement of the third, and the rising incredulity of the fourth, the verse (if I may borrow the phrase) "enacts the meaning." Perhaps one can hardly miss this kind of effect, but a development connected with it—the use of speech movement and idiom in the Sonnets to obtain a firmer command of tone (a matter of some importance in determining their meaning)—seems to have been fairly consistently overlooked. The sonnet form is a convention in which it is only too easy to adopt a special "poetic" attitude, and to the four "strong promises of the strength of Shakespeare's genius" which Coleridge found in the early poems might well be added a fifth: the way in which, in his Sonnets, he broke away from the formal and incantatory mode (conventions and precedent being what they were) to make the verse a more flexible and transparent medium. Sonnet 7 has a typically stylized opening:

> Loe in the Orient when the gracious light,
> Lifts up his burning head, each under eye
> Doth homage to his new appearing sight,
> Serving with lookes his sacred majesty.

Contrast, say, Sonnet 82:

> I grant thou wert not married to my Muse,
> And therefore maiest without attaint ore-looke

---

[1] "Surmise" is object to the imperative "accumilate"; the separating comma seems unnecessary.

> The dedicated words which writers use
> Of their faire subject, blessing every booke.

In the first line we hear the inflexion of the speaking voice, and it is the conversational movement that contributes the equivocal note of amused irony, directed towards the fulsome dedications and their—inevitably—fair subject. (Compare the "precious phrase by all the Muses filed" of Sonnet 85.) Sometimes a similar effect is used for deliberate contrast, as in

> Thus have I had thee as a dreame doth flatter,
> In sleepe a King, but waking no such matter,

where after a line and a half of yearning the offhand colloquialism shows us Shakespeare detached and critical. It is of course only by exploiting speech movement that any kind of delicacy of statement is possible (reservation is an obvious case, as in "I found —or thought I found—you did exceed . . ."), but it is the fairly frequent use of various ironic inflexions that it seems particularly important to stress:

> He nor that affable familiar ghost
> Which nightly gulls him with intelligence . . .

> Farewell thou art too deare for my possessing,
> And like enough thou knowst thy estimate . . .

—and there are other examples more or less immediately apparent.[1] To be alive to modulations of this kind is to recognize— which is what one would expect—that the *intelligence* that created, say, *Troilus and Cressida,* is also at work in the Sonnets.

I have already suggested that the critics who reconstruct a Shakespeare hopelessly and uncritically subjugated by a particular experience must be quite deaf to variations of tone. It is the same incapacity which causes them to read the Sonnets in which the touch is lightest with portentous solemnity and to perform various feats of legerdemain with the meaning. In Sonnet 94 the irony is serious and destructive.

[1] Of course the tone is not determined solely by the movement; often, for example, the degree of seriousness with which Shakespeare is writing is indicated by the imagery. Consider the roses of Sonnet 99 which "fearefully on thornes did stand," or the poet's thousand groans, "one on anothers necke," in Sonnet 131.

They that have powre to hurt, and will doe none,
That doe not do the thing, they most do showe,
Who moving others, are themselves as stone,
Unmooved, could, and to temptation slow:
They rightly do inherit heavens graces,
And husband natures ritches from expence,
They are the Lords and owners of their faces,
Others, but stewards of their excellence:
The sommers flowre is to the sommer sweet,
Though to itselfe, it onely live and die,
But if that flowre with base infection meete,
The basest weed out-braves his dignity:
    For sweetest things turne sowrest by their deedes,
    Lillies that fester, smell far worse then weeds.

This is commonly taken with Sonnet 95 and read as an exhortation to chastity—"'Tis a sign of greatness to be self-contained" is Gollancz's summary, and J. Q. Adams glosses: "The friend has fallen into a life of gross sensuality, and the poet finds it necessary to rebuke him in the strongest language." If nothing else, "Lillies that fester" (an image suggesting less the excesses of sensuality than "the distortions of ingrown virginity") might cast some doubts on this simple interpretation. The opening is coldly analytic (I at least am unable to detect any symptoms of moral fervour), and the unprepossessing virtues of those "who moving others, are themselves as stone" can hardly be held up for admiration; they remind us rather of Angelo, "whose blood was very snow-broth." If we remember Shakespeare's condemnation, in the early Sonnets, of those who husband their riches instead of acting as stewards of their excellence, we shall hardly be able to mistake the second quatrain for unambiguous praise; in any case the image suggested by "They are the Lords and owners of their faces" is unobtrusively comic, and the comma after "Others" suggests that Shakespeare is ironically repeating the opinion of the self-righteous. The Sonnet may have been intentionally equivocal, but there can be little doubt of Shakespeare's attitude—it is the attitude of *Measure for Measure*—and the poem (though not altogether successful) forms an interesting complement to the more famous Sonnet 129. Perhaps I had better add that I do not regard the earlier sonnet as an encouragement to incontinence.

The vivid and surprising "Lillies that fester" has been commented upon as typically Shakespearean, and indeed the image, whether borrowed or not, is typical of the way in which contrasted sets of associations are fused in the verse of the later plays. But it is hardly representative of the imagery of the Sonnets. In the later plays a wide range of relevant associations, both of thought and feeling ("relevant" being clearly a matter for specific illustration), are compressed into a single image ("The bank and shoal of time"). Images of sight, touch, muscular adjustment and so on follow in rapid succession (no catalogue of "visual," "tactile," etc., is sufficient to cover the variety), and different modes may be combined in our response at any one point. And there are those unexpected and startling juxtapositions of contrasted images:

> The *crown* o' the earth doth *melt*.

> This sensible warm *motion* to become
> A kneaded *clod*.

Now in the Sonnets not all of these characteristic uses of imagery are developed: it is largely this which justifies us in assigning them a date earlier than *Troilus and Cressida* or *Measure for Measure*. With the exception of the striking line, "Mine appetite I never more will grind On newer proof," we can find no parallels to "Lillies that fester." Such lines as

> Gor'd mine own thoughts . . .

and

> To bitter sawces did I frame my feeding

indicate an important line of development, but there is little of the intensely physical impact that we find in *Macbeth* ("The blanket of the dark," "We'd jump the life to come"). Most of the images—even when finely effective—arouse only one set of vibrations in the mind:

> Full many a glorious morning have I seene,
> Flatter the mountaine tops with soveraine eie

> My nature is subdu'd
> To what it workes in, like the Dyers hand.

If we place "the dust and injury of age" (108) and ". . . whose million'd accidents Creep in 'twixt vows . . ." (115) beside Macbeth's

> Tomorrow, and tomorrow, and tomorrow,
> Creeps in this petty pace from day to day . . .
> And all our yesterdays have lighted fools
> The way to dusty death

and ask ourselves exactly why "creep" and "dust" are used in each instance, we shall have a fair measure of the later development.

But even when we have made these qualifications the stress remains on the positive achievement; there is a clear advance on the early plays. In the Sonnets no image is *merely* decorative, as in Romeo's "Two of the fairest stars in all heaven . . ." Few are excessively developed, as in the laments of Richard II or even as in the Bastard's "Commodity, the bias of the world . . ." There is indeed a constant succession of varied images, which, because they are concrete and because they are drawn from the world of familiar experience, give precise expression to emotion:

> Beated and chopt with tand antiquitie.
>
> Incertenties now crowne them-selves assur'de.
>
> But makes antiquitie for aye his page.
>
> And captive-good attending Captaine ill.

What it comes to is this: in the Sonnets, as in the later plays, the imagery gives immediacy and precision, and it demands and fosters an alert attention. But the range of emotions liberated by any one image is narrower, though not always less intense. We have not yet reached the stage in which "the *maximum* amount of apparent incongruity is resolved simultaneously." [1] That is, the creating mind has not yet achieved that co-ordination of widely diverse (and, in the ordinary mind, often conflicting) experiences which is expressed in the imagery no less than in the total structure of the great tragedies. Put in this way the conclusion may

---

[1] The phrase is Edgell Rickword's (*Towards Standards of Criticism,* ed. F. R. Leavis, p. 120).

seem obvious, but it is a point to which I shall have to return when I deal with Shakespeare's treatment of the Time theme in the Sonnets.

A complete account of technical development in the Sonnets would include a detailed discussion of ambiguity—a technical device (if we may call it that) of which, since the publication of Mr. Empson's *Seven Types* and the Riding and Graves analysis of Sonnet 129, one can hardly fail to be aware; though the word seems to have caused some unnecessary critical shyness. But the argument would raise fundamental issues with which I do not feel competent to deal, and all that I have to offer—after a very brief indication of the way in which the language of the Sonnets is "charged" by means of overlaying meanings—is some caution.

There is a clear difference between the kind of compression that we find in "The steepe up heavenly hill" (7), "The world without end houre" (57), or "Th'imprison'd absence of your libertie" (58), and in such lines as "So thou, thy selfe out-going in thy noon" (7), or "That I have frequent binne with unknown mindes" (117). The first three are forms of elliptical construction requiring no unusual agility in the mind accustomed to English idiom. In the last two the context demands that we shall keep two or more meanings in mind simultaneously: "thy selfe out-going" means both "over-reaching yourself" and "you yourself going further on"; "unknown mindes" are "strangers," "nonentities," and perhaps "such minds as I am ashamed to mention" (the Arden Edition gives precedents for all these interpretations). In the same way as two or more meanings are fused in one word, different constructions may be run together, as in

> None else to me, nor I to none alive,
> That my steel'd sence or changes right or wrong. (112)

or they may be overlaid:

> My selfe corrupting salving thy amisse (35)

There can, I think, be no doubt that Shakespeare deliberately (though "deliberately" may be too strong a word) avails himself of the resources of the language in this way; I have chosen what seem to be the most incontrovertible examples, and they are clearly in line with his later development. In Sonnet 40 and one or two others we have something very like conscious experimenting with simple forms of ambiguous statement.

Now the important point is this: that when ambiguity occurs in successful verse it is valuable in much the same way as successful imagery is valuable, as representing a heightened, more inclusive and more unified form of consciousness. One need hardly say that the mere presence of ambiguities is not necessarily an indication of poetic value—they may equally represent unresolved contradictions in the poet's mind—or that the estimate of success is a more delicate matter (concerned with the whole poetic effect) than the working-out of alternative meanings. There is no need for me to praise Mr. Empson, though I may say that he is the only critic I know of who has detected the equivocal attitude which Shakespeare sometimes expresses towards his subject, and that some of his analyses (of Sonnet 58, for example) seem to me immediately convincing. But in perhaps the majority of cases (I am confining my attention entirely to the pages he devotes to the Sonnets [1]) his lists of meanings seem to me to be obtained by focussing upon a part of the poem, almost one might say by forgetting the poem, and considering the various grammatical possibilities of the part so isolated. His analysis of Sonnet 83, for example (pp. 168-175), is valuable as suggesting the conscious and subliminal meanings that may well have been in Shakespeare's mind at the time of writing, but only a few of them are there, in the poem. It is very unfair to make this charge without substantiating it in detail, but to do so would add many pages to the already excessive length of this essay; I can only hope that the reader will look up the analysis for himself—and my account of Sonnet 123, below, is relevant here. Mr. Eliot has remarked that the Sonnets are "full of some stuff that the writer could not drag to light, contemplate, or manipulate into art." [2] The sentence might be taken by the biographers to refer to an especially painful personal experience lying behind the Sonnets. But it suggests

[1] *Seven Types of Ambiguity*, pp. 65-78 and 168-175.
[2] *Selected Essays*, p. 144.

more profitable speculation if we interpret it *in the first place* as meaning that Shakespeare had not yet fully mastered the technique of complex expression.

IV

These imperfect considerations of technique will perhaps have been sufficient to establish the main point, that in the Sonnets, within the limitations of the imposed form, Shakespeare is working towards the maturity of expression of the great plays. But having said this we need to remind ourselves of two things. (The prevailing conception of technique as having something to do with the place of the caesura and hypermetric feet may justify the repetition.) The first is that the kind of technical development that we have been discussing is in itself an attempt to become more fully conscious (just as Spenser's technique is a method of exclusion), an attempt to secure more delicate discrimination and adjustment. The second is that technique does not function in a vacuum, it can only develop as the servant of an inner impulse. I shall conclude this essay by pointing to one or two of the major interests that lie behind the Sonnets.

I have already said that I do not think "The Sonnets" in any sense an ordered collection; they vary from the most trivial of occasional verses to poems in which a whole range of important emotions is involved, and in the latter we find in embryo many of the themes of the later plays; there is variety enough to make discussion difficult. But it seems to me that two interests predominate, making themselves felt, often, beneath the ostensible subject: they cannot be altogether disentangled from each other or from other interests, and they are not quite the same in kind; but the artificial grouping seems unavoidable. One is the exploration, discrimination and judgment of modes of being—attention consciously directed towards the kind of integration of personality that is implied by the development of technique. The second is an overwhelming concern with Time.

The first of these is not only expressed directly. Sonnet 30 is one of those concerned with "Friendship in Absence":

74

SHAKESPEARE'S SONNETS

When to the Sessions of sweet silent thought,
I summon up remembrance of things past,
I sigh the lack of many a thing I sought,
And with old woes new waile my deare times waste;
Then can I drowne an eye (un-us'd to flow)
For precious friends hid in deaths dateles night,
And weepe afresh loves long since canceld woe,
And mone th' expense of many a vannisht sight.

 .   .   .   .   .

But if the while I thinke on thee (deare friend)
All losses are restord, and sorrowes end.

The Sonnet seems to be an early one, but even here beneath the
main current of elegiac emotion (the tribute to friendship is
gracefully conventional) there is a counter-current of irony directed by the poet towards himself. In the eighth line Shakespeare
is conscious that the present moan, like the sighs [sights] previously expended, involves a fresh expense ("Every sigh shortens
life"), so that the line means, "I waste my time and energy regret-
ting the time and energy wasted in regrets"; and the slight over-
emphasis of the third quatrain adds to the irony. In other words
Shakespeare is aware of what he is doing (after all, "sessions" implies judgment), and therefore achieves a more stable equilibrium. This is a minor example, but the implicit self-criticism is
pervasive (we may compare the previous Sonnet: "Yet in these
thoughts myself almost despising"); and—although the poem
quoted is far enough from anything by Donne or Marvell—the
constant reference of the immediate emotion to a mature scale
of values reminds us that Shakespeare—Nature's Darling—is not
far removed from the Tradition of Wit.

In many of the Sonnets ostensibly concerned with a personal
relationship we find there is something of far greater interest to
Shakespeare than the compliments, complaints and pleas that
provide the occasion of writing. Sonnet 110 is in the form of a
plea for the restoration of friendship:

Alas 'tis true, I have gone here and there,
And made my selfe a motley to the view,
Gor'd mine owne thoughts, sold cheap what is most dear,
Made old offences of affections new.

75

Most true it is, that I have lookt on truth
Asconce and strangely: But by all above,
These blenches gave my heart an other youth,
And worse essaies prov'd thee my best of love,
Now all is done, have what shall have no end,
Mine appetite I never more will grin'de
On newer proofe, to trie an older friend,
A God in love, to whom I am confin'd.
    Then give me welcome, next my heaven the best,
    Even to thy pure and most most loving brest.

There can be no doubt that here the most powerful lines are those recording self-disgust,[1] and that there is a drop in intensity when Shakespeare turns to address the friend directly, as in the final couplet. The Sonnet is important as a direct approach to sincerity—it records the examination and integration of character. Indeed in many of the Sonnets in which the friend is given something more than perfunctory recognition it is hard to resist the conclusion that Shakespeare is addressing his own conscience.

You are my All the world, and I must strive,
To know my shames and praises from your tounge,
None else to me, nor I to none alive,
That my steel'd sence or changes right or wrong,
In so profound Abisme I throw all care
Of others voyces, that my Adders sence,
To cryttick and to flatterer stopped are . . .

—"Like the deaf adder that stoppeth her ear; which will not hearken to the voice of charmers, charming never so wisely." The reference is important; in the Sonnets Shakespeare is working out a morality based on his own finest perceptions and deepest impulses.[2] Sonnet 121, which has caused a good deal of perplexity, seems to me mainly a protest against any rigidly imposed moral scheme, a protest on behalf of a morality based on the nature of

[1] To take the first three lines as referring merely to the profession of actor and playwright is too narrow an interpretation; the reference seems to be to the way in which a sensitive intelligence has displayed its wares of wit and observation in common intercourse.

[2] "But we have to know ourselves pretty thoroughly before we can break the automatism of ideals and conventions. . . . Only through fine delicate knowledge can we recognize and release our impulses."—*Fantasia of the Unconscious*, p. 60.

the writer. But that morality can only be discussed in terms that the poetry supplies.

An essay might well be written on the Time theme in Shakespeare. Starting from an examination of *King Henry IV, Troilus and Cressida* and the Sonnets, it would illuminate some important aspects of Shakespeare's genius and of the Elizabethan mind. But before discussing Shakespeare's handling of this theme some distinctions must be made.

In the Sonnets Shakespeare's interest in the passage of time and the allied themes of death and mutability is sufficiently obvious. Not only does it provide the main theme of many of the more important Sonnets, it continually encroaches on other interests and overshadows them. And there is a clear difference in intensity, tone and treatment between Shakespeare's "Time" sonnets and other Elizabethan poems dealing with "Time's thievish progress to eternity"; between

> When I consider everything that growes
> Holds in perfection but a little moment (15)

or

> Like as the waves make towards the pibled shore . . . (60)

and such typically Elizabethan things as

> In time the strong and stately turrets fall,
> In time the rose and silver lilies die,
> In time the monarchs captive are, and thrall,
> In time the sea and rivers are made dry

or

> Soon doth it fade that makes the fairest flourish,
> Short is the glory of the blushing rose

or anything to be found in Spenser's Mutability Cantos.

Now "the problem of Time" is a metaphysical problem, and in various forms it is a preoccupation of some of the Metaphysical Poets. Moreover between Shakespeare's mature verse and Donne's there are similarities which it is important to recognize—the immediacy, the images generating intense mental activity ("the intellect at the tip of the senses"), the exploiting of speech rhythm and idiom, and so on: a good deal of Mr. Eliot's account of Metaphysical Poetry applies equally—as he points out—to the blank verse of Shakespeare and other late Elizabethans. This being so, it is all the more important to stress that in the Sonnets "the problem of Time" is not a metaphysical problem at all,—and the discussion of Platonic Forms and Ideal Beauty is irrelevant. Wherever we look, Shakespeare is concerned merely with the *effects* of time on animate and inanimate beings, on persons and personal relationships. As a poet, he reports and evaluates experiences, but he does not attempt to *explain* them, nor do they arouse speculation in his mind. So, too, the plays "explain" nothing; they are experiences to be lived. Indeed if Time had presented itself to Shakespeare as a metaphysical problem it could not have been dealt with in the verse of the Sonnets. Mr. James Smith has made a necessary distinction.[1] He points out that "verse properly called metaphysical is that to which the impulse is given by an overwhelming concern with metaphysical problems; with problems either deriving from, or closely resembling in the nature of their difficulty, the problem of the Many and the One," and that in Metaphysical Poetry it is the conflict arising out of the perception of such problems that is resolved by means of the metaphysical conceit, in which there is both unity and "high strain or tension, due to the sharpness with which its elements are opposed." Shakespeare's imagery in the Sonnets, as I have pointed out, rarely involves a high degree of tension; and when, in the later plays, we find images that not only possess richness of association but embrace conflicting elements, those elements are invariably drawn from experience and sensation, never from speculative thought: they make finer experience available for others, but they offer no resolution of metaphysical problems.

The temptation to look for the development of a metaphysical mode in the Sonnets is not perhaps very common. A second temptation has not proved so easy to resist, and most accounts of the Sonnets point to certain of them as showing "Love's Triumph over Time," without bothering to explain what this may mean.

---

[1] "The Metaphysical Note in Poetry" in *Determinations*.

Certainly, if we isolate those sonnets in which a reaction to the passage of time and the inevitability of death provides the main emotional drive it is permissible to look for a coherently developing attitude culminating in a solution that shall be at least emotionally satisfying. There is an obvious advance in maturity, an increasing delicacy in exposition, but unless we are prepared to accept assertion as poetry (that is, bare statement deliberately willed, instead of the communication in all its depth, fullness and complexity, of an experience that has been lived) we shall not find that solution in the Sonnets. An example may make my meaning clearer. Sonnet 123 is commonly taken to show that "Love conquers Time":

> No! Time, thou shalt not bost that I doe change,
> Thy pyramyds buylt up with newer might
> To me are nothing novell, nothing strange,
> They are but dressings of a former sight:
> Our dates are breefe, and therefor we admire,
> What thou dost foyst upon us that is ould,
> And rather make them borne to our desire,
> Then thinke that we before have heard them tould:
> Thy registers and thee I both defie,
> Not wondring at the present, nor the past,
> For thy records, and what we see doth lye,
> Made more or les by thy continuall hast:
>   This I doe vow and this shall ever be,
>   I will be true dispight thy syeth and thee.

It is upon the ambiguity of the first two quatrains that I wish to direct attention. *Sense 1:* "Time cannot make his boast that I change with his passage. The admired wonders of modern architecture are not novelties to me (since my conscious self is, in a sense, outside time); I have seen them all before, and I know that the modern examples are only variations on the old. Man's life is short; therefore he tends to wonder at things, foisted upon him by Time as novelties, which are really old, preferring to believe them newly created for his satisfaction [born to our desire] than to see them truly as repetitions of the old." *Sense 2* (Wyndham's interpretation): "Time cannot boast that I change. The pyramids —built with a skill that was new compared with my age-old self [with newer might to me]—were, I saw, no novelties even in ancient Egypt, but merely dressings of a former sight. Man's life is short; therefore he tends to wonder at the antiquities foisted upon him by Time, preferring to accept as absolute the limitations imposed by birth and death [to make them (dates) the bourn to his desire] than to think that the years of his life have been counted [told] before." A rough paraphrase of the last six lines is: "I refuse to accept as ultimate truth either history (recording that time has passed) or the present passage of time; neither novelty nor antiquity move me; the evidence of universal change given by history and the present time is false: only in appearance are past and present governed by time. I vow that I will be myself (and—perhaps—true to some person) in spite of death and time."

The purpose of the Sonnet is clear: to affirm the continuous identity of the self in spite of the passage of time. But, though a remarkable achievement, its failure is indicated by the unresolved ambiguity. That *Sense 1* is intended seems clear from line 10—"Not wondering *at the present,* nor the past"—as well as from the Elizabethan use of the word "pyramids"; and even if we do away with the maladroit pun on "borne" by interpreting it as "bourn" in *Sense 1* as well as in *Sense 2* (and I find it impossible to exclude the meaning "born to our desire") we are left with "that is old" fitting awkwardly into the first interpretation. Moreover—and perhaps it is more important to notice this than the conflicting meanings which somehow refuse to resolve themselves into unity —the poem *asserts* rather than expresses a resolved state of mind: "Thou shalt not boast," "I defy," "This I do vow," "I will be true."

In the manner of its assertion the Sonnet is in line with the more famous Sonnet 116 ("Love's not time's fool")—a poem of which the difficulties have never, I think, been squarely faced— and with those sonnets promising some form of immortality. And, we may remark in conclusion, in all the Sonnets of this last type, it is the contemplation of change, not the boasting and defiance, that produces the finest poetry; they draw their value entirely from the evocation of that which is said to be defied or triumphed over. In the plays—from *Henry IV* to *The Tempest*—in which the theme of Time occurs, there is no defiance; the conflict is resolved by the more or less explicit acceptance of mutability.[1] I should like to give this remark precision in terms of literary criticism by examining the second part of *King Henry IV*, a play of which the prelude is spoken by the dying Hotspur towards the end of Part I:

> But thought's the slave of life, and life time's fool . . .

But perhaps enough has been said to show that, in this respect as in all others, the Sonnets yield their proper significance only when seen in the context of Shakespeare's development as a dramatist.

[1] An acceptance, I should now (1944) add, that comes to be closely associated with the complementary recognition of new life and of values that are not subject to time. This has been admirably brought out by D. A. Traversi's *Approach to Shakespeare*, which also shows the essential continuity of development—a continuity of developing experience—between the Sonnets and the greater plays.

Chapter Three

PRINCE HAMLET

IT IS OFTEN NECESSARY for the reader of Shakespeare to remind himself that "Shakespearean Tragedy" is not all of one kind. In *Macbeth,* for example, the speeches of the protagonists refer not merely inwards to a hypothetical "character" behind them, but outward to the pattern of the play as a whole in which "character" is subordinate and often irrelevant. In *Othello,* on the other hand, the hero's character—in so far as we are intended to be aware of it, and we are aware of it only through the poetry— emerges from the pattern, and interest is centred there. In this respect, as in so many others, *Hamlet* is a difficult play to feel sure of; but it seems to me that here we are required, more explicitly and more continuously than in *Macbeth,* or *Lear* or *Antony and Cleopatra,* to be aware of, and therefore to assess, a particular state of mind and feeling embodied in the dramatic figure of the hero. The purpose of these notes is to suggest that most critical judgments concerning Prince Hamlet have ignored or misinterpreted some important parts of the evidence.

Recent criticism of *Hamlet,* recognizing the stubborn way in which the play resists attempts at consistent interpretation, has made much of the historical method of approach. We now know a good deal about the conventions of malcontent and revenge plays on the one hand and about the social background of late Elizabethan melancholy on the other; and we think we know something of the difficulties Shakespeare had to face in re-working a play already familiar to his audience.[1] But the accumulated knowledge of the context of the play, though it has corrected some obvious errors, has made remarkably little difference in the current estimate of the hero, which remains substantially the Romantic estimate. Thus Professor Dover Wilson, the play's latest learned editor, assures us that *Hamlet* is "a study of genius," and that the Prince is "the most adorable of heroes." "Shake-

[1] See J. M. Robertson, *The Problem of Hamlet,* and L. Schücking, *The Meaning of Hamlet* (tr. Graham Rawson).

speare asks every spectator, every reader, to *sympathize* with his hero, to feel with him, to place himself in his shoes." [1]

How far we are invited to sympathize with Hamlet is at least a debatable question, but I can find no evidence at all for the first of Professor Dover Wilson's assertions and little enough for the second. Hamlet's speeches, it is true, have at times a bookish flavour, and the range of his thoughts is often suggested though never demonstrated, but neither a familiarity with books nor a habit of philosophic musing is sufficient to rank a man as a genius. There is, it is true, considerable evidence of superior mental agility, expressing itself in wit and satire. But Hamlet's wit—and this seems the critical observation to start from—is of a peculiar and limited kind. With very few exceptions it is entirely destructive, malicious and sterile. When Hamlet bids the Player, "Follow that lord and look you mock him not," when he says, "We shall obey, were she ten times our mother," and when he demonstrates to Claudius how a king may go a progress through the guts of a beggar, the reader's reaction is not, I think, a sense of liberation but rather the feeling, "How I—in certain moods and in certain contexts—should have enjoyed saying that!" Santayana seems to be pointing to this quality of Hamlet's wit when he remarks of such "idealism" as Hamlet displays that it "is lame because it cannot conceive a better alternative to the thing it criticizes. It stops at bickerings and lamentations which, although we cannot deny the ample warrant they have in experience, leave us disconcerted and in an unstable equilibrium, ready to revert, when imagination falters, to all our old platitudes and conventional judgments." [2] The function of Hamlet's satirical girdings—think, for example, of the celebrated "fishmonger" scene with Polonius (II, ii)—is plainly to satisfy an emotional animus which exhausts itself in its own immediate gratification.

Now it seems to me that a similar self-indulgent quality lurks behind all of Hamlet's most pronounced attitudes, even when he is ostensibly on the side of the angels. As in many neurotics, Hamlet's exaggerated sense of unworthiness ("What should such

---

[1] Introduction to *Hamlet* (C.U.P.), p. lxiv; *What Happens in Hamlet?* pp. 44 and 229. Compare Coleridge, *Lectures on Shakespeare* (Bohn Edition), pp. 342ff. ("we see a great, an almost enormous intellectual activity . . .").

[2] *Obiter Scripta*, p. 40.

creatures as I do crawling between heaven and earth?") goes with considerable readiness to pronounce on the faults of other people. His reforming zeal, however, even when it is directed against the genuinely bad or despicable, is hardly remarkable for either charity or self-knowledge. Mr. Wilson Knight, in two interesting essays in *The Wheel of Fire,* has rightly emphasized the bitterness, cynicism and hatred which mark Hamlet's dealings with others in the middle scenes of the play, instancing his cruelty to Ophelia, his "demoniac pleasure" in the thought of ensuring the King's damnation, the callousness with which he sends Rosencrantz and Guildenstern to their death, "not shriving time allowed," and the "most withering, brutal and unnecessary sarcasm" which, towards the end of Act III, scene iv, he addresses to the Queen. What has to be added is that Hamlet's hectoring of the Queen is not only brutal, it is obstinately self-righteous:

> Forgive me this my virtue,
> For in the fatness of these pursy times
> Virtue itself of vice must pardon beg,
> Yea, curb and woo for leave to do him good.

Self-righteousness informs his forgiveness of himself for the murder of Polonius

> —For this same lord,
> I do repent; but heaven hath pleased it so,
> To punish me with this, and this with me—

and for the murder of Rosencrantz and Guildenstern—"They are not near my conscience"; and the same inability to admit that he, Hamlet, might have been wrong betrays itself in the too easy apology to Laertes for the hysterical outburst in the graveyard:

> If Hamlet from himself be ta'en away,
> And when he's not himself does wrong Laertes,
> Then Hamlet does it not; Hamlet denies it. . . .
> Hamlet is of the faction that is wrong'd;
> His madness is poor Hamlet's enemy.

What Hamlet's wit, his cruelty and his self-righteousness have in common is a quality of moral relaxation which more or less subtly distorts the values for which he professes to stand. His scourging of corruption is hardly ever impersonal. In his pretended concern for Ophelia's chastity (III, i), in the obscenities which he directs towards her in the play scene (III, ii), and in the fascinated insistence on lust in his long interview with his mother (III, iv), Hamlet seems intent not so much on exposing lust as on indulging an uncontrollable spite against the flesh.

> Nay, but to live
> In the rank sweat of an enseamed bed,
> Stew'd in corruption, honeying and making love
> Over the nasty sty.

The heated tone, the peculiar violence and limited range of the imagery in such lines as these sharply distinguish them from the vigorous impersonality of Vindice's meditations on the skull of his mistress.

That there is an intimate connexion between Hamlet's sexual nausea and his feelings about death is now commonly admitted; what seems to be less generally realized is the significance of this connexion. Mr. Wilson Knight, for example, after some pages of excellent analysis and evaluation, proceeds to attribute Hamlet's cynical bitterness simply to an overwhelming preoccupation with death which he tries to show as not merely touching but noble. "He is a superman among men. And he is a superman because he has walked and held converse with Death, and his consciousness works in terms of Death and the Negation of Cynicism." Forgetting his own injunction against sentimentalizing the personality of the Prince, Mr. Knight thus contrives a partial rehabilitation of the Romantic Hamlet. "We properly know Hamlet himself," he writes, "only when he is alone with Death: then he is lovable and gentle, then he is beautiful and noble, and, there being no trivial things of life to blur our vision, our minds are tuned to the exquisite beauty of his soul. We know the real Hamlet only in his address to the Ghost, in his 'To be or not to be ...' soliloquy, in the lyric prose of the graveyard scene. ... These touch a melody that holds no bitterness. Here, and when he is dying, we glimpse, perhaps, a thought wherein death, not life, holds the deeper assurance for humanity." [1]

[1] *The Wheel of Fire*, pp. 42 and 50.

EXPLORATIONS

Now whatever elements of beauty and pathos may be found in the expression of Hamlet's feelings about death it may be doubted whether his attitude is exactly that of a superman. A superman is, presumably, someone who is capable of making a sustained effort to grasp experiences beyond the reach of ordinary men; whereas what is most characteristic of Hamlet's meditations on death is something similar to the quality of moral relaxation that we have already noted,—a desire to lapse *back* from the level of adult consciousness. The "To be or not to be . . ." soliloquy has given rise to a vast amount of critical discussion, centring mainly on the question whether Hamlet is inspired primarily by thoughts of suicide or by thoughts of active opposition to the King. Certainly the specific reference is not clear, for if the "quietus" with "a bare bodkin" can only refer to suicide, the "enterprises of great pitch and moment" can only refer to stratagems against the King, whilst the act of "opposing" which ends all troubles is left ambiguous. That confusion, however, is of minor importance. What really matters is the quite unambiguous way in which Hamlet expresses what is, for him, the essential difference between life and death. The speech is built up on two contrasted sets of metaphors. Life, "this mortal coil," is at best something which hampers and impedes, imposing "fardels" under which we "grunt and sweat"; the "slings and arrows of outrageous fortune," "the thousand natural shocks," and "the whips and scorns of time" present it as an actively hostile force; and in "a sea of troubles" the power that it has to inflict pain is felt as continuous and irresistible, like the sea. Death, on the other hand, is presented simply as a relaxing of tension and an abandonment of the struggle. The reiterated "sleep," the soothing "quietus," and the smooth and weighted "consummation"

> —Quiet consummation have
> And renowned be thy grave—

make plain why death is so ardently desired by a spirit which, whether "suffering" or "opposing," feels itself continually on the defensive against a world conceived as entirely hostile.[1]

[1] It is perhaps significant that reason—stressed throughout the play as man's noblest and most godlike quality, "without the which we are pictures or mere

86

PRINCE HAMLET

The desire to escape from the complexities of adult living is central to Hamlet's character. It runs through the play from the opening lines of the first soliloquy, with their images of melting and yielding (I, ii, 129-130), to Hamlet's final welcoming of death as "felicity." The attitudes which appeal to Hamlet and in which he finds relief are all simplified attitudes, and he admires the uncomplicated forthrightness of Fortinbras—justifying his "divine ambition" by a sophistical argument [1]—for fundamentally the same reason that he finds the cloak of madness congenial. Even when he is alone, inspired by the Player's speech, he indulges himself in a fantasy in which to "cleave the general ear with horrid speech" seems like a genuine solution of difficulties; and his exaggerated play-acting soon takes on the obvious forms of melodrama:

> Am I a coward?
> Who calls me villain? breaks my pate across? . . .
> Who does me this? Ha! [2]

The distinguishing feature of melodrama is, of course, that it over-simplifies what are in reality complicated problems and relationships, and the tendency noted here is in line with Hamlet's most marked characteristics. His attitudes of hatred, revulsion, self-complacence and self-reproach, I have suggested, are, in their one-sided insistence, forms of escape from the difficult process of complex adjustment which normal living demands and which Hamlet finds beyond his powers.

Reflexions such as these lead inevitably to a further question. If, by any standards of maturity at all adequate to the later plays, Hamlet appears as fundamentally immature, may we suppose that Shakespeare, at the time of writing the play, deliberately intended

---

beasts"—is quite early referred to as beleaguered behind its "pales and forts" (I, iv, 28). On the general question of regressive tendencies and the longing for death there are some illuminating passages in D. W. Harding's "A Note on Nostalgia," in *Determinations*, pp. 67ff.

[1]   Rightly to be great
Is not to stir without great argument,
But greatly to find quarrel in a straw
When honour's at the stake. (IV, iv, 53-56).

—The word "honour" begs the question.

[2] Compare III, iii, 407-411 ("Now could I drink hot blood"), and V, i, 276-306 (the ranting in Ophelia's grave).

he should appear so? Is Hamlet an "objective" study, or is he—as a persistent tradition affirms—peculiarly near to his creator, whose first demand on spectators and readers is that they should "sympathize" with the Prince, "feel with him," and "place themselves in his shoes"?

This question, like most others concerning this puzzling play, does not admit of a simple answer. While Frank Harris's view of a complete identification of Shakespeare and Hamlet is obviously untenable, it is nevertheless difficult to believe that Hamlet is entirely objectified. It is not merely that in Hamlet's most characteristic speeches there is nothing positive, no technical device, to which one can point—as one can point to the sonorous, simplifying rhetoric of Othello or to the devices by which Jonson makes his figures express their own condemnation [1]—as clear proof of a critical intention. The speeches themselves, particularly the soliloquies, seem to focus a wide background of feeling which is not clearly defined. It is Francisco who sets the tone of the first scene, and of the play, with his terse

> 'tis bitter cold,
> And I am sick at heart

—a note that is echoed not only by Hamlet—"The time is out of joint"—but by Marcellus,—"Something is rotten in the state of Denmark." Fortinbras, we are told, supposes the state to be "disjoint and out of frame," and we hear of the common people, "muddied, thick and unwholesome in their thoughts and whispers." Such allusions have a cumulative effect in creating a rather sinister accompaniment to the main action, and the sinister tone is strongly reinforced by the prevailing imagery of physical corruption and disease, which appears as persistently in the speeches of the King as in the speeches of Hamlet himself.[2] The Ghost,

---

[1] See F. R. Leavis's essay on *Othello* in *Scrutiny* (VI, 8), December 1987, and my *Drama and Society in the Age of Jonson*, Chapter VI.

[2] It seems unnecessary to collect examples of metaphors drawn from the various ills of the body, but I should like to suggest that the disease imagery evidences a particular preoccupation with *unseen* corruption. The King twice refers to Hamlet as having, or being, a concealed disease (II, ii, 17-18; IV, i, 21-23), and Hamlet declares of Fortinbras' expedition (IV, iv, 27-29):

> This is the imposthume of much wealth and peace,
> That inward breaks, and shows no cause without
> Why the man dies.

moreover, expresses the same view of himself as Hamlet does—

> What a falling off was there!
> From me, whose love was of that dignity
> That it went hand in hand even with the vow
> I made to her in marriage; and to decline
> Upon a wretch, whose natural gifts were poor
> To those of mine.   (I, v, 47-52.)

And if it is objected that this is due simply to the conventional explicitness of the Elizabethan drama, one has still to explain the sweet, nostalgic ending of the play, when Horatio—responding exactly to the mood of Hamlet's "Absent thee from felicity awhile,"—speaks words of quiet reassurance such as one might use in putting a child to bed:

> Good night, sweet prince,
> And flights of angels sing thee to thy rest!

There is, finally, at least one point in the play where Hamlet is made the mouthpiece of sentiments that Shakespeare expresses in his non-dramatic verse. In the "To be or not to be . . ." soliloquy, the "whips and scorns of time" are particularized in a brief catalogue of ills

> —"The oppressors wrong, the proud man's contumely . . ."—

strongly reminiscent of the list of complaints against the world in Sonnet 66:

> Tir'd with all these, *for restful death I cry*,
> As, to behold desert a beggar born,
> And needy nothing trimm'd in jollity . . .[1]

Readers may differ about the significance to be attached to indica-

---

Professor Dover Wilson's notes (see his edition of *Hamlet*, p. 221) explain "imposthume" (abscess) in the context, but I can see no reason for the description "that inward breaks, and shows no cause without . . ." Shakespeare's mind seems to have unconsciously reverted to the image used by Hamlet a few short scenes previously (III, iv, 147-149):

> It will but skin and film the ulcerous place,
> Whilst rank corruption, mining all within,
> Infects unseen.

[1] Act III, iii, 58, "Offence's gilded hand" seems to echo the "gilded honour" of the Sonnet.

tions of this kind, but there does seem to be some ground for believing that Hamlet, in his recoil from the grossness of physical existence and his desire for death, expresses feelings that were personal to Shakespeare and not merely dramatically conceived. If this is so it may help to explain why the "negative" verse expressing loathing and recoil is, on the whole, so much more forceful than the passages in which any positive values are indicated. Ophelia's description of the earlier Hamlet (III, i, 158-168), like Hamlet's description of his hero-father (III, iv, 53-63), is weak and general compared with the astounding force and particularity of Hamlet's scathing comments on his mother's lust or on his uncle's guilt.

It is, however, impossible to believe that Hamlet is *merely* a mouthpiece, or to accept without qualification Ernest Jones's contention that, "The play is simply the form in which his [Shakespeare's] deepest unconscious feelings find their spontaneous expression, without any inquiry being possible on his part as to the essential nature or source of those feelings." [1] Apart from scattered passages of objective comment on Hamlet's "madness," his rashness, and his "bloody deeds," there are scenes where Shakespeare seems deliberately to point a contrast between the common sense and common kindliness of "normal" people and the obstinate self-centredness and suspicion of the maladjusted individual: Act I, scene ii, is, I think, such a scene, for the unfavourable impression made by Hamlet's sullen replies to the sensible suggestions of Claudius and Gertrude can hardly have been unintended. But the main evidence of Shakespeare's conscious, critical control is of another kind: it lies in the extraordinary dramatic and poetic power which, if it does not achieve the tight-knit unity of *Macbeth* or *Coriolanus,* expresses itself in a firm and flexible prose (prose which can be beautifully *spoken*) and, here and there, in imagery which can compare in force and vividness (though not in complexity) with anything in the later plays:

[1] *Essays in Applied Psycho-Analysis* ("The Oedipus Complex as an Explanation of Hamlet's Mystery"), pp. 59-60. I do not feel qualified to discuss the psychological issues involved in Dr. Jones's interesting essay, which is sometimes brushed aside too easily by literary critics. Although some modifications of the Freudian account of the play's genesis may suggest themselves to the non-specialist reader, there is no doubt that the essay helps to explain the persistence of the Hamlet legend from early times and the popularity of Shakespeare's play.

PRINCE HAMLET

> . . . if his occulted guilt
> Do not itself unkennel in one speech . . .
> . . . a vice of kings;
> A cut-purse of the empire and the rule,
> That from a shelf the precious diadem stole,
> And put it in his pocket!
> . . . and we ourselves compelled
> Even to the teeth and forehead of our faults
> To give in evidence.

One feels that lines such as these, which are free from the suggestion of mere emotional *relief* that clings to some of the equally
striking imagery of lust, are evidence enough of a mind playing
freely on its subject; just as one feels that the skilful delineation
of varied types within the play is incompatible with anything but
a high degree of self-possession on the part of the poet. Con-
centration on the figure of Hamlet is apt to make us overlook
such things as the speech in which Claudius is first presented to
us,—a perfect piece of dramatic self-revelation, modulating from
the unctuous and calculated hypocrisy of the opening lines

> —Though yet of Hamlet our dear brother's death
> The memory be green, and that it us befitted
> To bear our hearts in grief and our whole kingdom
> To be contracted in one brow of woe . . .—[1]

to the business-like efficiency of the close. Polonius has had more
attention, but it is pertinent to remark here how surely and consistently he is presented in terms of a gross and naïve self-assur-
ance which seems deliberately chosen to provide something more
than a simple ironic contrast to the doubt and uncertainty of
Hamlet. The lines in which Polonius explains his maxim, "To
thine own self be true," remind us that there is, after all, some
value in a more inquiring attitude towards the self and its duties.

Between the view that Hamlet is an objective study of a particular kind of immaturity and the view that it is a spontaneous

---

[1] Milton seems to have taken a hint from the tone and movement of these lines
in the presentation of Belial in *Paradise Lost*, Book II:

> I should be much for open war, O peers,
> As not behind in hate, if what was urged
> Main reason to persuade immediate war
> Did not dissuade me most . . .

and uncritical expression of Shakespeare's own unconscious feelings it seems necessary to make a compromise. To suppose—as one must—that Shakespeare was ignorant of the deeper sources of the malaise expressed by Hamlet does not commit us to believing him incapable of assessing the symptoms of that malaise in relation to a developed—or, it seems more accurate to say, developing—scale of values. But the implicit evaluation is not so subtle or so sure as in the later plays, and one is forced to the conclusion that this play contains within itself widely different levels of experience and insight which, since they cannot be assimilated into a whole, create a total effect of ambiguity. (This would help to explain why on different minds *Hamlet* can make such different impressions; since it offers unusually varied possibilities of interpretation you pick what pleases you and what your temperament demands.) That *Hamlet* does in fact represent successive stages of Shakespeare's development is suggested by the bibliographical evidence, and the literary evidence is even more conclusive. Probably no other play of Shakespeare's contains such an assortment of varied styles, ranging from an easy naturalism to a rather stiff formality; passages such as the Player's speech (II, ii) and the curious, almost Miltonic, description of Ophelia's death (IV, vii) suggest deliberate experiment. Anything like precise dating of the verse strata is of course impossible. It is sufficient to note that some of the verse is in Shakespeare's comparatively early manner —"Some say that ever 'gainst that season comes . . ." (I, i), or, for a different effect, "I could a tale unfold whose lightest word . . ." (I, v); that both the substance and style of the King's speech, "But that I know love is begun by time . . ." (IV, vii), would justify us, if we did not know the context, in attributing the lines to *Troilus and Cressida,* an obviously "transitional" play; and that there are passages of mature prose and authentically "Shakespearean" blank verse. If, as seems likely, the play was written and retouched over a number of years, that would help to account for the co-existence of the different levels of consciousness that one seems to find within it.

To those who like to feel wholehearted sympathy or antipathy for the characters of a play, and who like to feel assured that they are safely following clear moral judgments imposed by the author, the views that I have outlined will seem both inconclusive and perverse. To the charge of inconclusiveness I have already indicated a reply: *Hamlet* has always seemed something of a puzzle and the unusual discrepancies of critical opinion suggest that a certain ambivalence is inherent in the play itself. As for the charge of a perverse denigration of the character of Hamlet—"the most adorable of heroes"—there is at least one misunderstanding that can be guarded against. A clearsighted view of the fundamental weaknesses of Hamlet's personality is by no means incompatible with a lively dramatic sympathy, for the simple reason that for everyone Hamlet represents a possible kind of experience. Indeed for most of us it is more than merely possible; in a different sense from that intended by Coleridge, we have "a smack of Hamlet" ourselves, to say the least of it. It is in fact the strength of our own regressive impulses and unconscious confusions that tempts us to see the play in a false perspective. I would say that, read as it commonly is, with a large measure of identification between reader and hero, *Hamlet* can provide an indulgence for some of our most cherished weaknesses—so deeply cherished that we can persuade ourselves that they are virtues—but it is incapable of leading us far towards maturity and self-knowledge. It is only when Shakespeare's attitude is seen to be more critical than is commonly supposed, and when we ourselves make a determined effort to assess that attitude, that we are in a position to see *Hamlet* in relation to the supreme achievement—the achieved maturity—of the later plays.

Chapter Four

SHAKESPEARE AND SHAKESPEAREANS

I

IT WOULD BE interesting to know what proportion of the adult population of Great Britain, for private pleasure and profit, reads one play of Shakespeare a year. One is, at all events, fairly safe in assuming that it is a very small proportion indeed. Yet the books about Shakespeare go on accumulating in arithmetical progression, one "problem" begets another, and there are, we gather, plans for making intensive and highly co-ordinated attacks by trained bands of research workers upon all the problems of palaeography, transmission, divided authorship, staging and allusion that remain unsolved. Perhaps it is time to take stock, to suggest a few fundamental questions which, in the busy hum of industry, are not much attended to.

The occasion is provided by a book written, not for specialist scholars, but for intelligent laymen who want to increase their knowledge and understanding of Shakespeare. *A Companion to Shakespeare Studies* [1] contains fifteen essays by different writers, some of them authorities so eminent that it seems an impertinence for anyone lacking a combination of their various talents to criticize the book at all. Yet certain very important things must be said—things which the reviewers, tackling the book with the respectful timidity usual in such cases, forgot to say.

Mr. Eliot is the only contributor to the book to ask, or to imply, the important question, "Why should we read what has been written about Shakespeare?" And this, of course, in a world of obvious and urgent duties and distractions, involves some further questions: "Why should we read Shakespeare? Why should we read poetry at all?" If a centralizing conception of poetry and its function is lacking in this book, this is not because it is by fourteen different writers, but because Shakespeare studies, in com-

[1] *A Companion to Shakespeare Studies*, edited by H. Granville Barker and G. B. Harrison (C.U.P.), 1934.

94

mon with other intellectual pursuits, have suffered from the decay of a unifying tradition—have, in consequence, lost their life in becoming a specialism, or a collection of specialisms, with their own codes and standards. Whilst the tradition was alive, the answers to our questions were implicit within it. Some of the eighteenth-century critics are unimportant enough, but almost any paragraph of their work *implies* a social and moral world; and their appeal is to this world, not to "workers in the same field."

It was in the nineteenth century that the change took place. (There had been symptoms before then: Steevens, Mr. Isaacs tells us, "was one of the most learned in Elizabethan matters, an alert, shrewd and skittish scholar, enlivening his later editions with obscene annotations fathered facetiously on two respectable clergymen who had incurred his enmity.") That century saw the emergence of the Shakespearean, uncontaminated, as often as not, by any interest outside the Elizabethan field—a phenomenon which Dryden and Johnson—or even Kames and Richardson— would have found it hard to understand. Criticism was not only more and more closely associated with scholarship (which might have been all to the good) but dependent upon and subsidiary to it—a reversal of rôles which is responsible for the dismal spate of academic theses under which we suffer. (The thesis, it is worth remarking, is the key to a university teaching post.) Shakespeare scholarship progressed by *accumulation* rather than by a process of growth or development from a centre. It became a heavy industry, and to-day it has its monopolies and trusts, its extraordinarily efficient higher personnel, its shock-troopers and its navvies. "It would seem," says Mr. Isaacs, "as though the future of Shakespeare scholarship lies in the organization of new co-operative methods. . . . The new objectivity of research to-day is particularly favourable to such methods. By proper allocation and apportionment of tasks between the Shakespeare Association of England, the Shakespeare Association of America, and the German Shakespeare-Gesellschaft, and by organized University seminar work on specific problems, many of the problems at present beyond the individual's capacity could be brought to fruition." If we find this prospect depressing it is not because we are in-

different to the problems that Mr. Isaacs wants to see solved—
questions of authorship, patronage, literary groupings and so on
—but because the kind of mind that finds "the new objectivity of
research" congenial is likely to have a decisive effect upon the
future of Shakespeare criticism, and because that kind is, in
general, incapable of finding an answer to the questions that we
asked above, or indeed of realizing that they need be asked.

By an answer of course I do not mean a handy formula—a
motto for school editions—but an insight, a critical attitude
which will permeate and direct every word we write about
Shakespeare. It is something that reveals itself in the set of a
writer's interests—his points of emphasis—and it can be tested and
discussed in particular judgments. The true Shakespeare critic
will be concerned to make himself, as far as possible, a contemporary of Shakespeare's—as the editors of the *Companion* point
out. But, more important, he will also be concerned to make
Shakespeare a contemporary, to see his particular relevance for
our time. His essential qualification, then, is a lively interest in
the present and the immediate future of poetry, an ability to
make first-hand judgments here, coupled, I would add, with an
understanding of the extra-literary implications of poetry—its
relations to "the general situation"—*at present.* When this is lacking we can expect nothing but the worn counters that are shuffled
in every text-book.

For the scholarship of a Pollard or a Chambers we can only
feel respect, and gratitude. And a good deal of useful work in the
way of historical elucidation can, fortunately, be done by other
than first-class critics. But even here we demand that the Shakespeare commentator shall at least be able to recognize critical excellence, that he shall know what the real problems are that need
his elucidation. It is therefore significant that in the present volume the chapter on "Shakespeare the Poet" is both weak and
pretentious. Perhaps it is a temperamental difference that makes
me find Mr. Rylands's style exasperating:

> In *Antony and Cleopatra, Cymbeline* and *The Winter's Tale,*
> Shakespeare seems to gather in all the harvest of his poetic and dra-
> matic experience, to hark back and to adventure farther. He has

mastered style, but style has become an exacting and imperious mistress. Yet in *The Tempest* she ceases for a moment to be so whimsical, provocative and outrageous.

But such loose generalizations have nothing very firm in the way of particular judgments to support them. Mr. Rylands either makes his distinctions in the abstract—where they mean very little —or piles up words and phrases, out of their context and unanalysed, telling us nothing except that Shakespeare used them. (See, for example, the illustrations on page 99, where he attempts to show that in the later plays Shakespeare "returns to the old Elizabethan idiom, to the currency and coinage in which Spenser and his fellows had trafficked.") His comparisons are the opposite of illuminating:

> In the tragic period . . . Shakespeare's style has affinities with that of Webster and even Sir Thomas Browne . . . "Dark backward and abysm of time" may be *compared* [my italics] with "the Areopagy and dark tribunal of our hearts." [1]

And

> Shakespeare developed from the more elementary sequences of images of his Elizabethan period a far more subtle and profound use of imagery which is very near to that of the great poets of the romantic revival and not unlike the finest conceits of the metaphysicals. From the sweetness of his euphuisms came forth the strength of his metaphors. And metaphor, Aristotle tells us, is the poet's greatest gift, for it implies an eye for resemblances. Such an eye or such a wit Lyly possessed.

We may ignore the apotheosis of Lyly, and it is perhaps overfinicky to ask what is the common distinguishing mark of the imagery of Byron, Shelley, Keats, Coleridge and Wordsworth; but unless there is some occult distinction between "very near to" and "not unlike" we are justified in expecting little from the discussion of imagery that follows that amazing comparison. And failure here means so much more than merely local weakness; it

---

[1] Shakespeare's phrase has not only the suggestiveness of Browne's but also a sharpness of impact entirely its own: we momentarily *feel* the giddy horror (as though in danger of falling "backward") of the abyss that opens when time is considered solely as unending succession and the past, therefore, as infinitely receding.

explains the persistent dissatisfaction with which we read. For none of the recognized Shakespeareans—men whose knowledge of the Elizabethan period is vast and enviable—shows any indication that he could deal more successfully than Mr. Rylands with "Shakespeare the Poet" or that he would find Mr. Rylands's exposition unsatisfactory.[1]

Miss Willcock, who accepts, substantially, my own conclusions concerning the education of Shakespeare's audience, writes an admirable account of Elizabethan English, but when we are expecting the explanation that would throw a stream of light on the relations between language and living she fobs us off with a metaphor: "Acquisition was now in the air; there was a buccaneering spirit abroad in language as well as on the high seas. . . . The nature and quality of this late-Elizabethan achievement cannot be appreciated apart from the whole Tudor evolution in language of which it forms the second great phase. It is the thaw succeeding the frost." Three sentences on the last page of her essay provide a clue to this sudden slackening of tension. "While Shakespeare's plays remain the common study of English people," says Miss Willcock, "he will, it can be hoped, continue to exercise a centripetal, unifying influence on language. As a 'tradition' he will prevent our speech from suffering from a repetition of the mid-Tudor rootlessness. He keeps a certain amount of vivid Elizabethan word and phrase in popular circulation to-day." This facile observation could not have been written by anyone alive to the present. And a critic who is blind to contemporary rootlessness is—need we say?—thereby inhibited from explaining how Elizabethan idiom drew its life from a way of living that has vanished. But in Shakespeare criticism we have become habituated to explanations that do not explain.

With the exception of that on Marston all the essays in Mr. Eliot's latest volume [2] are reprinted from his *Selected Essays,* and there is no occasion for an extensive review. But the book comes

[1] In "Education and the Drama in the Age of Shakespeare," *The Criterion,* July 1932.

[2] *Elizabethan Essays,* by T. S. Eliot (Faber and Faber), 1934.

aptly to hand. Mr. Eliot, I once heard it disparagingly remarked, "is very clever; he can make a little go a long way." Exactly; Mr. Eliot's information does not outstrip his interests. It is unlikely that he could indicate "the specific contributions" to Shakespeare studies "of such men as Aronstein, Bolte, Brotanek, Cohn . . . Sievers, Vietor, Walzel, and Max J. Wolff"; his distinction, in this connexion, lies merely in the fact that he has given new life to Shakespeare criticism. Shakespeare is the specific subject of only two of the eleven essays before us, but when he writes of Marlowe and Jonson, of Middleton and Massinger, he not only isolates some essential quality of *their* genius, but, by implication or deliberate contrast, throws into relief a fresh aspect of Shakespeare.

The relevance of *Elizabethan Essays* to a lively interest in Shakespeare, compared with the irrelevance of so much that appears in *A Companion to Shakespeare Studies*, cannot be explained merely on the ground that Mr. Eliot is superior as a critic; most of the essays in the *Companion* do not profess to offer criticism. But Mr. Eliot is so much more successful in his way than the contributors to the *Companion* are in theirs, precisely because he possesses those interests in which we found them deficient. His approach is always the contemporary one. He is well aware of the remoteness of the Elizabethan period, but at the same time he sees his subjects as an *immediate* part of our experience; as he writes of Jonson, "We can even apply him, be aware of him as a part of our literary inheritance craving further expression." A second quality is harder to define. "Pure criticism" is nowhere urged and demonstrated more effectively than in *The Sacred Wood*. But the critical rigour, the faculty for isolating, is combined with an ability to see poetry as part of something larger than itself. He writes as a critic not a moralist, but an awareness of a *relation* between poetry and morals, poetry and living, is everywhere implicit. His start is from the careful analysis of particular arrangements of words, but from that he proceeds to problems of personal conduct, as in "Shakespeare and the Stoicism of Seneca," to questions of character and temperament, as in the essay on Jonson, to a discussion of the different moral outlook of two periods, as in the brilliant essay on Massinger, which perhaps exemplifies his method at its best. The great poet, he reminds us, is one whose works are "united by one significant, consistent, and developing personality." And, "Every vital development of language is a development of feeling as well." *Pour distraire les honnêtes gens* was perhaps rather more than a convenient battle-cry; but it is plain that for Mr. Eliot (he is explicit in the Preface in which the last quotation appears [1]) poetry is important because it has something to do with matters that cannot be discussed under the head of "aesthetics."

I do not mean that Mr. Eliot is always the critic described in ideal perfection. He has, it seems to me, an exaggerated respect for some of the minor Elizabethans; and a weakness for mysterious distinctions—odd in one whose literary conscience is so highly developed—is noticeable in some of the later essays. "The words in which Middleton expresses his tragedy," he says of *The Changeling*, "are as great as the tragedy," and two pages later "poetry, dramatic technique" is opposed to "the moral essence of tragedy"—blemishes which Mr. Eliot would have been quick to notice in the writings of another. We read of "poetry . . . in the general atmosphere" of Marston's tragedies, and there is a curious debility in his account of poetic drama in the same essay. What exactly, we should like to ask, is the "pattern behind the pattern into which the characters deliberately involve themselves"? It doesn't help to add, as Mr. Eliot does here, "the kind of pattern which we perceive in our own lives only at rare moments of inattention and detachment, drowsing in sunlight." From him we are accustomed to something a good deal nearer to precision than that.

But to play the reproving school-master to Mr. Eliot is no more part of my purpose than was wanton disparagement of the scholars. I am concerned with one point only—the function of Shakespeare criticism and Shakespeare scholarship. When we consider the part, actual or potential, of Shakespeare in the national life, we think first, I suppose, of the sensitiveness, the emotional development of each reader. But so much more than the individual sensibility is involved. Shakespeare exhibits, concretely, a particular relation between the individual poet and the language,

---

[1] *The Sacred Wood*, Second Edition, 1928.

a relation, that is to say, between the finest moments of experience, "united by one significant, consistent and developing personality," and a general social-economic situation—something which those who speak glibly of the relationship between "cultural superstructure" and "methods of production" have not been quick to investigate. Shakespeare criticism (including scholarship) has, then, a double function. It has to make the Shakespeare-experience available to each reader to the fullest possible extent, and it has to relate that experience to the possibilities of living at the present time and, therefore, at the time when Shakespeare wrote. All that does not perform one or other of these functions is lumber, and at a time when it is becoming more and more difficult to keep abreast of living issues—to find some answer to the question, How to live—it had better be recognized as such. Shakespeareanism, I would say, is, ultimately, a means of escaping that question and those issues.

II

Hamlet is the first of the tragedies to be published in the New Cambridge Shakespeare. Instead of the usual "Note on the Copy," Professor Dover Wilson has given us a separate monograph devoted to textual considerations,[1] and for this he deserves some gratitude; for he directs attention where, I think, it ought to be directed. Faced with the two volumes of *The Manuscript of Shakespeare's Hamlet and the Problems of its Transmission* the reviewer is, of course, exposed to obvious temptations. Even if he is not overcome by admiration for the detective ingenuity displayed, the labour that a careful reading involves makes him unwilling to question the assumptions on which the book is based; engaged in referring debatable words and passages to their context and weighing the evidence in relation to the conduct of an intricate argument, he tends merely to register local agreement or disagreement. But in the end he has to make some attempt to

---

[1] *Hamlet*, edited by J. Dover Wilson (Cambridge University Press), 1934. *The Manuscript of Shakespeare's Hamlet and the Problems of its Transmission. An Essay in Critical Bibliography.* By J. Dover Wilson. (Cambridge University Press.) Two Volumes, 1934.

assess the value of this study—of this kind of study—in relation to the ends which, presumably, it is meant to serve.

The bibliographical method employed by Dr. Wilson—if method is the word for a process which, in spite of explicit disclaimers, is tending to become an end in itself in Shakespearean circles—is very far removed from the hit or miss eclecticism of editors in "the pre-Pollardian era." Indeed the prestige which the new bibliography at present enjoys is largely due to the impression that it is able to convey of being an exact science, by means of which we can hope to approach "certainty" concerning what Shakespeare wrote, or intended to write. The apparatus is certainly impressive. In the present monograph a knowledge of Elizabethan handwriting, of (probably) Shakespeare's hand in *Sir Thomas More*, of the habits of Elizabethan compositors, and of the nature of Shakespearean quartos and the first Folio in general, is brought to bear to determine the character of the two main texts of *Hamlet*—the second (good) Quarto of 1605 and the Folio version of 1623. Principles based on the theory thus evolved are then applied to all the problems of the text. Roughly, Dr. Wilson's theory is this: Shakespeare's original autograph was first transcribed for the playhouse, undergoing some abridgment, alteration, and a general tidying up of "obscurities." This theatrical transcript is behind the Folio text, being copied for the printer by a careless playhouse scribe who thought he knew the play too well to attend very closely to the text before him. The original manuscript, on the other hand, was sent to Robert's office for the printing of the second Quarto. There it was set up by an unskilled compositor (a Welshman?), who had not yet learnt to carry large groups of words in his head, and who (apart from the lines that he left out and the words that he couldn't read and had to guess at) worked conscientiously from the manuscript, thus preserving, to a very large extent, the spelling and punctuation of the original copy. The second Quarto, therefore, must be taken as the basis of an edited text. An editor will use the Folio for filling in the omissions of the Quarto, but where there is a choice of readings "no F1 reading, however plausible, however long sanctioned by editorial approval, possesses any rights whatever unless it can be justified in the teeth of the Q2 variant"—justified, that is, by accounting for the possibility of Quarto misreading on "graphical principles," by a knowledge of the ways of scribes and compositors.

This bald summary gives no idea of the detailed elaboration of the argument—*The Manuscript of Shakespeare's Hamlet* contains some 350 pages of text besides a hundred pages of comparative tables as appendices—and it is the value of the apparatus that is in question. It seems best to take a particular example. In Chapter I, Dr. Wilson quotes three lines from Claudius's speech at the beginning of Act III, scene iii, which run, according to Q2,

> The termes of our estate may not endure
> Hazerd so neer's as doth hourely grow
> Out of his browes

—"which is on the face of it absurd." The Folio has "dangerous" instead of "neer's" and "lunacies" instead of "browes." Most modern editors reject "dangerous"—an obvious tautology—and accept "lunacies," but, says Dr. Wilson, they "do not enquire whether the readings in the variant pairs . . . may not be textually so closely knit that no editor should put them asunder." On the other hand,

> suppose, as we shall discover to be a fact, Q2 turns out to be the better copy of the two . . . we shall be encouraged to read "neer's," but we shall be left with the nonsense word "browes" on our hands. What are we to do with that? We may decide to emend it. But emendation in our day means something very different from the brilliant shots of a Theobald. Before we can even ask ourselves what word in Shakespeare's manuscript came to be misread "browes," we must know what Shakespearean manuscripts looked like, that is to say, how they were written and how spelt. We must know too, what kind of agents of transmission stood between that manuscript and the printed text of Q2, and how these agents were likely to depart from Shakespeare's intentions. In short, in order to emend the single word "browes," an editor must have made an extended study of Shakespeare's ways as a scribe in the texts of other plays and a close study of the idiosyncracies of the Q2 text. Nor is this all. He must further see to it that his lines of communication are secure; that is to say, he must explain "lunacies." In other words, he must make up his mind quite definitely on the composition of the F1 text of *Hamlet*, to say

nothing at the moment of Q1, if he does not wish to see his whole position, including his emendation of "browes," overthrown, or at any rate attacked from the rear, by some other scholar.

The upshot is (p. 324) that Dr. Wilson decides to read "brawls"— "which would make 'browes' a combined *a:o* and *l:e* error, that is to say, nothing at all out of the way"—and common sense and bibliographical principles are alike vindicated.

I have quoted the one passage at length not merely because it is a good example of the way in which Dr. Wilson goes to work. "Browes" is *not* a nonsense word. Presumably Hamlet had spent a good part of the play scene staring at the King, and "hazerd" may as well "grow out of his browes" as Banquo may "grow" and "harvest" in Duncan's bosom, or a sorrow be "rooted" in the memory. Moreover there is a particular appropriateness in the conjunction of "browes" (face—eyes—mind) with the organic suggestion of "grow": Hamlet is a continually hostile force, and it is of this that the King is thinking rather than of a particular exhibition of hostility. The bibliographical machinery has merely worked in the direction decided by the taste of the editor.

There is no need to collect instances where Dr. Wilson has plumped for a reading on the grounds that it is "completely and convincingly Shakespearean," and *then* brought the machinery to bear, since he is himself explicit: "It is true, as I have all along made clear . . . that the final arbiter in any particular textual decision must be the judgment and taste of the editor who makes it. . . . Yet [through the development of the new bibliographical methods] a definite corner has been turned." It seems to me a very indefinite corner. I have read § X, in which Dr. Wilson summarizes the benefits claimed for the method, several times, and I cannot see that he answers this objection, or proves that the method is in any way indispensable. Where, as an editor, he has done well—as in calling attention to the Quarto punctuation and stage directions [1]—he could have done as much in ignorance of

[1] This is an opportunity to comment on the irritating stage directions in the New Cambridge Shakespeare. The first scene of *Hamlet* is not improved by having "midnight, cold, very dark" put at its head; nor do we need to be told that Hamlet enters "in deep dejection" to speak the "To be, or not to be" soliloquy, or that "The King, very pale, totters to his feet" when he is caught in the mouse-trap. Shakespeare—and his readers—can do without this sort of thing.

the history of the copy. Perhaps I am only being wise after the event; but if, to take another example, we consider the particular instances of variation discussed on pp. 262-285, we find, in each case of any importance, that the bibliographical method is not merely subsidiary but irrelevant to a final judgment. It is true of course that "There are a large number of alternative readings of equal or almost equal aesthetic value, and it is just here that the new critical apparatus ought to prove most useful" (p. 177), but it is hard to see what relation this kind of utility has to reading *Hamlet*.

And Dr. Wilson makes larger claims for the bibliographical method than the one just quoted. Textual problems are, he tells us, "fundamental" (MSH, p. xii). "The establishment of the text comes first, then the interpretation of the dialogue, then the elucidation of the plot, and only after all these matters have been settled are we in a position to estimate character" (*Hamlet*, p. x). What Dr. Wilson seems to be aiming at is some kind of critical "certainty"—a concept that in any case needs examination. But even if we ignore the part played by taste in directing the machinery, and confine ourselves to bibliographical considerations, "certainty" remains elusive. Apart from emendation, which "involves in the last resort an effort of the imagination, or in plain English guess-work," there are endless possibilities of disagreement. Besides the two main transcribers standing between Shakespeare's autograph and the Folio text, a third makes a shadowy appearance on page 67, and on page 168 we learn that "some copyist" may have had the text before handing it over to the sharp fellow who prepared the theatrical copy. As for the second Quarto, we have to deal not only with the compositor but with the press corrector (what about the corrector for the Folio?), and problems involving double omission as well as double correction (cf. p. 143) leave scope enough for guessing.

The New Cambridge *Hamlet*—like every rehandling of the text —is an essay in taste. Dr. Wilson cites in this connexion the unfortunate Dr. Kellner, whose triumph was, I believe, the emendation, "As swift as volitation or the thoughts of love"—and one need hardly say that his own taste is far enough from that. But it is a taste with fairly obvious bias and limitations. We recall an improvement that he attempted in the first act of *The Tempest*, where Prospero, answering Miranda's agitated description of the wreck, declares,

> There is no soul
> No, not so much perdition as an hair
> Betid to any creature in the vessel
> Which thou heard'st cry. . . .

Dr. Wilson, shocked at the anacoluthon, decided that "soul" was a minim misprint for "soil"—and we have already had one instance of the kind of thing that he considers "nonsense." What saves him is his conservatism—he rightly brushes aside a dozen or so unnecessary emendations by modern editors—but the bias is there; and *Hamlet* does not offer so many temptations to the tidy-minded as *Macbeth* or *Lear*. He is right in preferring the Quarto punctuation (see pp. 198-199, for an excellent comparison), but he does not realize, in dealing with Hamlet's "What a piece of work is a man . . ." for example, that the sense derived from following the grammatical structure of the Quarto does not exhaust the meaning. And in the Preface to the play (p. xxxii) he explains that sometimes he has had to alter the Quarto punctuation "in order to avoid ambiguity and bewilderment on the part of the reader." (It is to be hoped that he realizes his wish and bewilders us—for our good—with a cheap edition of the Quarto.) One cannot indeed be sure that Dr. Wilson understands the nature of Elizabethan English or Shakespeare's handling of it His discussion of double meanings (*Hamlet*, pp. xxxiv-xxxviii) does little more than skim the surface. "So much had the use of double meaning become a second nature with Shakespeare," he says, "that in all probability it was generally involuntary on his part." But to a large extent it was in the language, which hadn't yet become completely separated out into different, distinguishable meanings: that process culminated after the Augustan period. "Involuntary," too, covers as many problems as the word "insensible," when we are told that the varied associations of Shakespeare's words are "generally . . . all the more potent for our being insensible of them" (p. xxxix). And perhaps we may add that even stage-quibbling was something more than "a kind of game, like the modern crossword puzzle" (p. xl).

It is not fair to judge the main critical remarks in the Preface to the play until the book that we are promised on *What Happens in Hamlet?* appears. But it is plain that Dr. Wilson's interest lies in the events and characters rather than in the poetry.[1] Nor is this surprising when we consider the last and the most serious objection that has to be made against "the new bibliography." "Emendation," Dr. Wilson tells us, "is a skilled game which can only be played successfully if all the rules are carefully observed" (MSH, p. 286), and one's opinion that the textual "rules" can only be learnt by a long and exclusive devotion is confirmed in the Preface to the play, where we read: "The problems raised by the text are quite as baffling as those belonging to character, and even more complicated. They are, indeed, fit subject for a lifetime of study. And another life might well be spent upon its exegesis."

> My vegetable love should grow
> Vaster than empires, and more slow.

Reminding ourselves what "Shakespeare" means at present, not only amongst the general reading public but—considering such things as school text-books and university examination papers— amongst the educated, we wonder if this kind of attachment can be justified. Bibliographical criticism is not only a highly specialized occupation, it is one of the most prominent branches of modern Shakespeare studies, and one to which a good deal of prestige—academic and other—is attached. It is also an escape from a more strenuous discipline: Dr. Wilson "counts himself more fortunate than most to have had for sixteen years Shakespeare's Elsinore to fly to and its enthralling and inexhaustible problems to ponder, as a refuge from the pressure of his ordinary duties and as a solace for world-hopes constantly deferred." Obviously there are years of labour behind these volumes, but the labour that poetry demands is of a different order.

[1] This was amply confirmed when *What Happens in Hamlet?* appeared.

Chapter Five

BACON AND THE SEVENTEENTH-CENTURY DISSOCIATION OF SENSIBILITY

THE LAST TWENTY or thirty years have seen a revolution in our attitudes towards the seventeenth century. To start with, we now know very much more about that period than was known a few decades ago. Whilst some historians have brought out the persistence of medieval modes of thought and action beyond the close of the medieval period, others have pushed back the beginnings of the Industrial Revolution and demonstrated a direct line of connexion between the commercial and industrial enterprise of Elizabethan and early Stuart times and the greater changes of the eighteenth century. And this increased knowledge of the economic life of the time has completely changed the picture of political development as drawn by the Whig historians—a picture in which the conflict between King and Parliament appeared simply as a struggle for civil and religious liberty. Indeed the reaction has gone so far that it is now fashionable to speak of the Civil War as nothing more than the necessary adjustment of political forms to those "progressive" economic forces which had grown up within the husk of the old order. Even if we find that formula misleading in its excessive simplicity we do now recognize the part played by economic pressure, in various forms, not only in moulding the constitutional development of the century but in helping to shape its dominant philosophies.

But the revolution that I referred to has not been caused merely by an increase in knowledge. It is due primarily to a shift in evaluation intimately related to the needs and interests of the present. We can see this most clearly in recent literary criticism. Metaphysical poetry has become a living force, felt directly as one feels contemporary poetry; of the Elizabethan-Jacobean dramatists one or two, such as Jonson and Tourneur, have obtained something very different from the inert and qualified approval of the text-books, whilst others, such as Beaumont and Fletcher, have slid quietly from their eminence; and the greatness of Shakespeare is estimated in terms radically different from those current forty years ago when Bradley published his *Shakespearean Tragedy*. These changes, and the reasons for them, are significant. The major change, however, is something that cannot be described purely in literary terms. The seventeenth century has long been recognized as marking in some ways the beginning of "the modern world." But the process is no longer felt as simple development, as unqualified progress. The literary splendours of the Shakespearean period are no longer explained solely in terms of the impingement of all that was new, free and "progressive" in the Renaissance; they are seen as the result of Renaissance turbulence and intellectual eagerness working on traditional ways of thinking and feeling and evaluating, the reflexion of a tension that can be observed in every sphere of the national life. That fruitful tension could not last; the new triumphed over the old, and the Civil War and the Restoration mark the ending of an historical period. The modern reassessment of the seventeenth century is largely a recognition of what was lost as well as gained by the transition to the modern world —a transition that took place not only in the spheres of practical achievement and conscious intellect but in those more subtle and more profound modes of perceiving and feeling that underlie men's conscious philosophies and explicit attitudes, and that have become so ingrained and habitual that it is only by a deliberate effort of the intelligence that we can recognize them as *not* inevitable, absolute and unchanging, the permanent *donnés* of "human nature": that is why they are best studied in our literature. It is as a contribution to our understanding of the seventeenth-century "dissociation of sensibility"—from which, as Mr. Eliot remarked in his brilliantly suggestive essay, "we have never recovered"—that I wish to consider some of the work of Francis Bacon.

I

Bacon's claim to be *"buccinator novi temporis,"* accepted for three hundred years, is not likely to be disputed. He was the

prophet, if he was not the founder, of modern scientific rationalism. Modern rationalism, of course, is not the only form that can
be taken by the exercise of the reason. It is the exercise of reason
towards a particular end in a particular way. The aim is the
understanding and mastery of the material world; the method is
a scrupulous examination of how things work and how they influence each other—what we now call the scientific method. Both
aim and general method were defined by Bacon. The purpose of
knowledge that he returns to repeatedly is "the benefit and use of
man," "the endowment and benefit of man's life," "the serious
use of business and occasions." The method proposed is "a laborious and sober inquiry of truth," "ascending from experiments to
the invention of causes, and descending from causes to the invention of new experiments"; and he notes as "the root of all error,"
"too untimely a departure and too remote a recess from particulars." And the scope of rational investigation is universal: "For
that nothing parcel of the world is denied to man's inquiry and
invention." These quotations from *The Advancement of Learning* (1605) sufficiently indicate the main directions of his thought.

We must, it is true, beware of exaggerating Bacon's *direct* influence on the development of modern science or of confounding
him with a nineteenth-century Rationalist. Not only was he not
himself an experimental scientist, he was either ignorant or con-
temptuous of the major scientific discoveries of his own time; and
he was without a glimmer of perception of what was to be the
supreme scientific achievement of the seventeenth century—the
development of mathematical physics.[1] But his ignorance of
science did not prevent him from clarifying the ideals that seventeenth-century scientists were to find congenial. Dr. Rudolf
Metz, who stresses Bacon's rôle as propagandist for the new science, writes: [2]

> Like almost all representative Renaissance thinkers, he was inspired
> with the Faustian urge. In this context may be mentioned one of the
> most significant and impressive elements of his doctrine; whose motto

[1] Spedding gives an account of Bacon's ignorance of some of the more important
aspects of scientific advance in his own day. See the collected *Works* (ed. Ellis,
Spedding and Heath), Vol. III, pp. 510ff. All page references are to this volume.
[2] In a valuable essay, "Bacon's Part in the Intellectual Movement of his Time,"
in *Seventeenth-Century Studies Presented to Sir Herbert Grierson.*

is "Knowledge is power," and its aim the *regnum hominis.* It is the pragmatic utilitarianism of the Baconian philosophy which is here first and most adequately stated. . . . For the first time the philosopher meets us not as a sedentary figure closeted away from the affairs of the world, not as a mere onlooker who seeks truth for its own sake, but as a being possessed by a passionate impulse to action, who places his knowledge at the service of practical ends and assigns to it as its greatest task the subjection of nature to the will of man . . . In this, Bacon's thought and feeling are entirely modern, and there is no vestige of medievalism left. . . . The science which is placed at the service of humanity has as its final aim technical mastery, which now supplants artistic culture. This shifting from art to technics repre sents, it seems to me, an important difference between early and late Renaissance thinking. Thus Bacon is one of the first to celebrate the coming of the technical age, and his doctrine is full of faith in future progress.

The combination of "the Faustian urge" and faith in progress with outstanding intellectual ability explains the respect, approaching veneration, felt for Bacon by the triumphant rationalists of the modern period. The early members of the Royal Society freely acknowledged their debt; and the Ode that Cowley contributed to Spratt's History of the Society (1667) is largely concerned to celebrate the champion of "Philosophy" and "the Mechanick way" against "Authority."

> From these and all long Errors of the way,
> In which our wandring Praedecessors went,
> And like th' old *Hebrews* many years did stray
> In Desarts but of small extent,
> *Bacon,* like *Moses,* led us forth at last,
> The barren Wilderness he past,
> Did on the very Border stand
> Of the blest promis'd Land,
> And from the Mountains Top of his Exalted Wit,
> Saw it himself, and shew'd us it.

Voltaire, speaking for the conscious Enlightenment of the eighteenth century, declared that the *Novum Organum* was the scaffolding on which "the new philosophy" had been built (*Lettres Philosophiques,* 12me. Lettre). A hundred years later, Macaulay acclaimed Bacon as "the greatest of English philosophers" —not, it must be admitted, for strictly philosophical reasons, but because, as he remarked, "two words form the key of the Baconian doctrine, Utility and Progress": "Turn where we may, the trophies of that mighty intellect are full in view."

What Macaulay's essay unconsciously serves to bring out is that Bacon was not only a directive force as a thinker. He was, in ways less obvious though intimately related to his philosophy, an early representative of that deeper change occurring in English life in the seventeenth century—a change in sensibility—to which I have referred. A short examination of Bacon's English prose style may help to reveal the partly unconscious habits of perceiving and feeling that underlie and give a particular tone to Bacon's own intellectual formulations and that, as the age of Utility and Progress advanced, were to become more and more "normal."

II

Some important aspects of Bacon's style were described by two of his contemporaries, by Dr. Rawley, his chaplain and literary executor, and by Ben Jonson. In his short *Life* of Bacon Rawley wrote:

> In the composing of his books he did rather drive at masculine and clear expression than at any fineness or affectation of phrases, and would often ask if the meaning were expressed plainly enough, as being one that accounted words to be but subservient or ministerial to matter, and not the principal. And if his style were polite, it was because he would do no otherwise. Neither was he given to any light conceits, or descanting upon words, but did ever purposely and industriously avoid them; for he held such things to be but digressions or diversions from the scope intended, and to derogate from the weight and dignity of the style.

Jonson's comment in *Discoveries* refers to Bacon's speeches, but it can be applied to his writings.

> Yet there happened in my time one noble speaker, who was full of gravity in his speaking. His language (where he could spare or pass by a jest) was nobly censorious. No man ever spake more neatly, more

pressly, more weightily, or suffered less emptiness, less idleness, in what he uttered. No member of his speech but consisted of his own graces. His hearers could not cough, or look aside from him, without loss.

Both Rawley and Jonson stress those elements in Bacon's style that make for a weighty and compact directness of meaning and that point forward to the "mathematical plainness" commended by Spratt and cultivated by the members of the Royal Society. His packed and aphoristic manner can be studied in the *Essays*. But these are rather consciously mannered performances, which do not seem to me to deserve the high place assigned to them by convention. In *The Advancement of Learning* a more direct and lively interest gives a keener edge to the close texture of the prose. The following extracts are from the section on medicine:

> In the inquiry of diseases, they do abandon the cures of many, some as in their nature incurable, and others as past the period of cure; So that Sylla and the triumvirs never proscribed so many men to die, as they do by their ignorant edicts; whereof numbers do escape with less difficulty than they did in the Roman proscriptions. Therefore I will not doubt to note as a deficience, that they inquire not the perfect cures of many diseases, or extremities of diseases, but pronouncing them incurable do enact a law of neglect, and exempt ignorance from discredit.

> But lest I grow to be more particular than is agreeable either to my intention or to proportion, I will conclude this part with the note of one deficience more, which seemeth to me of greatest consequence; which is, that the prescripts in use are too compendious to attain their end: for to my understanding, it is a vain and flattering opinion to think any medicine can be so sovereign or so happy, as that the receit or use of it can work any great effect upon the body of man. It were a strange speech which spoken, or spoken oft, should reclaim a man from a vice to which he were by nature subject. It is order, pursuit, sequence, and interchange of application, which is mighty in nature; which although it require more exact knowledge in prescribing and more precise obedience in observing, yet is recompensed with the magnitude of effects.

Such passages are characteristic, and they answer to the account given by Rawley and Jonson. But the account is not complete.

EXPLORATIONS

Bacon was not only a learned and weighty writer, he was also an Elizabethan with a eye for the literary possibilities of the spoken idiom. His *History of the Reign of King Henry VII* is full of phrases that one would not be surprised to meet in Nashe,[1] and *The Advancement of Learning* owes a good deal of its pungency to those pithy comparisons and muscular idioms that Elizabethan English threw up so readily:

> whereas reason does buckle and bow the mind unto the nature of things.

> As for the possibility, they are ill discoverers that think there is no land where they can see nothing but sea.

> Therefore I wish some collection to be made [of the opinions of ancient philosophers concerning nature], but here I must give warning, that it be done distinctly and severally; the philosophies of everyone throughout by themselves; and not by titles packed and faggoted up together, as hath been done by Plutarch. For it is the harmony of a philosophy in itself which giveth it light and credence; whereas if it be singled and broken, it will seem more foreign and dissonant.

> For it is in knowledges as it is in plants: if you mean to use the plant, it is no matter for the roots; but if you remove it to grow, then it is more assured to rest upon roots than slips.

There is, however, a significant difference between Bacon's use of Elizabethan idiom and that of the majority of his contemporaries. In the first place, the great majority of his figures of speech are simple *illustrations* of the ideas that he wishes to convey.

> It were good to divide natural philosophy into the mine and the furnace, and to make two professions or occupations of natural philosophers, some to be pioneers and some smiths; some to dig, and some to refine and hammer.

> And howsoever contention hath been moved touching an uniformity of method in multiformity of matter, yet we see how that opinion, beside the weakness of it, hath been of ill desert towards learning, as that which taketh the way to reduce learning to certain empty and barren generalities; being but the very husks and shell of

[1] Some especially lively passages will be found in the description of the Cornish rebellion, and in the account of the capture of Perkin Warbeck.

sciences, all the kernel being forced out and expulsed with the torture and press of the method . . .

For as in buildings there is great pleasure and use in the well-casting of the stair-cases, entries, doors, windows, and the like; so in speech the conveyances and passages are of special ornament and effect.

As for philosophers, they make imaginary laws for imaginary commonwealths; and their discourses are as the stars, which give little light because they are so high.

This same truth is a naked and open day-light, that doth not show the masques and mummeries and triumphs of the world, half so stately and daintily as candle-lights. Truth may perhaps come to the price of a pearl, that sheweth best by day; but it will not rise to the price of a diamond or carbuncle, that sheweth best in varied lights.

After these two noble fruits of friendship (peace in the affections, and support of the judgment) followeth the last fruit, which is like the pomegranate, full of many kernels; I mean aid and bearing a part in all actions and occasions.

In all these quotations (taken more or less at random from the *Advancement* and the *Essays*) the function of the images is not to intensify the meaning, to make it deeper or richer, but simply to make more effective a meaning that was already fully formed before the application of the illustrative device.[1] Shelley declared that Bacon was a poet. In reading his work what we are most frequently forced to remember is that he was a brilliant lawyer. Some analysis of a further example or two may make clear the distinction that I wish to establish.

Among the lesser diseases or "peccant humours" of learning Bacon lists the belief (which he considers erroneous) that time preserves what is most worth preserving and that what has been lost was not worth keeping:

[1] The process is seen most clearly when the illustration has not its usual aptness. "Shepherds of people had need know the kalendars of tempests in state; which are commonly greatest when things grow to equality; as natural tempests are greatest about the *Æquinoctia*" ("Of Seditions and Troubles"). As A. S. Caye points out in his edition of the *Essays*, "The analogy between the equality of classes in a state and the equality in length of day and night is very far fetched." It could not have been made if Bacon had not been intent on making his political point to the exclusion of any real interest in the natural phenomena involved in illustration.

as if the multitude, or the wisest for the multitude's sake, were not ready to give passage rather to that which is popular and superficial than to that which is substantial and profound; for the truth is, that time seemeth to be of the nature of a river or stream, which carrieth down to us that which is light and blown up, and sinketh and drowneth that which is weighty and solid (291-292).

This has so convincing an air that on a first reading we are not likely to question the legitimacy of the play on "light" and "solid." Closer inspection reveals that although the analogy appears to clinch the argument, it does not in fact prove anything. The comparison is *imposed*, and instead of possessing the validity that comes from the perception of similarity it is simply a rhetorical trick. We find something of the same kind in the famous attack on the elaboration of "vain matter":

> Surely, like as many substances in nature which are solid do putrefy and corrupt into worms, so it is the property of good and sound knowledge to putrefy and dissolve into a number of subtile, idle, unwholesome, and (as I may term them) vermiculate questions, which have indeed a kind of quickness and life of spirit, but no soundness of matter or goodness of quality. This kind of degenerate learning did chiefly reign amongst the schoolmen; who having sharp and strong wits, and abundance of leisure, and small variety of reading; but their wits being shut up in the cells of a few authors (chiefly Aristotle their dictator) as their persons were shut up in the cells of monasteries and colleges; and knowing little history, either of nature or time; did out of no great quantity of matter, and infinite agitation of wit, spin out unto us those laborious webs of learning which are extant in their books. For the wit and mind of man, if it work upon matter, which is the contemplation of the creatures of God, worketh according to the stuff, and is limited thereby; but if it work upon itself, as the spider worketh his web, then it is endless, and brings forth indeed cobwebs of learning, admirable for the fineness of thread and work, but of no substance or profit (285-286).

Bacon is here formulating one of the central doctrines of his philosophy, one, moreover, that has a permanent as well as an historical value. But it is simply on his method of argument that, for the moment, I wish to direct attention. The passage opens with a general truth: the study of "vain matter" is, by definition, a perversion of learning, and "vermiculate questions" defines aptly the relation of the diseased to the wholesome substance. The figures of the cell and the spider, on the other hand, although they apparently perform a similar function—namely, to define a particular example of the general kind—serve rather to weight the argument with feelings of contempt and to produce an air of finality that is not justified by any proof actually adduced. By combining a general truth with rhetoric Bacon has contrived to make *all* scholastic learning look silly and to recommend his own positivistic attitude as the only one possible for a reasonable man. The brilliance of the exposition should not blind us to the fact that what we have here is the enunciation of a partial truth as though it were the whole truth, the statement of a case intended to demolish opposite or complementary points of view. There are, after all, more ways in which the mind can "work upon itself" than in spinning vain theories from inadequate material, just as there are more kinds of "profit" than those envisaged by Bacon.

Bacon's figures of speech are forensic, intended to convince or confound. Some are used simply as apt illustrations of particular points; some serve to impose on the reader the required feeling or attitude. In neither kind is there any vivid feeling for *both* sides of the analogy such as we find in more representative Elizabethans. Elizabethan prose writers—from Hooker to Nashe, and from Nashe to Deloney and Dekker—also use figures to illustrate an argument or to support a case; but most of their similes and metaphors have a life of their own—sometimes too abundant and vigorous a life for the purpose of logical or "scientific" argument —whereas in Bacon the analogues only have value for the support they offer to his demonstration. I think it is true to say that Shakespeare's metaphorical complexity, by means of which a new meaning emerges from many tensions, is the development of modes of perception pervasive in the prose of the time and directly derived from the normal processes of living. But the characteristically Shakespearean manner, depending as it does on the maximum range of sensitive awareness, is diametrically opposed to the Baconian manner, which represents a development of assertive will and practical reason at the expense of the more

EXPLORATIONS

delicately perceptive elements of the sensibility. You see this especially in Bacon's images taken from Nature. In my own reading of Bacon I have found only one passage that indicates any sense of the creative life behind the natural phenomena that he observes.[1] And in this of course he points forward to the eighteenth century. To Shakespeare and the majority of his contemporaries "Nature" indicated a world of non-human life to which man was bound by intimate and essentially religious ties. By the beginning of the eighteenth century "Nature" had come to mean simply the daylight world of common sense and practical effort. Man had ceased to feel "the filial bond" binding him to all that is not human, and assumed without question that his part was simply to observe, to understand and to dominate the world of "matter." Almost as much as his explicit philosophy, Bacon's prose style is an index of the emergence of the modern world.

III

The findings of the last section can be reinforced and developed by some consideration of Bacon's explicit theory of the function of language, which in turn is closely related to his conception of the mind of man.

It is the "first distemper of learning, when men study words and not matter," for "words are but the images of matter; and except they have life of reason and invention, to fall in love with them is all one as to fall in love with a picture" (284). The more developed expression of these views in the second Book of the *Advancement* has some of the difficulty and confusion that is natural in a pioneer work; but it is clear that of the various functions of language Bacon attaches by far the greatest importance to what we should now call the referential function—that which is of primary importance in exact description and rational analy-

[1] "For if these two things be supposed, that a man set before him honest and good ends, and again that he be resolute, constant, and true unto them, it will follow that he shall mould himself into all virtue at once. And this is indeed like the work of nature; whereas the other course is like the work of the hand. For as when a carver makes an image, he shapes only that part whereupon he worketh; as if he be upon the face, that part which shall be the body is but a rude stone still, till such times as he comes to it; but contrariwise when nature makes a flower or living creature, she formeth rudiments of all the parts at one time" (441-442).

sis. Expressive function is relegated to a subordinate place and, as we shall see, rather curiously handled. Words are essentially "notes" (i.e. signs) of things or of "cogitations." "Words," he says, "are but the current tokens or marks of Popular Notions of things"; and he describes the second duty of grammar as "philosophical, examining the power and nature of words as they are footsteps and prints of reason" [1] (399-401).

This attitude to language has both positive and negative qualities. Some of the best passages in the *Advancement* concern the need for clarity in exposition and the avoidance of merely verbal quibbling. For Bacon "the great sophism of all sophisms" is "equivocation or ambiguity of words and phrase, specially of such words as are most general and intervene in every inquiry" (394); and all that is strong and valuable in his thinking comes out in his exposure of the mischief of ambiguity in what purports to be clear and rational argument.

> And lastly, let us consider the false appearances that are imposed upon us by words,[2] which are framed and applied according to the conceit and capacities of the vulgar sort: and although we think we govern our words, and prescribe it well, *Loquendum ut vulgus, sentiendum ut sapientes,* yet certain it is that words, as a Tartar's bow, do shoot back upon the understanding of the wisest, and mightily entangle and pervert the judgment; so as it is almost necessary in all controversies and disputations to imitate the wisdom of the Mathematicians, in setting down in the very beginning the definitions of our words and terms, that others may know how we accept and understand them, and whether they concur with us or no. For it cometh to pass for want of this, that we are sure to end there where we ought to have begun, which is in questions and differences about words (396-397).[3]

This excellent caution obviously looks forward to the prescriptions of the Royal Society ("reducing all things as near the mathe-

---

[1] In the lines from Cowley quoted above it is accepted as indisputable that words "are but Pictures of the Thought."

[2] These are the Idols of the Market-place, the name being given in the *De Augmentis.*

[3] A similar passage occurs in the essay, "Of Unity of Religion": "A man that is of judgment and understanding shall sometimes hear ignorant men differ, and know well within himself that those which so differ mean one thing, and yet they themselves would never agree. . . . Men create oppositions which are not; and put them into new terms so fixed, as whereas the meaning ought to govern the term, the term in effect governeth the meaning."

matical plainness as they can"), and it marks a necessary step forward if the English language was to be made, what it was not in Elizabethan times, a tool for scientific analysis and the construction of methodical systems. Debility set in when this one kind of usage came to be regarded as supreme, and the tyranny of grammar and dictionary meanings succeeded in ironing out the rich complexities of Elizabethan English—a process reflected in the handling of Shakespeare's text by his eighteenth-century editors, and their successors.

The negatve qualities of Bacon's attitude to words can be seen in his discussion of rhetoric and poetry, of language, that is, adapted to any other than a purely referential use. Rhetoric, in Bacon's eyes, was something of a deceitful art, for he speaks of "eloquence and other impressions of like nature, which do paint and disguise the true appearance of things" (382). Nevertheless, it is an "ornament" (326), it is useful "in civil occasions," and "sensible and plausible elocution" may be allowed "to clothe and adorn the obscurity even of philosophy itself" (284). In this Bacon is doing little more than repeat the commonplaces of contemporary rhetoricians, but we may notice that the metaphors of clothing and adorning that he applies to eloquence point forward to a view of *all* art as, at best, a decorative side-line increasingly held by practical men as the century advanced; [1] and in this they could find further support in Bacon's scattered comments on poetry and the imagination.

Bacon's use of the word "imagination" would provide the subject for an Exercise in Interpretation, but it is an exercise that I shrink from performing. It is clear, however, that in human

[1] Louis B. Wright, in his valuable book, *Middle-Class Culture in Elizabethan England*, gives some illuminating extracts from *Academiarum Examen*, by a certain John Webster (1654). Webster's view of "cultural subjects" is indicated by the following:

"Lastly, for *Rhetorick*, or *Oratory*, *Poesie*, and the like, which serve for adornation, and are as it were the outward dress, and attire of more solid sciences; first they might tollerably pass, if there were not too much affectation towards them, and too much pretious time spent about them, while more excellent and necessary learning lies neglected and passed by: . . ."

Chapter III of Mr. Wright's book ("The Concern over Learning") illustrates very clearly the pronounced utilitarian strain in Elizabethan and seventeenth-century writings on education. The philosophical current from Descartes was also influential in lowering the status of poetry. See Basil Willey, *The Seventeenth-Century Background*, Chap. V, Sect. 2, "Poetry and the Cartesian Spirit."

affairs [1] he assigns to imagination (however defined) a status decidedly inferior to that of the reason by means of which the mind reflects and works upon "matter." In the short section on poetry, included in the general survey of the branches of learning with which the second Book of the *Advancement* opens, the formal eulogy is less significant than the oddly limited function assigned to imaginative works.

> The use of this Feigned History [that is, poetry] hath been to give some shadow of satisfaction to the mind of man in those points wherein the nature of things doth deny it; the world being in proportion inferior to the soul; by reason whereof there is agreeable to the spirit of man a more ample greatness, a more exact goodness, and a more absolute variety, than can be found in the nature of things. . . . So as it appeareth that poesy serveth and conferreth to magnanimity, morality, and to delectation. And therefore it was ever thought to have some participation of divineness, because it doth raise and erect the mind, by submitting the shews of things to the desires of the mind; whereas reason doth buckle and bow the mind unto the nature of things (343-344).

After some examples of the moral value of poetical fables, the section concludes:

> But to ascribe unto it that which is due; for the expressing of affections, passions, corruptions, and customs, we are beholding to poets more than to the philosophers' works; and for wit and eloquence not much less than to orators' harangues. But it is not good to stay too long in the theatre. Let us now pass on to the judicial place or palace of the mind, which we are to approach and view with more reverence and attention (346).

This account is significant in various ways. In the first place, when Bacon descends from general encomium to an enumeration of the specific virtues of poetry he confines himself entirely (as elsewhere in the *Advancement*) to the explicit moral lessons and illustrations of human temperament that it affords. And in this his theory conforms to his practice; for although the *Advancement,* like the *Essays,* is studded with literary quotations and allu-

---

[1] For "in matters of Faith and Religion we raise our Imagination above our Reason"—but only because Imagination is an *instrument* of truths which unaided human reason cannot fully grasp.

sions, their purpose is invariably to point a moral or illustrate an argument: there is never any indication that Bacon has been *moved* by poetry or that he attaches any value to its power of deepening and refining the emotions. One sentence, it is true, allows to poetry "some participation of divineness, because it doth raise and erect the mind, by submitting the shews of things to the desires of the mind." But if this is a considered judgment it can only mean that poetry, when not explicitly "moral," is a kind of holiday play,[1] a temporary relief from the discipline of the sharply contrasted "reason." There is certainly no suggestion that poetry itself can be an exploration of emotion or a discipline of "desire." Bacon in fact sanctions that divorce between imagination and reason, emotion and intelligence, that—long before the Romantic Revival—was to have a bad effect on English poetry; and he passes with evident relief from the "theatre," where "feigned histories" are enacted, to "the judicial place or palace of the mind, which we are to approach and view with more reverence and attention."

The different kinds of emphasis that Bacon gives to the different uses of language—subordinating the emotional and expressive to the descriptive and analytic—are of course directly related to his conception of the mind of man as, primarily, an instrument for registering and manipulating the objects of the physical world. He was the first great exponent of pragmatic utilitarianism, and his practical and utilitarian attitude colours the whole of his work. A principal purpose of *The Advancement of Learning* was to break down the distrust of theoretical knowledge felt by "pragmatical men"[2] and to win for learning a place in the modern state—a place that could only be assured "if contemplation and action may be more nearly and straitly conjoined and united than they have been" (294). The direction of his thinking is indicated by the constant recurrence of such phrases as, "use and practice," the "use of such knowledge in civil occa-

---

[1] "For as for Poesy, it is rather a pleasure or play of imagination, than a work or duty thereof" (382).

[2] That "pragmatical men may not go away with an opinion that learning is like a lark, that can mount and sing and please herself, and nothing else" (456). It is noteworthy that most of the objections to learning that Bacon answers in the first Book of the *Advancement* are of the kind that might be brought by those in control of state affairs.

sions," "the serious use of business and occasions"; and the aim
was the development of "such natural philosophy as shall not
vanish in the fume of subtile, sublime or delectable speculations,
but such as shall be operative to the endowment and benefit of
man's life." [1] Bacon's exposition of this purpose has of course a
permanent value, and it has been properly acclaimed. What has
not been sufficiently remarked is that the central tenets of his
philosophy involve an attitude towards the emotions that makes
against wholeness of living. Discussing the need for inquiry concerning the affections or emotions, he remarks: "it followeth in
order to know the diseases and infirmities of the mind, which are
no other than the perturbations and distempers of the affections."
Although it is "the perturbations and distempers" of the emotions
that are noted as the diseases of the mind, the emotions themselves are regarded with some suspicion: "it may be fitly said, that
the mind in the nature thereof would be temperate and stayed,
if the affections, as winds, did not put it into tumult and perturbation" (437).[2] It is plain that for Bacon the ideal towards which
men should strive is expressed in the famous image of the mind
as "a clear and equal glass, wherein the beams of things should
reflect according to their true incidence." As things are, of course,
the mind "is rather like an enchanted glass, full of superstition
and imposture, if it be not delivered and reduced" (394-395), but
what is *desirable* is that it should approximate more and more to
the condition of a perfect reflector of "things." We have here the
germ of much later psychology in which the mind is conceived
primarily as something that "reacts" to external "stimuli." What
Bacon ignores completely is the creative and vital forces in the
mind itself; and it is relevant to notice the inadequacy and bar-
renness of his reflexions on subjects involving intimate and personal emotions in the *Essays* (they are naturally not much con-

[1] This last quotation is taken from a passage in which Bacon recommends "the
use of History Mechanical" as "of all others the most radical and fundamental
towards natural philosophy" (332).

[2] It is significant that at the end of the paragraph from which this is taken Bacon
comments on the "special use in moral and civil matters" of knowledge "how to set
affection against affection, and to master one by another . . . employing the predominant affections of *fear* and *hope* [i.e. punishment and reward] for the sup-
pressing and bridling the rest" (438). Shakespeare's metaphor for the relation of
law and natural impulse, in *Measure for Measure*—"the needful bits and curbs for
headstrong weeds"—is far more complex.

sidered in the *Advancement*). In the essays, "Of Parents and Children" and "Of Marriage and Single Life," for example, he reduces personal relations to schematic generalizations, handling them almost entirely from the "public" point of view. Although the tenth essay is headed, "Of Love," it is mainly concerned with the dangers attending "the mad degree of love," which in turn becomes confused with normal sexual feeling, for this too seems to come under the head of "weakness" or "folly." And not only does Bacon in this essay refuse to admit the validity of subjective estimates of worth—"It is a strange thing to note the excess of this passion, and how it braves the nature and value of things, by this, that the speaking in a perpetual hyperbole is comely in nothing but in love"—he seems to think it possible to compartmentalize one's feelings and actions: "They do best, who, if they cannot but admit love, yet make it keep quarter, and sever it wholly from their affairs and actions of life." This by itself would not have much significance (though Bacon was accustomed to weigh his words). But the whole trend of Bacon's work is to encourage the relegation of instinctive and emotional life to a sphere separate from and inferior to the sphere of "thought" and practical activity.

This derogation of instinct and emotion, although it has obvious affinities with "the puritan outlook," which in turn was an intensification of one strand in the complex pattern of medieval thought, was something new in the purely humanistic literature of the Renaissance; but it came to permeate more and more the accepted attitudes of the succeeding age. It is, in fact, one symptom of that shift in the direction of men's interests and attention that is reflected in the development of the English language at the time of the Restoration, and that was largely responsible for the divorce between "reason" on the one hand and creative perception and the feelings generally on the other—"reason" of course having the pre-eminence. The history of this dissociation of sensibility, like all important movements of the human mind and spirit, is far too complex to be summed up in a few unqualified generalizations. It can be studied however—although it was far more than a literary phenomenon—in the literature of the eighteenth century. And in this respect the so-called Romantic

Revival made no essential difference, for in spite of the great achievements of a few of the "Romantic" poets the general *effect* of their work was to perpetuate the division between "poetry" and "life," between those emotions that a sensitive person might wish to cultivate and the less lofty but (it was felt) more "real" equipment that served in practical affairs; and whilst poetry became more poetical material life reached a peak of dehumanizing ugliness. Yeats remarks in his *Discoveries* that by the beginning of the nineteenth century "the highest faculties had faded, taking the sense of beauty with them, into some sort of vague heaven and left the lower to lumber where they best could." [1] The process leading to that division within the mind and feelings—within the human psyche as a whole—began in the seventeenth century; and the work of Francis Bacon points forward to the conscious and unconscious utilitarianism of the nineteenth century of which we ourselves are the embarrassed heirs.

IV

The title-page of Bacon's *Novum Organum* shows a ship in full sail, setting out beyond the Pillars of Hercules towards the new and uncharted lands, and to-day—in "this American world" of scientific progress—the symbol is seen to have been especially appropriate. The dividends paid have been far beyond the dreams of the original projectors of the voyage, but, what was also not foreseen, technical mastery was accompanied by a spiritual impoverishment that has prevented the full realization even of the material gains. If we have learnt anything between the two wars it is that the period inaugurated by the Renaissance—with its buoyancy and belief in unlimited material progress—is coming to

[1] An extreme case of spiritual aridity resulting from a Hard Fact education is recorded in John Stuart Mill's *Autobiography*. Mill was saved from a break-down largely by a timely reading of Wordsworth, whom he, like Arnold, continued to value for his "healing-power" in "this iron time." It is in connexion with this period of his life that Mill comments: "In most other countries the paramount importance of the sympathies as a constituent of individual happiness is an axiom, taken for granted rather than needing any formal statement; but most English thinkers almost seem to regard them as necessary evils, required for keeping men's actions benevolent and compassionate. Roebuck was, or appeared to be, this kind of Englishman. He saw little good in any cultivation of the feelings, and none at all in cultivating them through the imagination, which he thought was only cultivating illusions."

an end, and that only in a new orientation of the spirit is there hope for a chaotic and bewildered world. The limitations of the particular kind of scientific rationalism established in the seventeenth century have been recognized by scientists themselves; and it is beginning to be recognized that to regard nature *simply* as a storehouse of material for the human workshop and man *simply* as a manipulator has disastrous effects (soil erosion is the most obvious instance) even in the material sphere.[1] And it is now pretty generally accepted that the protests of isolated men of genius—Blake, Baudelaire or Lawrence—against the values of a world dominated by Progress were not merely aberrations expected from poets.

But, busy as we must be in overhauling the values of the last three hundred years, it is as well to remind ourselves that there is little use in proceeding in a blindly "reactionary"[2] spirit. It is no use simply trying to reverse the direction of Bacon's symbolic ship and sail back. Perhaps to-day we are in a position to understand why Blake wrote on the title-page of his copy of Bacon's *Essays*, "Good advice from Satan's kingdom"; but to make Bacon a villain in the drama of the post-Renaissance world and to abandon the hard-won and precarious rationalism that he helped to found and on which, until recently, Europe prided itself—to do this would be not only silly but disastrous. W. H. Auden in his *New Year Letter*—a kind of Hundred Points of Good Husbandry for contemporary intellectuals—has remarked:

> We know no fuss or pain or lying
> Can stop the moribund from dying,
> That all the special tasks begun
> By the Renaissance have been done.

This is a thought-blurring over-simplification. Some of the tasks

[1] On which see *The Discipline of Peace* by K. E. Barlow (1942). The best analysis for the non-scientific reader of the assumptions of seventeenth-century science is still that contained in E. A. Burtt's *The Metaphysical Foundations of Modern Science* (1925), and Basil Willey's *The Seventeenth-Century Background* (1934) is of course also relevant. A. Wolf concludes the Preface to his *History of Science, Technology and Philosophy in the Sixteenth and Seventeenth Centuries* (1935) with these words: "What has sustained him [the author] throughout the long and laborious exercise, apart from the intrinsic interest of the subject, is his belief that the world has need of a new intellectual re-orientation, and that to this end a close study of the history of human thought in its most objective spheres would be the best beginning."

[2] This word has been so misused in recent years that I feel quotation marks are necessary to indicate that my use of it is here purely descriptive.

begun by the Renaissance have still to be pushed a bit further—though not necessarily in the spirit of the eighteenth or nineteenth century. And if we ask what, in Bacon, is of high and permanent value the answer is, the disinterested and disciplined inquiring spirit—what Bacon called "the laborious and sober inquiry of truth." It is this, the genuinely scientific spirit, that gives life to many fine pages in *The Advancement of Learning*, which, when all is said, is likely to remain a permanent inspiration to "those that seek truth and not magistrality."

Liberal learning "taketh away all levity, temerity, and insolency, by copious suggestion of all doubts and difficulties, and acquainting the mind to balance reasons on both sides, and to turn back the first offers and conceits of the mind, and to accept of nothing but examined and tried."

"For as knowledges are now delivered, there is a kind of contract of error between the deliverer and the receiver: for he that delivereth knowledge desireth to deliver it in such form as may be best believed, and not as may be best examined; and he that receiveth knowledge desireth rather present satisfaction than expectant inquiry; and so rather not to doubt than not to err: glory making the author not to open his weakness, and sloth making the disciple not to know his strength."

"If it be truth . . . the voice of nature will consent, whether the voice of man do or no . . . I like better that entry of truth which cometh peaceably . . . than that which cometh with pugnacity and contention." For, "in learning, where there is much controversy there is many times little inquiry."

It is with these reminders of what is truly admirable in the *Advancement* that I wish to conclude; for the account that I have given of the limitations of attitude inherent in Bacon's work will have been completely misunderstood if it is taken to support any kind of "anti-scientific" hocus-pocus. Aware of the limitations of scientific rationalism, dissatisfied with the forms of existence created by modern materialism, a large part of Europe has shown itself willing to abandon the gains altogether (the gains, that is, on the spiritual side, for even the most fanatical believers in Blood and Race show no signs of abandoning the internal-combustion engine) and to fall back on the irrational. What we need, on the contrary, is not to abandon reason, but simply to recognize that reason in the last three centuries has worked within a field which is not the whole of experience, that it has mistaken the part for the whole, and imposed arbitrary limits on its own working. Both within those limits and outside them there are still gains to be won *by reason,* but by a reason, or intelligence, that recognizes the claims of the sensibility as a whole and tries to work in harmony with it.

Chapter Six

GEORGE HERBERT

I

THE POETRY of George Herbert is so intimately bound up with his beliefs as a Christian and his practice as a priest of the Church of England that those who enjoy the poetry without sharing the beliefs may well feel some presumption in attempting to define the human, as distinguished from the specifically Christian, value of his work. The excuse for such an attempt can only be the conviction that there is much more in Herbert's poetry for readers of *all* kinds than is recognized in the common estimate. That his appeal is a wide one is implicit in the accepted claim that he is a poet and not simply a writer of devotional verse; but I think I am right in saying that discussion of him tends to take for granted that admirers are likely to be drawn from a smaller circle than admirers of, say, Donne or Marvell. Even Canon Hutchinson, whose superbly edited and annotated edition of the complete Works is not likely to be superseded [1]—it would be difficult to imagine a better qualified editor and introducer—even Canon Hutchinson remarks that, "if to-day there is a less general sympathy with Herbert's religion, the beauty and sincerity of its expression are appreciated by those who do not share it." True; but there is also much more than the "expression" that we appreciate, as I shall try to show. Herbert's poetry is an integral part of the great English tradition.

It is, however, with expression, with form and manner, that appreciation must begin, and Dr. Hutchinson directs our attention to what are unquestionably the most important features of Herbert's style. "His craftsmanship is conspicuous. Almost any poem of his has its object well defined," he says. And again:

> Few English poets have been able to use the plain words of ordinary speech with a greater effect of simple dignity than Herbert.

[1] *The Works of George Herbert*, edited with a Commentary by F. E. Hutchinson (Oxford University Press, 30s.). Canon Hutchinson's essay on Herbert in *Seventeenth-Century Studies Presented to Sir Herbert Grierson* should also be consulted.

From Donne he had learnt the use of the conversational tone, which establishes an intimacy between poet and reader; and when his poems are read aloud, the emphasis falls easily on the natural order of the speaking idiom.

In other words, Herbert, like Donne, is a realist in literature. The first *Jordan* poem ("Who says that fictions only and false hair Become a verse?") is not only an expression of personal dedication, it is also, as the second poem of the same title is explicitly, a literary manifesto:

> Is it no verse, except enchanted groves
> And sudden arbours shadow course-spunne lines?
> Must purling streams refresh a lovers loves?
> Must all be vail'd, while he that reades, divines,
>   Catching the sense at two removes?
>
> Shepherds are honest people; let them sing:
> Riddle who list, for me, and pull for Prime. . . .

The "pure, manly and unaffected" diction that Coleridge noted, the rhythm that, though musical, is close to the rhythm of living speech, the construction that almost always follows the evolution of thought and feeling, even in the most intricate of the stanza forms that he used in such variety—these elements of Herbert's style show his determination to make his verse sincere and direct, to avoid even the slightest degree of the distortion that occurs when a preconceived idea of "the poetical" takes charge of the matter. And the effort of craftsmanship involved was one with the moral effort to know himself, to bring his conflicts into the daylight and, so far as possible, to resolve them. It is in the wide application of Herbert's self-discovery that the value of his poetry lies; but before approaching the substance of his verse I should like to examine some aspects of his style that have had less attention than those so far glanced at. For the "definition of the object" that Dr. Hutchinson rightly puts in the forefront of Herbert's achievement as a poet is not simply a matter of surface purity and naturalness; it has depth and solidity, and we need to become conscious of the variety of resources brought to bear in the process—simple only in appearance—that the defining is.

It is here that literary criticism necessarily joins hands with

GEORGE HERBERT

"the sociology of literature," since what we are concerned with is the personal use of a more than personal idiom with its roots in tradition and the general life. To the critic no less than to the student of English civilization in the first half of the seventeenth century it is of considerable significance that Herbert, as man and artist, is not the product of one social class alone. An aristocrat by birth, and related to some of the more prominent figures at court, the protégé of James I, the friend of Donne and Bacon, he has also that ingrained sense of "common" English life which in so many representative figures of the time blends with and modifies the intellectual currents from the world of courtly refinement, learning and public affairs. His poetry has plainly an upper-class background. The Metaphysical subtlety and intellectual analysis that he learnt from Donne,[1] the skill in music—so pleasantly attested by Walton—that one senses even in his handling of the spoken word, the easy and unostentatious references to science and learning, all imply a cultivated milieu.[2] And although the rightness of tone that keeps even his most intimate poetry free from sentimentality or over-insistence springs from deeply personal characteristics, it is also related to the well-bred ease of manner of "the gentleman."[3]

Turn, however, to that poem with the characteristic title, *The Quip,* and a different aspect of Herbert's genius, implying a different source of strength, is at once apparent.

> The merrie world did on a day
> With his train-bands and mates agree

[1] Herbert's metaphysical wit has marked differences from Donne's as well as affinities with it. It tends in one direction towards humour, which is saved by its intellectual quality from anything like whimsicality. The following verse from *Vanitie* (i) shows his amused play of mind:

> The subtil Chymick can devest
> And strip the creature naked, till he finde
> The callow principles within their nest:
> There he imparts to them his minde,
> Admitted to their bed-chamber, before
> They appeare trim and drest
> To ordinarie suitours at the doore.

[2] See in this connexion his fine poem, *The Pearl.*
[3] That Herbert's invariable courtesy is based on a genuine responsiveness to other people—that it is not simply "good manners"—is plain from the advice given in *The Church Porch,* e.g. stanzas 52-55. See also Letter XII in Dr. Hutchinson's edition, where Herbert discusses the needs of his orphan nieces.

To meet together, where I lay,
And all in sport to geere at me.

First, Beautie crept into a rose,
Which when I pluckt not, Sir, said she,
Tell me, I pray, Whose hands are those?
But thou shalt answer, Lord for me.

Then Money came, and chinking still,
What tune is this, poore man? said he:
I heard in Musick you had skill.
But thou shalt answer, Lord, for me.

Then came brave Glorie puffing by
In silks that whistled, who but he?
He scarce allow'd me half an eie.
But thou shalt answer, Lord, for me. . . .

The personifications here have nothing in common either with
Spenser's allegorical figures or with the capitalized abstractions of
the eighteenth century: "Brave Glorie puffing by In silks that
whistled" might have come straight from *The Pilgrim's Progress*.
And Bunyan, as Dr. G. R. Owst has shown,[1] had behind him not
only the rich folk-culture that produced the ballads, but also a
long line of preachers in the vernacular. Again and again Herbert
reminds us of the popular preacher addressing his audience—
without a shade of condescension in doing so—in the homely
manner that they themselves use. There is humour, mimicry and
sarcasm, seen most clearly when the verses are read aloud with
the inflexions they demand.

He doth not like this vertue, no;
Give him his dirt to wallow in all night:
These Preachers make
His head to shoot and ake.   (*Miserie*)

Love God, and love your neighbour. Watch and pray.
Do as ye would be done unto.
O dark instructions; ev'n as dark as day!
Who can these Gordian knots undo?   (*Divinitie*)

[1] In *Literature and Pulpit in Medieval England*.

GEORGE HERBERT

> To be in both worlds full
> Is more then God was, who was hungrie here.
> Wouldst thou his laws of fasting disanull?
> Enact good cheer?
> Lay out thy joy, yet hope to save it?
> Wouldst thou both eat thy cake, and have it?
> (*The Size*)

Herbert, we know, made a collection of "Outlandish [*sc.* foreign] Proverbs" for the community at Little Gidding, and although he does not often, as in the last quotation, incorporate a popular saying, many of his terse sentences have a proverbial ring.

Herbert's "popular" manner is, however, far more deeply grounded—and serves a more important purpose in his poetry—than these last examples might suggest.

> Let forrain nations of their language boast,
> What fine varietie each tongue affords:
> I like our language, as our men and coast:
> Who cannot dresse it well, want wit, not words.

This, from *The Sonne,* is explicit,—"I like our language": and one way of enforcing the judgment that he is in the great English tradition is to point out how surely he uses the native idiom to give the effect of something immediately present, something going on under one's eyes. In the colloquial expostulation of *Conscience* an over-active scrupulousness comes to life as it is rebuked:

> Peace pratler, do not lowre:
> Not a fair look, but thou dost call it foul:
> Not a sweet dish, but thou dost call it sowre:
> Musick to thee doth howl.
> By listning to thy chatting fears
> I have both lost mine eyes and eares.

The opening of *The Discharge* has a similar, almost dramatic, effect:

> Busie enquiring heart, what wouldst thou know?
> Why dost thou prie,
> And turn, and leer, and with a licorous eye

EXPLORATIONS

Look high and low:
And in thy lookings stretch and grow?

Even his simplest poems have a muscular force, an almost physical impact, as in the description of "the honest man" (in *Constancie*):

> Whom neither force nor fawning can
> Unpinne, or wrench from giving all their due.

He uses alliteration and assonance in the native Elizabethan way, not, that is, as a poetic or musical device, but as a means of controlling emphasis and movement so as to obtain the maximum immediacy. To the examples already given may be added these lines from *The Flower*:

> Many a spring I shoot up fair,
> Offring at heav'n, growing and groning thither,

where the effect is, in Shakespearean fashion, to assimilate the participles to each other, so that the groans seem an intrinsic part of the growing. It is the artist's feeling for *all* the resources of "our language" that gives to the greater poems of spiritual conflict their disturbing immediacy.

Herbert's style, then, is "popular" as well as courtly and Metaphysical, and his leaning towards the manner of common Elizabethan speech is further emphasized by his well-known liking for homely illustrations, analogies and metaphors. His poems contain plenty of learned allusions (especially, as was natural in that age, to astronomy), but he certainly "goes less far afield for his analogies than Donne and finds most that will serve his purpose from common life,"—from carpentry, gardening and everyday domestic activity: Redemption "spreads the plaister equal to the crime," after the refreshment of sleep, day will "give new wheels to our disorder'd clocks," and so on. But although this feature of Herbert's style is so commonly recognized that further illustration is unnecessary, its function is sometimes misinterpreted, as though Herbert's experience were somehow *limited* by his interest in the commonplace. Even Professor Grierson, after listing some of Herbert's comparisons, remarks:

GEORGE HERBERT

These are the "mean" similes which in Dr. Johnson's view were fatal to poetic effect even in Shakespeare. We have learned not to be so fastidious, yet when they are not purified by the passionate heat of the poet's dramatic imagination the effect is a little stuffy, for the analogies and symbols are more fanciful or traditional than natural and imaginative.

The last sentence, it is true, contains a qualifying clause, "*when they are not purified by . . . imagination*"; but since Professor Grierson goes on to describe Herbert as a "sincere and sensitive" rather than a "greatly imaginative" poet, some undue emphasis remains on the phrase "a little stuffy." [1]

The significance of Herbert's "homely" imagery—pointing as it does to some of the central preoccupations of his poetry—is something that we need to get clear. But before taking up this question—or, rather, as a way of taking it up—I should like to bring into focus another aspect of his imagery. As well as metaphor and simile Herbert uses symbols and allegory. Now whereas metaphor conveys its meaning directly from common experience, in symbolism there is usually an element of the arbitrary. *The Church-floore* is an obvious example:

> Mark you the floore? that square & speckled stone,
>   Which looks so firm and strong,
>   Is *Patience.*

But this arbitrary use of symbols is not characteristic of Herbert. Much more often his verse (like Bunyan's prose) gives life to his symbolic figures and allegorical situations, so that they appear as something immediately experienced, and carry their meaning with them. Even the highly emblematic poem, *Love Unknown*, has a matter-of-fact quality that makes it something more than a monument to a bygone taste. In *The Pilgrimage* the allegory is completely realized in terms of the actual.

> I travell'd on, seeing the hill, where lay
>   My expectation.
>   A long it was and weary way.

---

[1] "But if not a greatly imaginative, Herbert is a sincere and sensitive poet, and an accomplished artist elaborating his argumentative strain or little allegories and conceits with felicitous completeness, and managing his variously patterned stanzas . . . with a finished and delicate harmony."—*Metaphysical Lyrics and Poems of the Seventeenth Century*, pp. xliii-xliv.

The gloomy cave of Desperation
I left on th' one, and on the other side
The rock of Pride.

And so I came to Fancies medow strow'd
With many a flower:
Fain would I here have made abode,
But I was quicken'd by my houre.
So to Cares cops I came, and there got through
With much ado.

That led me to the wilde of Passion, which
Some call the wold;
A wasted place, but sometimes rich.
Here I was robb'd of all my gold,
Save one good Angell, which a friend had ti'd
Close to my side.

Mr. Empson, analysing the rich meaning of the third verse,[1] remarks that Herbert's manner is that of a traveller, "long after-
wards, mentioning where he has been and what happened to him,
as if only to pass the time." But the air of verisimilitude, the impression of a difficult journey actually undertaken, is not only an
effect of the sober tone; it springs also from the sensitive and
subtle movement. In reading the second verse we feel that we
ourselves have been in "Cares cops" and scrambled out

—got through
With much ado—

as best we might. The fourth verse, making skilful use of the
varied lengths of line and of the slight end-of-line pauses, repro-
duces the sensations of the traveller, as expectation—rather out
of breath, but eager and confident—gives way abruptly to flat
disappointment:

At length I got unto the gladsome hill,
Where lay my hope,
Where lay my heart; and climbing still,
When I had gain'd the brow and top,
A lake of brackish waters on the ground
Was all I found.

[1] *Seven Types of Ambiguity*, pp. 163-165. Mr. Empson also has some excellent
criticism of other poems by Herbert.

GEORGE HERBERT

The allegorical form is of course a reminder that what we are concerned with is a graph of more than one kind of experience, but at no point in the poem are we simply interpreting an allegory; the bitter poignancy of the conclusion springs from deeply personal feelings that we have been made to share.

> With that abash'd and struck with many a sting
> Of swarming fears,
> I fell, and cry'd, Alas my King!
> Can both the way and end be tears?
> Yet taking heart I rose, and then perceiv'd
> I was deceiv'd:
>
> My hill was further: so I flung away,
> Yet heard a crie
> Just as I went, *None goes that way*
> *And lives*: If that be all, said I,
> After so foul a journey death is fair,
> And but a chair.

This use of vivid allegory—tied down, as it were, to the actual and immediate—represents one aspect of Herbert's method. In poems such as *Vertue* and *Life* ("I made a posie, while the day ran by") we have the opposite and complementary process, where natural objects, without ceasing to be natural, have a rich symbolic meaning. In the lovely lines of *Vertue* the rose is no less a real rose, "angrie and brave," for being at the same time a symbol of life rooted in death. It is here that we see something of the significance of Herbert's consistent use of homely and familiar imagery. We may recall Coleridge's account of the genesis of the *Lyrical Ballads*: "Mr. Wordsworth was to propose to himself as his object to give the charm of novelty to things of every day, and to excite a feeling analogous to the supernatural, by awakening the mind's attention from the lethargy of custom, and directing it to the loveliness and wonder of the world before us." It is "the things of every day" that Herbert's poetry keeps consistently before us; but instead of invoking a rather adventitious "charm of novelty" or exciting "a feeling analogous to the supernatural" (one thinks of *Peter Bell*), he sees them in direct relation to a supernatural order in which he firmly believes. Thus in his poetry, just as the supernatural is apprehended in terms of the familiar, so common things—*whilst remaining common things,* clearly observed, and deeply felt—have a supernatural significance, and the familiar is perpetually new. "This is the skill, and doubtless the Holy Scripture intends thus much," he says, "when it condescends to the naming of a plough, a hatchett, a bushell, leaven, boyes piping and dancing; shewing that things of ordinary use are not only to serve in the way of drudgery, but to be washed and cleansed, and serve for lights even of Heavenly Truths." [1] Once more we are reminded of Bunyan, in whose blend of Biblical language and native idiom the august events of the Bible seem to be transacted in a familiar world, and the humble doings of every day are placed in a context that reveals how momentous they are.

II

Herbert's message to Nicholas Ferrar when, a few weeks before his death, he sent him the manuscript of *The Temple,* is well known.

> Sir, I pray deliver this little book to my dear brother Ferrar, and tell him he shall find in it a picture of the many spiritual conflicts that have passed betwixt God and my soul, before I could subject mine to the will of Jesus my Master; in whose service I have now found perfect freedom; desire him to read it: and then, if he can think it may turn to the advantage of any dejected poor soul, let it be made public; if not let him burn it; for I and it are less than the least of God's mercies.

Herbert's poetry was for him very largely a way of working out his conflicts. But it does not, like some religious poetry, simply *express* conflict; it is consciously and steadily directed towards resolution and integration. Dr. Hutchinson rightly describes the poems as "colloquies of the soul with God or self-communings which seek to bring order into that complex personality of his which he analyses so unsparingly."

This general account of conflict and resolution as the stuff of Herbert's poetry is, I believe, commonly accepted. But the con-

[1] *A Priest to the Temple or, The Country Parson,* Chapter XXI.

flict that gets most—indeed almost exclusive—attention is the struggle between the ambitious man of the world and the priest. Dr. Huchinson rightly insists that Herbert's conflict of mind was not simply about the priesthood, that his spiritual struggle "was over the more general issue of his submission to the Divine will" (p. lxviii); but he elsewhere records the opinion that "his principal temptation, the 'one cunning bosome-sin' which is apt to break through all his fences, is ambition."[1] Now it would certainly be unwise to underestimate Herbert's worldly ambitions, or the severity of the struggle that took place in one "not exempt from passion and choler," who liked fine clothes and good company, before he could renounce his hopes of courtly preferment and, finally, become a country parson. But it seems to me that if we focus all our attention there, seeing the struggle simply as one between "ambition" and "renunciation," we ignore some even more fundamental aspects of Herbert's self-division and at the same time obscure the more general relevance of his experience. Most criticism of the poet tends to suggest that we are simply watching someone else's conflict—sympathetic, no doubt, but not intimately involved ourselves.

Behind the more obvious temptation of "success" was one more deeply rooted—a dejection of spirit that tended to make him regard his own life, the life he was actually leading, as worthless and unprofitable. Part of the cause was undoubtedly persistent ill-health. "For my self," he said, "I alwaies fear'd sickness more then death, because sickness hath made me unable to perform those Offices for which I came into the world, and must yet be kept in it" (p. 373); and this sense of the frustration of his best purposes through illness is expressed in *The Crosse* and other poems:

> And then when after much delay,
> Much wrastling, many a combate, this deare end,
> So much desir'd, is giv'n, to take away
>   My power to serve thee; to unbend
> All my abilities, my designes confound,
> And lay my threatnings bleeding on the ground

---

[1] *Seventeenth-Century Studies Presented to Sir Herbert Grierson*, p. 154.

It is, however, difficult to resist the impression that his agues and consumption only intensified a more ingrained self-distrust. Commenting on some lines from *The Temper* (i),

—O let me, when thy roof my soul hath hid,
O let me roost and nestle there—

Dr. Hutchinson remarks that "Herbert often shows a fear of unlimited space and loves the shelter of an enclosure"; and his shrinking from the kind of experience that was possible for him shows itself now in the frequently recorded moods of despondency, now in the desire for a simpler and apparently more desirable form of existence:

My stock lies dead, and no increase
Doth my dull husbandrie improve. (*Grace*)

All things are busie; onely I
Neither bring hony with the bees,
Nor flowres to make that, nor the husbandrie
To water these.

I am no link of thy great chain,
But all my companie is a weed. . . . (*Employment* [i])

Oh that I were an Orenge-tree,
That busie plant!
Then should I ever laden be,
And never want
Some fruit for him that dressed me. (*Employment* [ii])

Now this feeling of uselessness and self-distrust has two further consequences: one is a preoccupation with time and death,

—So we freeze on,
Untill the grave increase our cold; (*Employment* [ii])

the other is a sense that life, real life, is going on elsewhere, where he happens not to be himself. It was his weakness, as well as his more positive qualities of "birth and spirit," that made a career at court seem so intensely desirable: "the town" was where other people lived active and successful lives. Certainly, then, it was not a small achievement to "behold the court with an impartial eye, and see plainly that it is made up of fraud, and titles, and

flattery, and many other such empty, imaginary, painted pleasures; pleasures that are so empty, as not to satisfy when they are
enjoyed." [1] But it was an even greater achievement to rid himself
of the torturing sense of frustration and impotence and to accept
the validity of his own experience. His poems come home to us
because they give new meanings to "acceptance."

The first condition of development was that the disturbing
elements in experience should be honestly recognized; and here
we see the significance of Herbert's technical achievement, of his
realism, of his ability to make his feelings immediately present.
In the masterly verse of *Affliction* (i) we have one of the most
remarkable records in the language of the achievement of maturity and of the inevitable pains of the process. In the opening
stanzas movement and imagery combine to evoke the enchanted
world of early manhood, when to follow the immediate dictates
of the soul seems both duty and pleasure.

> When first thou didst entice to thee my heart,
> 　　　　I thought the service brave:
> So many joyes I writ down for my part,
> 　　　　Besides what I might have
> Out of my stock of naturall delights,
> Augmented with thy gracious benefits.
>
> I looked on thy furniture so fine,
> 　　　　And made it fine to me:
> Thy glorious houshold-stuffe did me entwine,
> 　　　　And 'tice me unto thee.
> Such starres I counted mine: both heav'n and earth
> Payd me my wages in a world of mirth.
>
> What pleasures could I want, whose King I served,
> 　　　　Where joyes my fellows were?
> Thus argu'd into hopes, my thoughts reserved
> 　　　　No place for grief or fear.
> Therefore my sudden soul caught at the place,
> And made her youth and fierceness seek thy face.
>
> At first thou gav'st me milk and sweetnesses;
> 　　　　I had my wish and way:

[1] Herbert to Woodnot, on the night of his induction to Bemerton: recorded by Walton.

EXPLORATIONS

> My dayes were straw'd with flow'rs and happinesse;
> There was no moneth but May.

But implicit in the description—as we see from "entice" and "entwine" [1] and the phrase, "argu'd into hopes"—is the admission that there *is* enchantment, an element of illusion in the "naturall delights," and we are not surprised when the triumphant fourth verse ends with the sudden bleak recognition of ills previously unperceived but inherent in the processes of life:

> But with my yeares sorrow did twist and grow,
> And made a partie unawares for wo.

The three central verses not merely describe the "woes"—sickness, the death of friends, disappointed hopes—they evoke with painful immediacy the feelings of the sufferer.

> Sorrow was all my soul; I scarce beleeved,
> Till grief did tell me roundly, that I lived.

With characteristic honesty Herbert admits the palliative of "Academick praise"—something that temporarily "dissolves" the mounting "rage"; but the current of feeling is now flowing in a direction completely opposite to that of the opening.

> Whereas my birth and spirit rather took
>   The way that takes the town;
> Thou didst betray me to a lingring book,
>   And wrap me in a gown.
> I was entangled in the world of strife,
> Before I had the power to change my life.

"Betray" and "entangle" make explicit a sense already present but not openly acknowledged in "entice" and "entwine"; and instead of direct spontaneity—"I had my wish and way"—there is division and uncertainty:

> I took thy sweetned pill, till I came where
> I could not go away, not persevere.

---

[1] The earlier reading, in the Williams MS., is more explicit:

> I looked on thy furniture so rich,
>   And made it rich to me:
> Thy glorious houshold-stuffe did me bewitch
>   Into thy familie.

In the eighth stanza the potentialities of emphasis latent in the spoken language are used to evoke the full sense of frustration and conflict:

> Yet lest perchance I should too happie be
> > In my unhappinesse,
> Turning my purge to food, thou throwest me
> > Into more sicknesses.
> Thus doth thy power crosse-bias me, not making
> Thine own gift good, yet me from my wayes taking.

Verse nine is quieter in tone, bringing into prominence an element in the whole complex attitude of the poet previously expressed only in the quiet control of the verse in which such turbulent feelings have been presented:

> Now I am here, what thou wilt do with me
> > None of my books will show:
> I reade, and sigh, and wish I were a tree;
> > For sure then I should grow
> To fruit or shade: at least some bird would trust
> Her household to me, and I should be just.

The opening lines of the last stanza can be read in two ways according as we bring into prominence the resigned or the rebellious tone:

> Yet, though thou troublest me, I must be meek;
> > In weaknesse must be stout . . .

But resignation and rebellion are alike half-measures, and it is here, where the feelings are so subtly poised, that the need for an absolute decision makes itself felt. Return for a moment to the eighth stanza. There the last line, with its strong alliterative emphasis, makes plain that the problem of the will ("*my* wayes") is the central theme of the poem. What we call happiness ("no moneth but May") is the result of events meeting our desires,— "I had my wish and way"; but the universe is not constructed on our plan, and when the will cannot bring itself to accept the cross-bias of existence frustration is inevitable. This commonplace is something that everyone admits in a general way; to accept it fully, in terms of our own personal experience, is another matter. It is because Herbert has faced the issues so honestly and completely that the first alternative that presents itself in the moment of decision has only to be brought into focus to be seen as no real solution at all; and it is because its rejection has behind it the whole weight of the poem that the sudden reversal of feeling is so unforced, the undivided acceptance of the ending so inevitable.

> Yet, though thou troublest me, I must be meek;
>   In weaknesse must be stout.
> Well, I will change the service, and go seek
>   Some other master out.
> Ah my deare God! though I am clean forgot,
> Let me not love thee, if I love thee not.

In *The Collar* the same problem is approached from a slightly different angle.

> I struck the 'board, and cry'd, No more.
>   I will abroad.
>   What? shall I ever sigh and pine?
> My lines and life are free; free as the rode,
>   Loose as the winde, as large as store. . . .
>
> But as I rav'd and grew more fierce and wilde
>   At every word,
>   Me thoughts I heard one calling, Child!
>   And I reply'd, *My Lord.*

At one time I felt that in this well-known ending—a similar sudden "return" to that of *Affliction* (i)—Herbert was evading the issue by simply throwing up the conflict and relapsing into the naïve simplicity of childhood. But of course I was wrong. The really childish behaviour is the storm of rage in which the tempestuous desires—superbly evoked in the free movement of the verse—are directed towards an undefined "freedom." What the poem enforces is that to be "loose as the wind" is to be as incoherent and purposeless; that freedom is to be found not in some undefined "abroad," but, in Ben Jonson's phrase, "here in my bosom, and at home."

The mature "acceptance" that one finds in Herbert's poetry has little in common with a mere disillusioned resignation. The effort towards it is positive in direction. Just as Herbert shows no fear of any imposed punishment for sin—of Hell—but only of the inevitable consequences of sin's "venome," [1] so the recurring stress of his poetry is on life. That "nothing performs the task of life" is the complaint of *Affliction* (iv);

> O give me quicknesse, that I may with mirth
> Praise thee brim-full

is his prayer when "drooping and dull" (*Dulnesse*). And one reason why his religion appears so humane, in a century tending more and more to associate religion with fear and gloom, is that his God is a God of the living.

> Wherefore be cheer'd, and praise him to the full
> Each day, each houre, each moment of the week,
> Who fain would have you be new, tender, quick.
>
> (*Love Unknown*)

It is because he actually did learn from experience to find life "at hand," [2] life realized in the commonplace details of every day, that so many of his "homely" metaphors have such freshness and are the opposite of "stuffy." But acceptance has a further, final meaning. It involves the recognition not only of one's limited sphere but (the paradox is only apparent) of one's own value. It is this that gives such wide significance to the poem, "Love bade me welcome: yet my soul drew back," placed deliberately at the end of the poems in "The Church":

> You must sit down, sayes Love, and taste my meat:
> So I did sit and eat.

The achieved attitude—"accepted and accepting"—marks the final release from anxiety.

With this release not only is significance restored to the present ("Onely the present is thy part and fee . . ." [3]), but death is robbed

---

[1] See the second verse of the poem, *Nature*, in which it is not, I think, fanciful to see some resemblance to the far more searching analysis of evil in *Macbeth*.
[2]   Poore man, thou searchest round
    To finde out *death*, but missest *life* at hand. (*Vanitie* [i]).
[3] *The Discharge.*

of its more extreme terrors.[1] The ending of the poem *Death* (which begins, "Death, thou wast once an uncouth hideous thing") is entirely unforced:

> Therefore we can go die as sleep, and trust
> Half that we have
> Unto an honest faithfull grave;
> Making our pillows either down, or dust.

The integration of attitude thus achieved lies behind the poetry of *Life* ("I made a posie while the day ran by"), and of the well-known *Vertue*—a poem that shows in a quite personal way the characteristically Metaphysical "reconciliation of opposites": the day has lost none of its freshness because its end is freely recognized as implicit in its beginning. But it is in *The Flower* that the sense of new life springing from the resolution of conflict is most beautifully expressed.[2]

> How fresh, O Lord, how sweet and clean
> Are thy returns! ev'n as the flowers in spring;
> To which, besides their own demean,
> The late-past frosts tributes of pleasure bring.
> Grief melts away
> Like snow in May,
> As if there were no such cold thing.
>
> Who would have thought my shrivel'd heart
> Could have recover'd greenesse? It was gone
> Quite under ground; as flowers depart
> To see their mother-root, when they have blown;
> Where they together
> All the hard weather,
> Dead to the world, keep house unknown.

He still feels the need for security, for a guaranteed permanence:

[1] I should like to refer to D. W. Harding's review of *Little Gidding* in this journal (Spring, 1943): "For the man convinced of spiritual values life is a coherent pattern in which the ending has its due place and, because it is part of a pattern, itself leads into the beginning. An over-strong terror of death is often one expression of the fear of living, for death is one of the life-processes that seem too terrifying to be borne."

[2] I think it should be noticed that in the original order, apparently Herbert's own, *The Flower* is immediately preceded by *The Crosse*, another poem on the theme of acceptance, ending, *"Thy will be done."*

GEORGE HERBERT

> O that I once past changing were,
> Fast in thy Paradise, where no flower can wither.

But in the poem as a whole even the fact that the good hours do not last, that they are bound to alternate with "frosts" and depression, is acceped without bitterness:

> These are thy wonders, Lord of power,
> Killing and quickning. . . .

As a result the renewed vitality, waited for without fret or fuss, has something of the naturalness and inevitability of the mounting sap. The sixth stanza takes up the spring imagery:

> And now in age I bud again,
> After so many deaths I live and write;
> I once more smell the dew and rain,
> And relish versing: O my onely light,
> It cannot be
> That I am he
> On whom thy tempests fell all night.

The sense of refreshment, conveyed in imagery of extraordinary sensuous delicacy, is as completely realized as the suffering expressed in the poems of conflict. And like the flower it comes from "under ground," from the deeper levels of the personality.

The account I have given of the positive direction of Herbert's poetry is not meant to imply that anything like a continuous development can be traced in the poems, few of which can be dated with any precision.[1] In any case, development—when it is of the whole man, not simply of a line of thought—rarely shows the smooth curve that biographers like to imagine. We do know, however, that his life at Bemerton was one of uncommon sweetness and serenity, expressing what Dr. Hutchinson calls "an achieved character of humility, tenderness, moral sensitiveness, and personal consecration, which he was very far from having attained or even envisaged when he was dazzled by the attractions

[1] A few seem to be early work, some contain references to the priesthood, and poems that appear in the Bodleian, but not in the Williams, Manuscript may be assumed to be later than the others: see Dr. Hutchinson's Introduction, pp. l-lvi, and pp. lxvii-lxix. It is worth remarking that *The Pilgrimage, Vertue, Life* and *The Flower* are among the poems found only in the Bodleian MS.

of the great world." The poems in which the fluctuating stages of this progress are recorded are important human documents because they handle with honesty and insight questions that, in one form or another, we all have to meet if we wish to come to terms with life.

Chapter Seven

RESTORATION COMEDY:
THE REALITY AND THE MYTH

I

HENRY JAMES—whose "social comedy" may be allowed to provide a standard of maturity—once remarked that he found Congreve "insufferable," [1] and perhaps the first thing to say of Restoration drama—tragedy as well as comedy—is that the bulk of it is insufferably dull. There are long stretches of boredom to be found in the lower ranges of Elizabethan drama, but there is nothing comparable to the unmitigated fatigue that awaits the reader of *Love in a Tub, Sir Martin Mar-all, Mr. Limberham, The Relapse,* or *The Mourning Bride.* And who returns to Dryden's heroic plays with renewed zest? The superiority of the common runs of plays in the first period to that of the second is, at all events, a commonplace. It should be equally commonplace that the strength of the Elizabethan drama lies partly in the kind and scope—the quality and variety—of the interests that the playwrights were able to enlist, partly in the idiom that they had at their command: the drama drew on a vigorous non-dramatic literature, and literature in general was in close relation with non-literary interests and a rich common language. That is not the whole story, but it is an important part of it, and it seems profitable, in a discussion of Restoration comedy, to keep these facts in mind for comparison. Ever since Collier published *A Short View of the Profaneness and Immorality of the English Stage* opponents of Restoration comedy have conducted their case almost entirely in moral terms, and it has been easy for recent critics, rightly discarding Lamb's obvious subterfuge, to turn the moral argument upside down, to find freedom of manners where Macaulay found licentiousness. "Morals" are, in the long run, decidedly relevant—but only in the long run: literary criticism has prior claims. If, to start with, we try to see the comedy of

[1] *Letters,* Vol. I, p. 140.

manners in relation to its contemporary non-dramatic literature—
to take its bearings in the general culture of the time—we may
at least make possible a free and critical approach.

During the forty years that followed the Restoration, English
literature, English culture, was "upper-class" to an extent that it
had never been before, and was not, after Addison, to be again.
"Now if they ask me," said Dryden, "whence it is that our conversation is so much refined? I must freely and without flattery,
ascribe it to the court," and his insistence, as a writer, on "the
benefit of converse" with his courtly patrons was not merely
dedicatory fulsomeness; the influence of the current conception
of "the gentleman" is shown plainly enough by the urbane ease
of his critical prefaces; and Dryden's non-dramatic prose is fairly
representative of the new age.[1]

It is this that explains why, if one comes to Restoration literature after some familiarity with the Elizabethans, the first impression made by the language is likely to be a sense of what has
been lost; the disintegration of the old cultural unity has plainly
resulted in impoverishment. The speech of the educated is now
remote from the speech of the people (Bunyan's huge sales were,
until the eighteenth century, outside "the circumference of wit"),
and idiomatic vigour and evocative power seem to have gone out
of the literary medium. But there was gain as well as loss. The
common mode of Restoration prose—for there is now a common
mode, a norm—was not evolved merely in the interests of good
form and polite intercourse; it had behind it a more serious
pressure. When, in 1667, Sprat attacked "this vicious abundance
of phrase . . . this volubility of tongue, which makes so great a
noise in the world," he had in mind the needs of scientific inquiry and rational discussion. "They have therefore," he said of
the Royal Society, "been most rigorous in putting in execution
the only remedy that can be found for this *extravagance,* and that
has been a constant resolution to reject all amplifications, digres-
sions, and swellings of style; to return back to the primitive
purity and shortness, when men delivered so many *things* almost

---

[1] On "the last and greatest advantage of our writing, which proceeds from
conversation," see in particular the *Defence of the Epilogue.* And the dialogue form
in which Dryden cast the *Essay of Dramatic Poesy* was not unrecognizably far from
actuality.

in an equal number of *words.* They have exacted from all their members a close, naked, natural way of speaking, positive expressions, clear senses, a native easiness, bringing all things as near the mathematical plainness as they can." [1] For the first time the English language was made—and to some extent made consciously —an instrument for rational dissection.

> When once the aversion to bear uneasiness taketh place in a man's mind, it doth so check all the passions, that they are dampt into a kind of indifference; they grow faint and languishing, and come to be subordinate to that fundamental maxim, of not purchasing any thing at the price of a difficulty. This made that he had as little eagerness to oblige, as he had to hurt men; the motive of his giving bounties was rather to make men less uneasy to him, than more easy to themselves; and yet no ill-nature all this while. He would slide from an asking face, and could guess very well. It was throwing a man off from his shoulders, that leaned upon them with his whole weight; so that the party was not gladder to receive, than he was to give.

This is from Halifax's *Character of Charles II,* and the even tone, the sinuous ease of movement and the clarity of the analysis mark the passage as unmistakably post-Restoration. Halifax, of course, is in some ways an unusually handsome representative of his age; he is racy (the apt adjective is supplied by his editor, H. C. Foxcroft) as well as polite. But the achievement represented by his style was far from being a merely individual achievement. The shrewd and subtle portrait of Charles II is unlike anything that had appeared in English before his time, and it could only have appeared when it did.

Now an upper-class culture that produced *Absalom and Achitophel, The Character of a Trimmer,* Dryden's critical prefaces and Locke's *Second Treatise of Government,* may have been limited, but it was not altogether decadent. If the drama is inferior it is not because it represents—by Elizabethan standards—a limited culture, but because it represents contemporary culture so inadequately; it has no significant relation with the best thought of the time. Heroic tragedy is decadent because it is factitious;

---

[1] *The History of the Royal Society of London:* Spingarn, *Critical Essays of the Seventeenth Century,* Vol. II, pp. 112ff.

it substitutes violent emotionalism for emotion, the purple patch for poetry, and its rhetoric, unlike Elizabethan dramatic rhetoric, has no connexion with the congenial non-dramatic modes of the age; it is artificial in a completely damaging sense, *and by contemporary standards.* If we look for an early illustration of the bad mid-eighteenth-century conception of poetry as something applied from the outside [1] we find it in Dryden's verse plays, where he adopts canons of style that he would not have dreamed of applying—apart from his Odes—in his non-dramatic verse. Tragedy, he said, "is naturally pompous and magnificent." Nothing in English literature is more surprising—if we stop to consider—than the complete discrepancy between the sinewy ease of Dryden's satires and the stiff opaqueness of his dramatic verse; and "the lofty style," since it cannot modulate, is always coming down with a bump.

> I'm pleased and pained, since first her eyes I saw,
> As I were stung with some tarantula.
> Arms, and the dusty field, I less admire,
> And soften strangely in some new desire;
> Honour burns in me not so fiercely bright,
> But pales as fires when mastered by the light:
> Even while I speak and look, I change yet more,
> And now am nothing that I was before.
> I'm numbed, and fixed, and scarce my eyeballs move;
> I fear it is the lethargy of love! [2]

It is only in the easy strength of occasional lines ("A good, luxurious, palatable faith") that we hear his natural voice. In the plays as a whole—each made up of a succession of "great" moments and heroic postures—the "nature" that is "wrought up to a higher pitch" [3] bears little resemblance to the Nature that was to figure so largely in the Augustan code.

This, or a similar account, would probably be accepted by all critics of the Restoration heroic play. What is not commonly

---

"... enriching every subject (otherwise dry and barren) with a pomp of diction and luxuriant harmony of numbers."—Gray's note to *The Progress of Poesy*, 1754.
[2] *The Conquest of Granada*, Part I, III, i.
[3] "... the nature of a serious play; this last is indeed the representation of nature, but 'tis nature wrought up to a higher pitch."—*Of Dramatic Poesy.* The final paragraph of the Preface to *Religio Laici* has some interesting remarks in this connexion; e.g. "The florid, elevated, and figurative way is for the passions."

recognized (it is, at all events, not said) is that the comedy of manners exhibits a parallel attenuation and enfeeblement of what the age, taken as a whole, had to offer. I am not, for the moment, referring to the moral or social code expressed. The observation to start from is that the prose in which Restoration comedy is written—select which dramatist you like—is poor and inexpressive in comparison with the staple non-dramatic prose.

Congreve is usually accepted as the most brilliant stylist of the five or six comic dramatists who count. But place beside the extract quoted from Halifax a passage or two from *Love for Love* or *The Way of the World* (it makes no difference whether the speaker is Scandal or Mirabell), and Congreve's style shows as nerveless in the comparison:

> A mender of reputations! ay, just as he is a keeper of secrets, another virtue that he sets up for in the same manner. For the rogue will speak aloud in the posture of a whisper; and deny a woman's name, while he gives you the marks of her person: he will forswear receiving a letter from her, and at the same time show you her hand in the superscription; and yet perhaps he has counterfeited the hand too, and sworn to a truth; but he hopes not to be believed; and refuses the reputation of a lady's favour, as a doctor says *No* to a bishopric, only that it may be granted him. In short, he is a public professor of secrecy, and makes proclamation that he holds private intelligence.

> *A.* To give t' other his due, he has something of good nature, and does not always want wit.

> *B.* Not always: but as often as his memory fails him, and his common-place of comparisons. He is a fool with a good memory, and some few scraps of other folks' wit. He is one whose conversation can never be approved, yet it is now and then to be endured. He has indeed one good quality, he is not exceptious; for he so passionately affects the reputation of understanding raillery, that he will construe an affront into a jest; and call down-right rudeness and ill language, satire and fire.

This reminds me of Arnold's definition of Macaulayese, "the external characteristic being a hard metallic movement with nothing of the soft play of life, and the internal characteristic being a perpetual semblance of hitting the right nail on the head without the reality." Both construction and movement are so far from being expressive *of* anything in particular that the main function of some words is, it seems, to complete an antithesis or to display a riddling wit.[1] The verbal pattern appears at times to be completely unrelated to a mode of perceiving. The passages quoted have an air of preening themselves on their acute discriminations, but the antitheses are mechanical, and the pattern is monotonously repeated: "She has beauty enough to make any man think she has wit; and complaisance enough not to contradict him who should tell her so"—the common form soon loses the sting of surprise. Burnet can write in an antithetical style which also penetrates:

> And tho' he desired to become absolute, and to overturn both our religion and our laws, yet he would neither run the risk, nor give himself the trouble, which so great a design required. He had an appearance of gentleness in his outward deportment: but he seemed to have no bowels nor tenderness in his nature: and in the end of his life he became cruel.[2]

The nearest approach to subtlety that Congreve's style allows is represented by such things as this:

> *Fainall.* You are a gallant man, Mirabell; and though you may have cruelty enough not to satisfy a lady's longing, you have too much generosity not to be tender of her honour. Yet you speak with an indifference which seems to be affected, and confesses you are conscious of a negligence.
>
> *Mirabell.* You pursue the argument with a distrust that seems to be unaffected, and confess you are conscious of a concern for which the lady is more indebted to you than is your wife.

It isn't, really, very subtle. As for the "wit," when it isn't merely verbal and obvious ("Fruitful, the head fruitful;—that bodes horns; the fruit of the head is horns," etc.) it is hopelessly dependent on convention.

---

[1] *The Old Bachelor* shows the riddles in the process of manufacture. *Bellmour:* He is the drum to his own praise—the only implement of a soldier he resembles; like that, being full of blustering noise and emptiness. *Sharper:* And like that, of no use but to be beaten, etc.

[2] I quote from Professor Nichol Smith's excellent anthology, *Characters from the Histories and Memoirs of the Seventeenth Century* (Clarendon Press).

> She that marries a fool, Sir Sampson, forfeits the reputation of her honesty or understanding: and she that marries a very witty man is a slave to the severity and insolent conduct of her husband. I should like a man of wit for a lover, because I would have such a man in my power; but I would no more be his wife than his enemy. For his malice is not a more terrible consequence of his aversion than his jealousy is of his love.

An intelligent husband, you see, must be jealous; take away that entertaining assumption and the point is blunted. Halifax is a witty writer, but his wit springs naturally from the situation he is concerned with and illuminates it. "A partner in government is so unnatural a thing that it is a squint-eyed allegiance which must be paid to such a double-bottomed monarchy."[1] Congreve's wit is entirely self-regarding.

If there were space to discuss the manner of Wycherley, Etherege and Vanbrugh, it is a similar account that would have to be given. I am not suggesting that they write in a completely indistinguishable common mode (though they all have passages that might come from any play); but in essentials—in the way in which they use their similes and antitheses, in the conception of "style" and "wit" that they exhibit—they all stand together. Not one of them has achieved a genuinely sensitive and individual mode of expression; and in each the pattern of the prose inhibits any but the narrowest—and the most devastatingly *expected*—response. That, I should claim, is the judgment to which an analysis of their prose inevitably leads. The trouble is not that the Restoration comic writers deal with a limited number of themes, but that they bring to bear a miserably limited set of attitudes. And these, in turn, are factitious to exactly the same degree as the prose is artificial and non-representative of the current non-dramatic medium.

II

Apart from the presentation of incidental and unrelated "wit" (which soon becomes as tiring as the epigrams of the "good talker"), Restoration comedy has two main interests—the be-

---

[1] Also from *The Character of a Trimmer*:—". . . the indecent courtship of some silken divines, who, one would think, did practise to bow at the altar, only to learn to make the better legs at Court."

haviour of the polite and of pretenders to politeness, and some aspects of sexual relationships. Critics have made out a case for finding· in one or other of these themes a unifying principle and a serious base for the comedy of manners. According to Miss Lynch, the "thoroughly conventionalized social mode" of the courtly circle "was discovered to have manifestly comic aspects, both when awkwardly misinterpreted, and when completely fulfilled through personalities to which, however, it could not give complete expression," [1] and both these discrepancies were exploited by Etherege and his successors. Bonamy Dobrée, attributing to the comic dramatists "a deep curiosity, and a desire to try new ways of living," finds that "the distinguishing characteristic of Restoration comedy down to Congreve is that it is concerned with the attempt to rationalize sexual relationships. It is this that makes it different from any other comedy that has ever been written. . . . It said in effect, 'Here is life lived upon certain assumptions; see what it becomes.' It also dealt, as no other comedy has ever done, with a subject that arose directly out of this, namely sex-antagonism, a consequence of the experimental freedom allowed to women, which gave matter for some of its most brilliant scenes." [2]

These accounts, as developed, certainly look impressive, and if Restoration comedy really answered to them—if it had something fresh and penetrating to say on sex and social relations—there would be no need to complain, even if one found the "solutions" distasteful. But Miss Lynch's case, at all events, depends on a vigorous reading into the plays of values which are not there, values which could not possibly be expressed, in fact, in the prose of any of the dramatists. (The candid reader can turn up the passages selected by Miss Lynch in support of her argument, and see if they are not all in the factitious, superficial mode that I have described.)

We may consider, by way of illustration, Etherege's *The Man of Mode*. When the play opens, Dorimant ("the finest of all fine gentlemen in Restoration comedy") is trying to rid himself of an old mistress, Mrs. Loveit, before taking up with a new, Bellinda,

[1] K. M. Lynch, *The Social Mode of Restoration Comedy*, p. 216.
[2] Bonamy Dobrée, *Restoration Comedy*, pp. 22-23.

whilst Young Bellair, in love with Emilia, is trying to find some way out of marrying Harriet, an heiress whom his father has brought to town for him. The entertainment is made up of these two sets of complications, together with an exhibition of the would-be modishness of Sir Fopling Flutter. Events move fast. After a night spent in various sociabilities Dorimant keeps an appointment with Bellinda at 5 A.M. Letting her out of his lodgings an hour or so later, and swearing to be discreet "By all the Joys I have had, and those you keep in store," he is surprised by his companions, and in the resulting confusion Bellinda finds herself paying an unwilling visit to Mrs. Loveit. Dorimant appears and is rated by the women before he "flings off." Meanwhile Young Bellair and Emilia have secretly married. Dorimant, his equanimity recovered, turns up for the exposure, followed by his mistresses. The lovers are forgiven, the mistresses are huddled off the stage, and it is decided that Dorimant, who, the previous day, had ingratiated himself with Harriet's mother, and whose "soul has quite given up her liberty," shall be allowed to pay court to the heiress.

It seems to me that what the play provides—apart from the briskly handled intrigue—is a demonstration of the physical stamina of Dorimant. But Miss Lynch sees further. For her, Dorimant is "the fine flowering of Restoration culture." Illustrating her theory of the double standard, she remarks: "We laugh at Sir Fopling Flutter because he so clumsily parodies social fashions which Dorimant interprets with unfailing grace and distinction. We laugh at Dorimant because his assumed affectation admits of so poor and incomplete an expression of an attractive and vigorous personality." [1] The "unfailing grace and distinction" are perhaps not much in evidence in Dorimant's spiteful treatment of Mrs. Loveit; [2] but even if we ignore those brutish scenes we are

---

[1] *The Social Mode of Restoration Comedy*, p. 181.

[2] See II, ii, and V, i, where Dorimant, trying to force a quarrel with Mrs. Loveit, attributes to her a fondness for Sir Fopling. The first of these scenes was too much for Etherege, and he makes Bellinda say:

> He's given me the proof which I desired of his love,
> But 'tis a proof of his ill nature too.
> I wish I had not seen him use her so.

But this is soon forgotten, and we are not, of course, called on to register an unfavourable judgment of Dorimant.

forced to ask, How do we know that there *is* this "attractive and vigorous personality" beneath the conventional forms? Dorimant's' intrigues are of no more human significance than those of a barn-yard cock, and as for what Miss Lynch calls "his really serious affair with Harriet" (I feel this deserves a *sic*), it is purely theatrical, and the "pangs of love" are expressed in nothing but the conventional formulae: "She's gone, but she has left a pleasing Image of herself behind that wanders in my Soul." The answer to the question posed is that Miss Lynch's account is a mere assumption. Nothing that Dorimant actually *says* will warrant it —and nothing in the whole of Restoration comedy—in the words actually spoken—allows us a glimpse of those other "personalities" to which the conventional social modes "could not give complete expression." The "real values" [1] simply are not there.

A minor point can be made in passing. It is just possible to claim that Restoration comedy contains "social criticism" in its handling of "the vulgar." "Come Mr. Sharper," says Congreve's Belinda, "you and I will take a turn, and laugh at the vulgar; both the great vulgar and the small," and Etherege's Lady Townley expresses the common attitude of the polite towards the social nuisances: "We should love wit, but for variety be able to divert ourselves with the extravagancies of those who want it." The butts, unfortunately, are only shown as fools by the discrepancy between their ambitions and their achievements, not because their ambitions are puerile. The subject is hardly worth discussing, since it is obviously nothing but an easily satisfied sense of superiority that is diverted by the "variety" of a constant succession of Dapperwits, Froths and Fopling Flutters. "When a humour takes in London," Tom Brown remarked, "they ride it to death ere they leave it. The primitive Christians were not persecuted with half that variety as the poor unthinking beaus are tormented with upon the theatre . . . A huge great muff, and a gaudy ribbon hanging at a bully's backside, is an excellent jest, and new-invented curses, as, Stap my vitals, damn my diaphragm, slit my wind pipe, sink me ten thousand fathom deep, rig up

---

[1] "The love affairs of Courtal and Ariana, Freeman and Gatty [in *She Wou'd if She Cou'd*] are similarly embarrassed by social convention. . . . The conduct of these polite lovers acquires comic vitality through the continually suggested opposition of artificial and real values."—*Op. cit.*, p. 152.

a new beau, though in the main 'tis but the same everlasting cox-comb." [1]

III

In the matter of sexual relations Restoration comedy is entirely dominated by a narrow set of conventions. The objection that it is only certain characters, not the dramatists themselves, who accept them can be more freely encountered when the assumptions that are expressed most frequently have been briefly illustrated.

The first convention is, of course, that constancy in love, especially in marriage, is a bore. Vanbrugh, who was the most uneasy if not the most honest of the comic dramatists (I think that in *The Provok'd Wife* he shows as unusually honest), unambiguously attributes this attitude to Sir John Brute:

> What cloying meat is love—when matrimony's the sauce to it! Two years marriage has debauch'd my five senses. . . . No boy was ever so weary of his tutor, no girl of her bib, no nun of doing penance, or old maid of being chaste, as I am of being married. Sure there's a secret curse entail'd upon the very name of wife!
>
> The woman's well enough; she has no vice that I know of, but she's a wife, and—damn a wife! [2]

What Vanbrugh saw as a fit sentiment for Sir John had by that time (1697) served the Restoration stage—without change—for thirty years. In *She Wou'd if She Cou'd* Etherege had exhibited Sir Oliver Cockwood in an identical vein: "A pox of this tying man and woman together, for better, for worse." "To have a mistress love thee entirely" is "a damn'd trouble." "There are sots that would think themselves happy in such a Lady; but to a true bred Gentleman all lawful solace is abomination." [3] If Sir Oliver is a fool it is only because he is a trifle gross in his expression. "If you did but know, Madam," says the polite Freeman, "what an odious thing it is to be thought to love a Wife in good Company." [4] And the convention is constantly turning up in Con-

[1] Tom Brown, *Works*, Vol. III, *Amusements Comical and Serious*, "At the Playhouse," p. 39.
[2] *The Provok'd Wife*, I, i; II, i.
[3] *She Wou'd if She Cou'd*, I, i; III, iii.
[4] *Ibid.*, III, iii.

greve. "There is no creature perfectly civil but a husband," explains Mrs. Frail, "for in a little time he grows only rude to his wife, and that is the highest good breeding, for it begets his civility to other people." [1] "Marry her! Marry her!" Fainall advises Mirabell, "Be half as well acquainted with her charms, as you are with her defects, and my life on't, you are your own man again." [2] And Witwoud: "A wit should no more be sincere than a woman constant; one argues a decay of parts, as t'other of beauty." [3] Appetite, it seems (and this is the second assumption), needs perpetually fresh stimulus. This is the faith of Rhodophil in *Marriage à la Mode* and of Constant in *The Provok'd Wife*, as well as of Wycherley's old procuress, Mrs. Joyner. "If our wives would suffer us but now and then to make excursions," Rhodophil explains to Palamede, "the benefit of our variety would be theirs; instead of one continued, lazy, tired love, they would, in their turns, have twenty vigorous, fresh, and active lovers." [4] "Would anything but a madman complain of uncertainty?" asks Congreve's Angelica, for "security is an insipid thing, and the overtaking and possessing of a wish, discovers the folly of the chase." [5] And Fainall, in *The Way of the World,* speaks for a large class when he hints at a liking for sauce—a little gentleman's relish—to his seductions: "I'd no more play with a man that slighted his ill fortune than I'd make love to a woman who under-valued the loss of her reputation." [6] Fainall, of course, is what he is, but the attitude that makes sexual pleasure "the bliss," that makes woman "delicious"—something to be savoured—as well as "damned" and "destructive," demands, for its support, "the pleasure of a chase." [7]

> Would you long preserve your lover?
> Would you still his goddess reign?

[1] *Love for Love,* I, ii.
[2] *The Way of the World,* I, ii.
[3] *Ibid.*
[4] *Marriage à la Mode,* II, i. Cf. *The Provok'd Wife,* III, i: *Constant,* "There's a poor sordid slavery in marriage, that turns the flowing tide of honour, and sinks us to the lowest ebb of infamy. 'Tis a corrupted soil: Ill-nature, sloth, cowardice, and dirt, are all its product."
[5] *Love for Love,* IV, iii.
[6] *The Way of the World,* I, i.
[7] *The Old Bachelor,* I, i; III, ii ("O thou delicious, damned, dear, destructive woman!"); IV, ii.

RESTORATION COMEDY

Never let him all discover,
Never let him much obtain.[1]

Restoration comedy used to be considered outrageously out-spoken, but such stuff as this, far from being "outspoken," hovers on the outskirts of sexual relations, and sees nothing but the titillation of appetite (" 'Tis not the success," Collier observed, "but the manner of gaining it which is all in all").[2] Sex is a hook baited with tempting morsels; [3] it is a thirst quencher; [4] it is a cordial; [5] it is a dish to feed on; [6] it is a bunch of grapes; [7] it is anything but sex. (This, of course, explains why some people can combine a delighted approval of Restoration comedy with an un-balanced repugnance for such modern literature as deals sincerely and realistically with sexual relationships.)

Now the objection referred to above was that sentiments such as these are not offered for straightforward acceptance. Many of them are attributed to characters plainly marked as Wicked (Maskwell, for example, is the black-à-vised villain of melo-drama), or, more frequently, as trivial, and the dramatist can therefore dissociate himself. He may even be engaged in showing his audience the explicit, logical consequences of the half-con-scious premises on which they base their own lives, saying, as Mr. Dobrée has it, "Here is life lived upon certain assumptions; see what it becomes." To this there are several answers. The first is that reflexions of the kind that I have quoted are indistinguish-able in tone and style from the general epigrammatic stock-in-

[1] *Ibid.*, II, ii.
[2] *A Short View of the Profaneness and Immorality of the English Stage*, Fifth Edition, 1738, p. 116.
[3] " 'Tis true you are so eager in pursuit of the temptation, that you save the devil the trouble of leading you into it: nor is it out of discretion that you don't swallow the very hook yourselves have baited, but . . . what you meant for a whet turns the edge of your puny stomachs."—*The Old Bachelor*, I, i. "Strike Heartwell home, before the bait's worn off the hook. Age will come. He nibbled fairly yesterday, and no doubt will be eager enough to-day to swallow the temptation."—*Ibid.*, III, i.
[4] "What was my pleasure is become my duty: and I have as little stomach to her now as if I were her husband. . . . Pox on't! that a man can't drink without quench-ing his thirst."—*The Double-Dealer*, III, i.
[5] You must get you a mistress, Rhodophil. That, indeed, is living upon cor-dials; but as fast as one fails, you must supply it with another."—*Marriage à la Mode*, I, i.
[6] "Because our husbands cannot feed on one dish, therefore we must be starved."—*Ibid.*, III, i.
[7] "The only way to keep us new to one another, is never to enjoy, as they keep grapes, by hanging them upon a line; they must touch nothing, if you would preserve them fresh."—*Ibid.*, V, i.

trade (the audience was not altogether to be blamed if, as Congreve complained, they could not at first "distinguish betwixt the character of a Witwoud and a Lovewit"); and they are largely "exhibited," just as all the self-conscious witticisms are exhibited, for the sake of their immediate "comic" effect. One has only to note the laughter of a contemporary audience at a revival, and the places where the splutters occur, to realize how much of the fun provides a rather gross example of tendency wit.[1] The same attitudes, moreover, are manipulated again and again, turning up with the stale monotony of jokes on postcards, and the play that is made with them demands only the easiest, the most superficial, response. But it is, after all, useless to argue about the degree of detachment, the angle at which these attitudes and assumptions are presented. As soon as one selects a particular comedy for that exercise one realizes that all is equally grist to the mill and that the dramatist (there is no need, here, to make distinctions) has no coherent attitude of his own. A consistent artistic purpose would not be content to express itself in a style that allows so limited, so local an effect.

But it is the triviality that one comes back to. In Dryden's *Marriage à la Mode* the characters accept the usual conventions: constancy is dull, and love only thrives on variety.

> *Palamede.* O, now I have found it! you dislike her for no other reason but because she's your wife.
>
> *Rhodophil.* And is not that enough? All that I know of her perfections now, is only by memory . . . At last we arrived at that point, that there was nothing left in us to make us new to one another . . .
>
> *Palamede.* The truth is, your disease is very desperate; but, though you cannot be cured, you may be patched up a little: you must get you a mistress, Rhodophil. That, indeed, is living upon cordials; but, as fast as one fails, you must supply it with another.

---

[1] The Freudian "censor" is at times projected in the form of the stage puritan. The plays written soon after the Commonwealth period appealed to Royalist prejudice by satirizing the "seemingly precise"; and even later, when "the bonfires of devotion," "the bellows of zeal," were forgotten, a good deal of the self-conscious swagger of indecency seems to have been directed against "our protestant husbands," city merchants, aldermen and the like; the "daring" effect was intensified by postulating a shockable audience somewhere—not necessarily in the theatre. Not that the really obscene jokes were merely bravado: Collier quite rightly remarked that "the modern poets seem to use smut as the old ones did Machines, to relieve a fainting situation."—*A Short View*, Fifth Edition, p. 4.

RESTORATION COMEDY

The mistress that Rhodophil selects is Melantha, whom Palamede is to marry; Palamede falls in love with Doralice, Rhodophil's wife, and the ensuing complications provide sufficient entertainment (the grotto scene, III, ii, is really funny). Mr. Dobrée, however, regards the play as a witty exposure of the impossibility of rationalizing sex relations, as Palamede and Rhodophil attempt to rationalize them. Dryden "laughs morality back into its rightful place, as the scheme which ultimately makes life most comfortable." [1] But what Dryden actually does is to *use* the conventions for the amusement they afford, not to examine them. The level at which the play works is fairly indicated by the opening song:

> Why should a foolish marriage vow,
>   Which long ago was made,
> Oblige us to each other now,
>   When passion is decayed?
> We loved, and we loved, as long as we could,
>   'Till our love was loved out in us both;
> But our marriage is dead, when the pleasure is fled:
>   'Twas pleasure first made it an oath.
>
> If I have pleasures for a friend,
>   And further love in store,
> What wrong has he, whose joys did end,
>   And who could give no more?
> 'Tis a madness that he should be jealous of me,
>   Or that I should bar him of another:
> For all we can gain, is to give ourselves pain,
>   When neither can hinder the other.

The lovers make no attempt to "rationalize sex" for the simple reason that genuine sexual feelings no more enter into the play as a whole than feelings of any kind enter into the song. (The obviously faked emotions of the heroic plot are, after all, relevant —and betraying.) And according to Mr. Dobrée, "In one sense the whole idea of Restoration comedy is summed up in the opening song of *Marriage à la Mode*.[2]

In a sense, too, Mr. Dobrée is right. Restoration comedy no-

---

[1] *Restoration Comedy*, p. 133.
[2] *Ibid.*, p. 106.

where provides us with much more of the essential stuff of human experience than we have there. Even Congreve, by common account the best of the comic writers, is no exception. I have said that his verbal pattern often seems to be quite unrelated to an individual mode of perceiving. At best it registers a very limited mode. Restoration prose is all "social" in its tone, implications and general tenor, but Congreve's observation is *merely* of the public surface. And Congreve's, too, relies on the conventional assumptions. In *The Way of the World,* it is true, they are mainly given to the bad and the foolish to express: it is Fainall who discourses on the pleasures of disliking one's wife, and Witwoud who maintains that only old age and ugliness ensure constancy. And Mirabell, who is explicitly opposed to some aspects of contemporary manners, goes through the common forms in a tone of rather weary aloofness: "I wonder, Fainall, that you who are married, and of consequence should be discreet, will suffer your wife to be of such a party." But Congreve himself is not above raising a cheap snigger; [1] and, above all, the characters with some life in them have nothing to fall back on— nothing, that is, except the conventional, and conventionally limited, pleasures of sex. Millamant, who says she loathes the country and hates the town, expects to draw vitality from the excitement of incessant solicitation:

> I'll be solicited to the very last, nay, and afterwards . . . I should think I was poor and had nothing to bestow, if I were reduced to an inglorious ease, and freed from the agreeable fatigues of solicitation. . . . Oh, I hate a lover that can dare to think he draws a moment's air, independent of the bounty of his mistress. There is not so impudent a thing in nature, as the saucy look of an assured man, confident of success. The pedantic arrogance of a very husband has not so pragmatical an air.

Everyone seems to have found Millamant intelligent and attractive, but her attitude is not far removed from that expressed in

> Would you long preserve your lover?
> Would you still his goddess reign?

[1] Ay there's my grief; that's the sad change of life,
To lose my title, and yet keep my wife.
The Way of the World, II, ii.

and she shares with characters who are decidedly not attractive a disproportionate belief in "the pleasure of a chase." Which is not surprising in view of her other occupations and resources; visiting, writing and receiving letters, tea-parties and small talk make up a round that is never for a moment enlivened by the play of genuine intelligence.[1] And although Congreve recognizes, at times, the triviality of his characters,[2] it is to the world whose confines were the Court, the drawing-room, the play-house and the park—a world completely lacking the real sophistication and self-knowledge that might, in some measure, have redeemed it— that he limits his appeal.

It is, indeed, hard to resist the conclusion that "society"—the smart town society that sought entertainment at the theatres— was fundamentally bored.[3] In *The Man of Mode* Emilia remarks of Medley, "I love to hear him talk o' the intrigues, let 'em be never so dull in themselves, he'll make 'em pleasant i' the relation," and the idiotic conversation that follows (II, i), affording us a glimpse of what Miss Lynch calls "the most brilliant society which Restoration comedy has to offer," [4] suggests in more than one way how badly society *needed* to be entertained. It is the boredom—the constant need for titillation—that helps to explain not only the heroic "heightening" of emotion, but the various scenic effects, the devices of staging and costume that became popular at this period. (Charles II "almost died of laughing" at Nell Gwynn's enormous hat.) The conventions—of sexual pursuit, and so on—were an attempt to make life interesting—an impossible job for those who were aware of so limited a range of human potentialities.

The dominating mood of Restoration comedy is, by common

---

[1] As Lady Brute remarks. "After all, a woman's life would be a dull business, if it were not for the men . . . We shou'd never blame Fate for the shortness of our days; our time would hang wretchedly upon our hands."—*The Provok'd Wife*, III, iii.

[2] *Mirabell:* You had the leisure to entertain a herd of fools; things who visit you from their excessive idleness; bestowing on your easiness that time which is the encumbrance of their lives. How can you find delight in such society?—*The Way of the World*, II, i.

[3] The constitution, habits and demands of the theatre audience are admirably illustrated by Alexandre Beljame in that neglected classic of scholarship, *Le Public et les Hommes de Lettres en Angleterre au Dix-Huitième Siècle*, 1660-1740. See also C. V. Deane, *Dramatic Theory and the Rhymed Heroic Play*, Chapter I, Section 6.

[4] *The Social Mode of Restoration Comedy*, p. 177.

account, a cynical one. But one cannot even say that there is here, in contrast to naïve Romantic fervours, the tough strength of disillusion. If—recognizing that there is a place in the educational process for, say, La Rochfoucauld—one finds the "cynicism" of the plays distasteful, it is because it is easy and superficial; the attitudes that we are presented with are based on so meagre an amount of observation and experience. Thus, "Elle retrouvait dans l'adultère toutes les platitudes du mariage" has, superficially, much the same meaning as, "I find now, by sad experience, that a mistress is much more chargeable than a wife, and after a little time too, grows full as dull and insignificant." But whereas the first sentence has behind it the whole of *Madame Bovary,* the second comes from *Sir Martin Mar-all,* which (although Dryden shares the honours with the Duke of Newcastle) is perhaps the stupidest play I have ever read, and the context is imbecility.

But the superficiality is betrayed at every turn—by the obvious rhythms of the interspersed songs, as well as by the artificial elegance of the prose. And the cynicism is closely allied with—merges into—sentimentality. One thinks of the sentimentally conceived Fidelia in the resolutely "tough" *Plain Dealer;* and there is no doubt that the audience was meant to respond sympathetically when, at the end of *Love for Love,* Angelica declared her love for Valentine: "Had I the world to give you, it could not make me worthy of so generous a passion; here's my hand, my heart was always yours, and struggled very hard to make this utmost trial of your virtue." There is, of course, a good deal of loose emotion in the heroic plays, written—it is useful to remember—for the same audience:

> I'm numbed, and fixed, and scarce my eyeballs move;
> I fear it is the lethargy of love!
> 'Tis he; I feel him now in every part:
> Like a new lord he vaunts about my heart;
> Surveys, in state, each corner of my breast,
> While poor fierce I, that was, am dispossessed.[1]

[1] *The Conquest of Granada,* Part I, III, i.

RESTORATION COMEDY

A secret pleasure trickles through my veins:
It works about the inlets of my soul,
To feel thy touch, and pity tempts the pass:
But the tough metal of my heart resists;
'Tis warmed with the soft fire, not melted down.[1]

"Feeling," in Dryden's serious plays, is fairly represented by such passages as these, and Dryden, we know, was not alone in admiring the Fletcherian "pathos." But it is the lyric verse of the period that provides the strongest confirmatory evidence of the kind of bad taste that is in question. It is not merely that in Etherege, Sedley and Dorset the feeling comes from much nearer the surface than in the Metaphysicals and the Caroline poets, intellectual "wit" no longer strengthens and controls the feeling. Conventional attitudes are rigged out in a conventional vocabulary and conventional images. (The stock outfit—the "fair eyes" that "wound," the "pleasing pains," the "sighs and tears," the "bleeding hearts" and "flaming darts"—can be studied in any anthology.[2] There is, in consequence, a pervasive strain of sentimental vulgarity.

> Farewell, ungrateful traitor!
> Farewell, my perjured swain!
> Let never injured creature
> Believe a man again.
> The pleasure of possessing
> Surpasses all expressing,
> But 'tis too short a blessing,
> And love too long a pain.
>
> .   .   .   .   .
>
> The passion you pretended,
> Was only to obtain;
> But when the charm is ended,
> The charmer you disdain.

[1] *Don Sebastian*, III, i.
[2] See, for example, Aphra Behn's "Love in fantastic triumph sate," Buckingham's *To his Mistress* ("Phyllis, though your all powerful charms"), Dryden's "Ask not the cause why sullen spring," and "Ah, how sweet it is to love," and Sedley's *To Chloris*—all in *The Oxford Book of English Verse*, or Ault's *Seventeenth Century Lyrics*.

EXPLORATIONS

Your love by ours we measure
Till we have lost our treasure,
But dying is a pleasure
When living is a pain.

This piece of music-hall sentiment comes from Dryden's *The Spanish Friar,* and it does not stand alone. The mode that was to produce, among other things of equal merit, "When lovely woman stoops to folly," had its origin in the lyrics of the Restoration period. Most of these were written by the group connected with the theatres, and they serve to underline the essential criticism of the plays. The criticism that defenders of Restoration comedy need to answer is not that the comedies are "immoral," but that they are trivial, gross and dull.

Chapter Eight

NOTE ON A MARXIAN VIEW OF THE SEVENTEENTH CENTURY

THE FIRST of the books listed below [1] contains three essays, written from the Marxist point of view, on different aspects of the English Revolution—"perhaps the most important event that has yet occurred in English history"—and of them Mr. Hill's is the one that most demands attention. Writing for a non-specialist audience Mr. Hill avoids most of the pitfalls of "popular" history, and, drawing on large resources of information, he orders his material in a remarkably workmanlike way. In some seventy pages he exhibits the social forces behind the constitutional opposition to the early Stuarts, disentangles the conflicts of interest and policy on the parliamentary side, and gives a lucid summary of the results of the struggle by which the economically dominant classes adapted the political organization of the country to their needs. If, in spite of these merits, one feels that the total picture is over-simplified it is not because Mr. Hill has in any way twisted the evidence that is relevant for assessing political action in general. It is rather a question of whether another kind of evaluation is not also necessary if the common conviction of the three authors, "that an understanding of the problems and ideas of the seventeenth century will help us to solve the problems of to-day," is to be justified.

My uneasiness centres on the use of the word "progressive," which, together with its complement "reactionary," is freely scattered about some part of the essay. (Progressive—the trading and industrial classes and those landowners who treated their lands as a commercial investment; reactionary—James and Charles, the Church, the gilds, and gentry who wanted to live in the old style.) Progressive seems to be used in three ways which ought to be, but are not, distinguished. As a neutral descriptive term it is applied

[1] *The English Revolution,* 1640, Three Essays in Interpretation, edited by Christopher Hill (Lawrence and Wishart, 1940). *The Role of the Individual in History,* by G. V. Plekhanov (Lawrence and Wishart, 1940).

to anything making for "the full development of all the resources [sc. economic resources] of the country." An intermediate meaning is found in the assumption that anything progressive in the first sense was also progressive as representing an extension of the general good: "the struggle of the bourgeoisie was progressive, representing the interests of the country as a whole"; and "free capitalist development was of much more benefit to the masses of the population than the maintenance of an outmoded, unproductive and parasitic feudalism." Finally the term is invested with a sense of general, moral approval: "the middle-class struggle to shake off the control of this [court] group was not merely selfish, not reactionary, but progressive"; it was "the essential preliminary condition of social and intellectual advance."

No one is likely to deny that the struggle of the seventeenth-century bourgeoisie was progressive in the first sense; and since their attempt to make political forms correspond with economic power was inevitable we may understand the phrase, "the historical necessity and progressiveness of their task" (the collocation has important implications). Why, and in what ways, this movement was of "benefit to the masses of the population" is something that should perhaps have been explained. Since the progressive merchants and industrialists of the Civil War period were the direct ancestors of the capitalists of the eighteenth century whose outlook was expressed in such progressive maxims as, "In a free Nation where slaves are not allowed of, the surest Wealth consists in a Multitude of Laborious Poor," and, "In a certain class of people too much well-being lessens industriousness and encourages idleness with all its attendant evils," one cannot suppose Mr. Hill to refer to the immediate benefits accruing to the wage-earners as a body.[1] (Since Mr. Hill is certainly well aware of the effects of "primary accumulation" on many thousands of workers, eloquently described by Marx in the twenty-

---

[1] The attitude of eighteenth-century employers towards "the laborious poor" is well described by Heckscher, *Mercantilism*, Vol. II, pp. 152ff., from which the above quotations are taken. Heckscher remarks that in England in the eighteenth century "there is no doubt at all that the State everywhere exerted its influence on the side of low wages and unfavourable conditions of work." The degraded condition of workers in the rapidly expanding coal industry in the seventeenth century—an industry in many ways foreshadowing the more general economic developments—is described by J. U. Nef in *The Rise of the British Coal Industry*, Part IV, Chapter IV.

fourth chapter of *Capital,* one is almost tempted to believe that he had in mind the ultimate benefits to mankind when the historical process, helped on by the seventeenth-century bourgeoisie, should have completed itself.) Even at the economic level the advance in productiveness brought attendant evils which, together with the beginnings of change in methods of work, in the status of the workers and in the simpler kinds of enjoyment available, should have qualified the simple formula. But even more disturbing is the way in which "progressive" in its third sense slurs over all activities not immediately connected with economics. Charles I's financial methods were corrupt and impossible, but why is it that a minor Caroline court poet like Carew (thoroughly representative of his class and its tradition) is so much finer than a minor Augustan poet like Prior? The old, semifeudal agricultural order was bound to pass, but how was it that that order could produce *The Pilgrim's Progress?* (Mr. Badman, one remembers, was thoroughly progressive.) The English language necessarily developed in certain ways to meet the needs of an increasingly scientific and practical age, but what qualities were lost—and, since language is an index of deep-seated habits of feeling and observing, what was the significance of that loss— about the time of the Restoration? Mr. Hill may say that it was not his purpose to raise the issues indicated here, but consideration of them is not only important in connexion with the question of motive in the participants in the seventeenth-century struggle, it is essential if by "the problems of to-day"—towards a solution of which Mr. Hill explicitly offers his essay—we are to understand not only political problems but the problems that lie beyond politics.

> It is struggle that wins reforms [the essay concludes], just as it is struggle that will retain the liberties which our ancestors won for us. And if the people find the legal system "not suitable to freedom as it is," then it can be changed by united action. That is the lesson of the seventeenth century for to-day.

It seems to me that the lesson of the seventeenth century is a more difficult lesson than that, and to learn it we need to be aware of many factors that the Marxist philosophy of "historical necessity and progressiveness" is content to ignore. Since I have no wish to incur a charge of "bias against liberalism in general" perhaps I may invoke here the name of that distinguished associate of the Commonwealth leaders and exemplary M.P., Andrew Marvell. There is no doubting Marvell's conviction of the inevitability of the major political movement of his time ("For men may spare their pains where nature is at work, and the world will not go the faster for our driving"), but it is a fact to ponder that his greatest poems draw on a tradition more closely associated with the "reactionary" than with the "progressive" side. The qualities of the historian who will bring out the full significance of the vast changes—economic, social and cultural—marked by the Civil War should, one feels, include a sense of complexities such as informs that triumphantly civilized poem, *An Horatian Ode.*

Of the remaining essays little need be said. Miss Margaret James, in "Contemporary Materialist Interpretations of Society in the English Revolution," shows that some mid-century writers, notably Harrington and Winstanley, were aware of the relation between economics and politics. Mr. Edgell Rickword's essay on "Milton: the Revolutionary Intellectual" is a more academic piece of work than one would have expected, and it makes no attempt to relate the principles expressed in Milton's political writing to the sensibility expressed in his poetry. The claim, therefore, that it is because of his revolutionary principles that Milton's fame "is still the battle-ground of conflicting interests, and each book about him tends to turn into a polemic with its predecessors" is simply unwarranted dogmatism. Plekhanov's *The Role of the Individual in History* (1898) answers the ill-informed charge that Marxist philosophy reduces the function of the individual to insignificance. (Cf. Engels: "We make our own history, but in the first place under very definite presuppositions and conditions. Among these the economic ones are finally decisive.") It may be remarked that the anonymous introduction to the present translation displays features that must often puzzle the non-Marxist reader of some Marxist writings. Plekhanov's essay is said not merely to deny a charge but to "expose" a "slanderous argument"; it "delivered a crushing blow" to Narodnik (terrorist) theory, and three times in eight lines we are told that it "shattered"—once "utterly"—various anti-Marxist arguments; "our young people" are required to read this "obligatory text" in order to "combat the survivals of Narodnik and Socialist Revolutionary views." It is odd to find a serious political theory presented in the language of a dissenting conventicle. Confronted with such fundamentally self-distrustful aggressiveness we are reminded not of Marx but

> —Lord, hear my earnest cry an' pray'r
> Against that presbyt'ry o' Ayr—

of Holy Willy.

Chapter Nine

HENRY JAMES AND THE
TRAPPED SPECTATOR

I

IN EVEN THE MOST persistent admirers of Henry James admiration
is tempered by serious qualifications. It is not altogether a superficial view that, regarding James as primarily a satirist—destructive—sees something unsatisfactory about the positives he offers,
and I suppose that most readers would agree with F. R. Leavis
when he speaks [1] of "some failure about the roots and at the
lower levels of life." "He came to live in his art—and not the less
so for living strenuously—the life of a spiritual recluse; a recluse
in a sense in which not only no novelist but no good artist of any
kind can afford to be one." It is easy—too easy, we shall see—to
account for this sense of isolation, for the impression—more
marked of course in the later novels—that there are bars between
the artist and necessary kinds of experiences, by referring to
James's upbringing, his early environment, and the mode of life
he adopted. There was, to start with, the influence of Henry
James, Senior, behind whom, in spite of his cosmopolitan ease
and enlightenment, one senses the Genteel Tradition. "What was
marked in our father's prime uneasiness in presence of any form
of success we might, according to our lights, propose to invoke
was that it bravely . . . dispensed with any suggestion of an alternative. What we were to do instead was just to *be* something,
something unconnected with specific doing, something free and
uncommitted, something finer in short than being *that,* whatever
it was, might consist of." It was sufficient for the sons "to be
liberally 'good,'" and although they owed their father a great
deal it may be questioned whether he did not too successfully
cultivate in his second son the faculty of detachment. And "detachment," Henry James was to note, was even more markedly
the result of "the experience of Europe." After the four years

[1] In an article in *Scrutiny,* March 1937.

spent in Europe whilst James was in his early adolescence, the family was "insidiously, fatally disconnected," and some of the most interesting passages in *Notes of a Son and Brother* describe their "almost distressfully uninvolved and unconnected state." In America of the 1860's—the modern America that was just taking shape—the Jameses found nothing to connect on to. Whatever was not business didn't exist: "Disconnected from business we could only be connected with the negation of it, which had as yet no affirmative, no figurative side." Henry James stood it for some years, and then in 1875—when he was thirty-two—left America for good.

Even as readers of the novels we need to know these facts, and we need to know too the thesis which Mr. Van Wyck Brooks—more consistently than anyone else—has evolved in *The Pilgrimage of Henry James* to explain James's development in terms of his uprooting. According to Mr. Brooks, James drew his strength as a novelist from the land that, after all, he knew best: he is the painter of the American scene in a certain phase of its development; he is "the historian and the poet" of those Americans who, "released from the compulsions of poverty and custom, . . . become aware of a thousand requirements for which the world about them offers no scope," and who—at home or abroad—pay the penalty of their divided state. James settled in England (the thesis continues) but he never became at home there, and his persistent attempts to acclimatize himself only served to sap his genius. "In adapting himself to this world he was to lose his instinctive judgment of men and things; and this explains his 'virtuosity of vision' . . . the gradual decomposition, more and more marked the more his talent grew, of his sense of human values." "James had strayed so far from his natural world that the tree of knowledge had withered and died in his mind." As the source of his inspiration recedes he becomes more and more "the watcher from afar," unable "to conceive a major moment" or to "go behind his characters," preoccupied with technical devices which are "simply rationalizations of his exiguities."

Now no one would wish to deny James's achievement in his handling of "the American theme"—an achievement which, ranging from the magnificent satire of *The Bostonians* to the lighter, but still serious, comedy of *The Reverberator,* includes successes of such different kinds as *Washington Square, Daisy Miller,* and *Four Meetings.* But one may guess that it is simply the requirements of his thesis that leads Mr. Brooks to balance his justifiable enthusiasm for the novels and stories of James's first period—the period, that is, in which he devotes most attention to the American theme—with such sweeping disparagement of the products of the second. It is one thing to suggest, as Mr. Leavis does—and this simply in qualification of his discerning praise—that "something went wrong with James's development"; it is quite another thing to assert, as Mr. Brooks asserts, that "those for whom formal significance . . . is not the cardinal virtue of prose literature, for whom the world of fiction is to be judged by the vitality, the depth, and the variety of its content, will never be satisfied with the novels of the later James." So many objections to this comprehensive indictment come to mind. The later novels contain sustained passages of lively, concrete writing which are sufficient proof that vitality has not altogether departed: one can point to the satiric verve of the portrait of Sarah Pocock in *The Ambassadors* and of Mrs. Lowder in *The Wings of the Dove,* or to the crisp skill of the dialogue in *The Awkward Age,* dialogue which is "witty" and "dramatic" but which firmly defines James's attitude towards his characters and—without explanatory asides— shows them up for what they essentially are. And one could point to a good many other signs of life. But what I wish to do in this paper is simply to take up Mr. Brooks's remarks about "the avid eye," "the watcher from afar," and to examine a few of the ways in which James, in some of his later work, treats the subject of the man or woman who, for some reason or another, is merely a watcher, unable to participate freely and fully in human experience. This may prove a way of disengaging elements of real value in James's later work, and—a secondary point—it may throw some light on the old question concerning the relation between the artist's "life" and his successful work.

II

One way of approaching the subject is to observe that Henry James's "villains" have one characteristic in common: they all, in some way, *use* other people. They may prey on others for their money, but James is not much interested in common robbery, and usually their predatoriness takes forms that are less obvious and more gross. They make excessive demands for sympathy and try to absorb their victims' life into their own, as Olive Chancellor attempts to absorb Verena Tarrant in *The Bostonians*; they are "primed with a moral scheme of the most approved pattern" which—like the representatives of Woollett in *The Ambassadors*—they apply as a universal yardstick; or—like the relatives of Owen Wingrave—they demand a course of conduct that cuts across the essential nature of the individual; or they display a gross insensitiveness to the feelings of others, like the crude young reporter in *The Reverberator* or the cultivated literary gentleman of *The Aspern Papers*. As these references indicate, the "villainy" that James is interested in is rarely simple wickedness; it is quite often an unholy righteousness, and it is no accident that the phrase "the brutality of her good conscience," from *The Middle Years,* turns up again as "a high brutality of good intentions" in *The Spoils of Poynton*. The context of the second of these—a passage describing Mrs. Gereth's relations with Fleda Vetch—is worth quoting (James's judgment of the relationship is of course given by the metaphors):

> There were ways in which she could sharply incommode such a person, and not only with the best conscience in the world but with a high brutality of good intentions. One of the straightest of these strokes, Fleda saw, would be the dance of delight over the mystery she, terrible woman, had profaned; the loud, lawful tactless joy of the explorer leaping upon the strand. Like any other lucky discoverer she would take possession of the fortunate island. She was nothing if not practical: almost the only thing she took account of in her young friend's soft secret was the excellent use she could make of it. . . . She had no imagination about anybody's life save on the side she bumped against . . . Mrs. Gereth had really no perception of anybody's nature.

EXPLORATIONS

Few novelists have so fully explored the recesses and refinements of egotism as Henry James, and his egotists—whether they are calculating or frivolous or insensitive or armed with righteousness or compounded of a mixture of these qualities—are condemned because, as moral parasites, they thwart the free development of another's life.

In *The Portrait of a Lady*, for example, Gilbert Osmond marries Isabel Archer for her money, but the use she has for him is not of course merely a matter of pounds and shillings.

> The real offence, as she ultimately perceived, was her having a mind of her own at all. Her mind was to be his—attached to his own like a small garden-plot to a deer-park. He would rake the soil gently and water the flowers; he would weed the beds and gather an occasional nosegay. It would be a pretty piece of property for a proprietor already far-reaching. He didn't wish her to be stupid. On the contrary, it was because she was clever that she had pleased him. But he expected her intelligence to operate altogether in his favour, and so far from desiring her mind to be a blank he had flattered himself that it would be richly receptive. He had expected his wife to feel with him and for him, to enter into his opinions, his ambitions and his preferences.

When Isabel finally realizes that she has been *used*—"an applied handled hung-up tool, as senseless and convenient as mere wood and iron"—the full consciousness of her plight is put before us in a single brilliant chapter.

> She had taken all the first steps in the purest confidence, and then she had suddenly found the infinite vista of a multiplied life to be a dark, narrow alley with a dead wall at the end. Instead of leading to the high places of happiness, from which the world would seem to lie below one, so that one could look down with a sense of exaltation and advantage, and judge and choose and pity, it led rather downward and earthward, into realms of restriction and depression where the sound of other lives, easier and freer, was heard as from above.
>
> There were certain things they must do, a certain posture they must take, certain people they must know and not know. When she saw this rigid system close about her, draped though it was in pictured tapestries, that sense of darkness and suffocation of which I

178

have spoken took possession of her; she seemed to be shut up with an odour of mould and decay.

I have referred especially to this chapter of *The Portrait of a Lady* because it indicates so clearly what was, in various forms, one of James's main preoccupations—a preoccupation with the plight of the trapped creature. Isabel Archer is trapped by Osmond just as Nanda Brookenham in *The Awkward Age* is trapped by the greedy gossiping crew who surround her. But there are other stories in which this preoccupation takes a different form. They produce a kindred sense of suffocation, of being in some way shut off from the free enjoyment of living, but in them the central character is not trapped by others but by "circumstances" or by something in his own nature or his own past history. In these stories our immediate interest is not so much in a series of relations, in the action and reaction of personalities; it has shifted almost entirely to the consciousness of the trapped spectator of life.[1]

One of the strongest feelings evoked in that long meditation of Isabel Archer's is a feeling as of being buried alive, and the strength of the book comes largely from the evoked contrast of the heroine's "fund of life"—"her delighted spirit"—and the "cold obstruction" that thwarts it. This is a feeling that runs through James's work from first to last. We find it in *The Princess Casamassima,* in which the hero, Hyacinth Robinson, "was liable to moods in which the sense of exclusion from all he would have liked most to enjoy in life settled on him like a pall . . . *he* was above all out of it"; and we sense something similar in *The Ambassadors* when Strether—exhorting little Bilham to "live, live all

---

[1] This point needs to be stressed since Mr. Brooks has made it a reproach to James that in his later work he tends to "see" his story "through the opportunity and sensibility of some more or less detached, some not strictly involved, though thoroughly initiated and intelligent, witness or reporter" (James's words). Mr. Brooks seems to regard this device as evidence of "the evasiveness, the hesitancy, the scrupulosity of an habitually embarrassed man" (*The Pilgrimage of Henry James*). What he fails to notice is that, in most of the stories he mentions, the "observer" is not really "detached." He—or she—may be detached inasmuch as he is unable to influence the course of the action, but in other ways he is passionately committed. *His* reaction to persons and events is precisely what we are required to feel, so that to present the story as it appears to him is not at all a mere mechanical device for reporting. As James says in the preface to the volume containing *What Maisie Knew*, "The just remark for each of these small exhibited lives is . . . that they are actively, are luxuriously lived. The luxury is that of the number of their moral vibrations, well-nigh unrestricted—not that of an account at the grocer's." But there are a few stories that justify Mr. Brooks's strictures.

you can!"—realizes that he himself has "missed the train." When this sense of exclusion is presented, not as the result of human machinations but as inherent in a character's situation, it is only too easy to assume that James—"insidiously, fatally disconnected" as he knew himself to be—is interested solely in presenting the excluded, the caged and thwarted consciousness as a kind of personal relief, and that the reader is invited merely to share a narrow though intense range of feeling.

The assumption, however, would be misleading. In the Preface to *The Lesson of the Master* James remarks that, "The strength of applied irony" is "in the sincerities, the lucidities, the utilities that stand behind it. When it's not a campaign, of a sort, on behalf of something better (better than the obnoxious, the provoking object) that blessedly, as is assumed, *might* be, it's not worth speaking of. But this is exactly what we mean by operative irony. It implies and projects the possible other case, the case rich and edifying where the actuality is pretentious and vain." This is something to keep in mind when examining those stories in which our immediate interest is in the consciousness of an apparently "detached" spectator or of an observer in whom the sense of exclusion operates—*The Sacred Fount, In the Cage, What Maisie Knew, The Beast in the Jungle,* or *The Ambassadors.* We should look for the value of each of these not merely in the representation of the trapped state of mind (which may or may not represent James's personal predicament) but in the projection of "the possible other case, the case rich and edifying"; we should seek, that is, *the sense of life* that is released by the story of frustration. In other words, our fundamental concern (as distinguished from the immediate interest I have mentioned) is not simply with the nature of the "speculative thread," the "mental reactions" of the central character, but with the quality of *James's own* "moral vibrations" as these inform each novel as a whole. "The question comes back thus, obviously" (I am quoting from the Preface to *The Portrait of a Lady*), "to the kind and degree of the artist's prime sensibility, which is the soil out of which his subject springs," although, the passage continues, "one is far from contending that this enveloping air of the artist's humanity—which gives the last touch to the worth of his work—is not a widely and wondrously varying element; being on the one occasion a rich and magnificent medium and on another a comparatively poor and ungenerous one." [1] And the moral of this is simply that the value of James's stories of "detached" or "excluded" observers of life—the extent to which their irony does succeed in projecting "sincerities and lucidities," in releasing, in short, a sense of life— is something to be determined by the methods of literary criticism. This may seem a platitude, but it is a platitude which discussions about James, some portions of his Prefaces and— occasionally—his practice tend to obscure.

III

At this point it seems necessary to draw together the threads of a rather discursive paper. What I have tried to say is this:— From an early period James was interested in persons whose free and normal development—the development that, given their endowment, one might have expected—is thwarted by the egotism of others. As he grew older that preoccupation was joined (though never entirely superseded) by another—a preoccupation with the plight of the creature trapped not by others but—shall we say? —by Fate; and some of his most notable stories present the trapped, the caged, the excluded consciousness. Since it was in his later period too that James developed the technical device of "seeing" his stories through the eyes of one of his characters, the critic is presented with two different but related opportunities for going astray. He may regard the central consciousness as merely "detached" (as in *The Sacred Fount,* in which the narrator is a mere observer and James isn't interested in him except as a detective device), without realizing that it may be itself the central point of interest (as it is in *What Maisie Knew*). On the

---

[1] "There is, I think, no more nutritive or suggestive truth in this connexion than that of the perfect dependence of the 'moral' sense of a work of art on the amount of felt life concerned in producing it. The question comes back thus, obviously, to the kind and the degree of the artist's prime sensibility, which is the soil out of which his subject springs. The quality and capacity of that soil, its ability to 'grow' with due freshness and straightness any vision of life, represents, strongly or weakly, the projected morality. That element is but another name for the more or less close connexion of the subject with some mark made on the intelligence, with some sincere experience. By which, at the same time, of course, one is far from contending . . ." etc.—Preface to *The Portrait of a Lady*.

other hand, he may concentrate on the evoked sense of exclusion from experience, without realizing that it is the vitality, the qualities making for life, that the reader has most reason to be grateful for. To expose and establish those qualities is the main business of criticism.

Two examples may make these contentions clear. *In the Cage* (1898) concerns a young woman employed as telegraphist in the postal department of a Mayfair grocery store. She is literally, as well as figuratively, "caged," and the question James posed himself was "what it might 'mean,' wherever the admirable service was installed, for confined and cramped and yet considerably tutored young officials of either sex to be made so free, intellectually, of a range of experience otherwise quite closed to them."

> It had occurred to her early that in her position—that of a young person spending, in framed and wired confinement, the life of a guinea-pig or magpie—that she should know a great many persons without their recognizing the acquaintance. . . . Her function was to sit there with two young men—the other telegraphist and the counter clerk; to mind the "sounder" which was always going, to dole out stamps and postal-orders, weigh letters, answer stupid questions, give difficult change, and, more than anything else, count words as numberless as the sands of the sea, the words of the telegrams thrust, from morning to night, through the gap left in the high lattice, across the encumbered shelf that her fore-arm ached with rubbing. This transparent screen fenced out or fenced in, according to the side of the narrow counter on which the human lot was cast, the duskiest corner of a shop pervaded not a little, in winter, by the poison of perpetual gas, and at all times by the presence of hams, cheese, dried fish, soap, varnish, paraffin, and other solids and fluids that she came to know perfectly by their smells without consenting to know them by their names.

In this position she employs her curiosity—the spare mental energy not absorbed by her work—to speculate on the "outside" lives of some of her more frequent customers, using as clues the telegrams which they lavishly commit to her. "The amusements of captives," James remarks, "are full of a desperate contrivance," and another of this young woman's amusements is to establish something which might be called a personal relationship with some of those whom she serves—a relationship so slight, however, that it is measured by her sticking on the stamps for those she likes and merely pushing them across to the peremptory. Her attention is particularly engaged by two handsome products of the leisured class—Lady Bradeen and Captain Everard—who are engaged in an "affair" which, since the woman is married, involves some element of danger. Lady Bradeen spends most of her time away from Mayfair, so it is through her lover's innumerable telegrams that the Telegraphist is able to keep track of the relationship, and it becomes of the greatest importance to her that the Captain shall give some sign of recognizing the devotion— the speed and intelligence—with which she handles his business. On one occasion when she has contrived to meet him "outside," the Captain declares that he does recognize it, and her fantasy soars to the level of half-formulated desire: "It was more and more between them that if he might convey to her he was free, with all the impossible locked away into a closed chapter, her own case might become different for her, she might understand and meet him and listen." It is at this pitch of devotion and delusion that she has an opportunity of doing the aristocratic pair a genuine service, by recalling the contents of a telegram that has gone astray; but when Captain Everard, relieved of his anxiety, hurries out of the post office her share in the relationship is abruptly ended. "And without another look, without a word of thanks, without time for anything or anybody, he turned on them the broad back of his great stature, straightened his triumphant shoulders and strode out of the place."

Since one critic, whom Mr. Van Wyck Brooks quotes apparently with approval, has remarked that, "Reading *In the Cage* was like watching Henry James watching through a knot-hole somebody who was watching somebody else through a knot-hole," it may not be out of place to say that to watch through a knot-hole is exactly what the reader isn't required to do. It isn't a question here of detective work, of sifting clues and piecing together evidence in order to come at "the truth" concerning Captain Everard and Lady Bradeen. The ups and downs of that couple are purposely left vague, only the main lines are established, and James indicates again and again that, however much the Telegraphist may divine, her guesses are only guesses: they have a subjective rather than an objective reference. The purpose of the story is, in short (the Preface is explicit), to display the mind of the Telegraphist. The various pressures that reduce the girl to guessing, that determine the form of her fantasies, are vividly created. There is the pressure of her own and her mother's period of poverty,

> when, as conscious and incredulous ladies, suddenly bereft, betrayed, overwhelmed, they had slipped faster and faster down the steep slope at the bottom of which she alone had rebounded. Her mother had never rebounded any more at the bottom than on the way; had only rumbled and grumbled down and down, making, in respect of caps, topics and "habits," no effort whatever—which simply meant smelling much of the time of whisky.

There is the pressure of the solid presence and limiting imagination of her betrothed, Mr. Mudge, a rising young man in the grocery trade, who offers her the snug prospect of a "sweet little home." And there is the pressure of her friend, Mrs. Jordan, the "reduced" widow of a clergyman, who "does the flowers" in the houses of the well-to-do, and whose intimations of the higher life provide a setting for adventures read of in novels. That these persons, and to some extent the Telegraphist herself, are presented ironically in no way detracts from the seriousness of James's theme. (His intensely *moral* concern is explicit in the opening paragraph of Chapter V where the lives of "the two nations" are contrasted.) If James is to be blamed for anything it can only be for a misleading phrase in the Preface, where he speaks of the "solution" depending on the girl's "winged wit." "The action of the drama is simply the girl's 'subjective' adventure—that of her quite definitely winged intelligence; just as the catastrophe, just as the solution, depends on her winged wit." The "solution" is not, as this might suggest, the solution of Captain Everard's perplexities; it is simply the Telegraphist's recognition—her final acceptance—of the bleakness of reality. Mrs. Jordan has just announced the death of Lady Bradeen's husband and her approaching marriage to the Captain:

HENRY JAMES AND THE TRAPPED SPECTATOR

They sat there together; they looked out, hand in hand, into the damp dusky shabby little room and into the future, of no such very different complexion, at last accepted by each. There was no definite utterance, on either side, of Mr. Drake's position in the great world [Mrs. Jordan is to marry Lady Bradeen's butler], but the temporary collapse of his prospective bride threw all further necessary light; and what our heroine saw and felt for in the whole business was the vivid reflexion of her own dreams and delusions and her own return to reality. Reality, for the poor things they both were, could only be ugliness and obscurity, could never be the escape, the rise.

One does not need to peep through a knot-hole to observe that caged consciousness; it is firmly and lucidly presented, and the reader is made to feel the full weight of the circumstances that mould it.

The Beast in the Jungle (1903) may also serve to show that in James's later period subtlety is sometimes far from being evidence of evasiveness, hesitancy, or scrupulosity. It is the story of a man, John Marcher, trapped and made impotent—reduced to being a mere spectator of life—by an obsession, the belief, namely, "that experience will be marked for him, and whether for good or for ill, by some rare distinction, some incalculable violence or unprecedented stroke." The only person to whom Marcher confides this secret is a woman, May Bartram, whom he persuades to watch with him—to watch, that is, for the spring of the lurking beast in the jungle. It is May Bartram who first sees the truth concerning Marcher and who, offering him an opportunity to recognize and respond to her love, offers him also the chance to escape his doom. He, however, remains fixed in his obsession— never thinks of her "but in the chill of his egotism and the light of her use"—and when she dies, assuring him that the beast *has* sprung and begging him not to seek further illumination, it is only over her grave that he can persuade himself that he has lived at all. It is there, on one of his periodic visits to the cemetery, that illumination finally comes to him. The occasion is the passing of an unknown mourner whose glimpsed face shows the marks of inconsolable grief, and whom Marcher is surprised to find himself looking after with envy.

EXPLORATIONS

The sight that had just met his eyes named to him, as in letters of
quick flame, something he had utterly, insanely missed, and what he
had missed made these things a train of fire, made them mark themselves in an anguish of inward throbs. He had seen *outside* of his life,
not learned it within, the way a woman was mourned when she had
been loved for herself: . . . Now that illumination had begun, however, it blazed to the zenith, and what he presently stood there gazing
at was the sounded void of his life. . . . The name on the table
smote him as the passing of his neighbour had done, and what it said
to him, full in the face, was that *she* was what he had missed. . . .
The fate he had been marked for he had met with a vengeance—he
had emptied the cup to the lees; he had been the man of his time, *the*
man, to whom nothing on earth was to have happened. . . . It was
the truth, vivid and monstrous, that all the while he had waited, the
wait itself was his portion.

In summary the story may appear unimpressive. But all that
an admirer needs to do is to indicate the subtle firmness with
which James presents his "case," to demonstrate, that is, the mode
which he established for the telling. Things are "seen" largely
through the eyes of Marcher, but the seeing is flecked with un-
obtrusive irony so that we are aware of two views—Marcher's,
and that of James himself—existing simultaneously.

He had thought himself, so long as nobody knew, the most disinterested person in the world, carrying his concentrated burden, his
perpetual suspense, ever so quietly, holding his tongue about it, giv-
ing others no glimpse of it nor of its effect upon his life, asking of
them no allowance and only making on his side all those that were
asked. He hadn't disturbed people with the queerness of their having
to know a haunted man, though he had had moments of rather special temptation on hearing them say they were forsooth "unsettled."
If they were as unsettled as he was—he who had never been settled
for an hour in his life—they would know what it meant. Yet it wasn't,
all the same, for him to make them, and he listened to them civilly
enough. This was why he had such good—though possibly such rather
colourless—manners; this was why, above all, he could regard himself,
in a greedy world, as decently—as in fact perhaps even a little sub-
limely—unselfish. Our point is accordingly that he valued this character quite sufficiently to measure his present danger of letting it lapse,
against which he promised himself to be much on his guard. He was

186

quite ready, none the less, to be selfish just a little, since surely no more charming occasion for it had come to him. "Just a little," in a word, was just as much as Miss Bartram, taking one day with another, would let him.

"His concentrated burden," "his perpetual suspense," "a haunted man"—these phrases, and a good deal besides, represent Marcher's view. James only allows himself a few asides—" 'Just a little,' in a word, was just as much as Miss Bartram, taking one day with another, would let him"—but these are sufficient to give an angle on Marcher's attitude towards himself, on his egotism, his calculated unselfishness,[1] and on his exalted view of his own refinements, even when we are given what are apparently his own thoughts: "A man of feeling didn't cause himself to be accompanied by a lady on a tiger hunt." And the two points of view—the subjective and the objectively critical—not only alternate swiftly and with almost unnoticed transitions, they are often presented simultaneously:

> The real form it [their relationship] should have taken on the basis that stood out large was the form of their marrying. But the devil in this was that the very basis itself put marrying out of the question. His conviction, his apprehension, his obsession, in short, wasn't a privilege he could invite a woman to share: and that consequence of it was precisely what was the matter with him. Something or other lay in wait for him, amid the twists and the turns of the months and the years, like a crouching beast in the jungle.

Almost every word, there, bears the double burden. And the advantage of this method is that it enables James to present Marcher's case with a degree of sympathy—for the theme is a common human feeling, though isolated and magnified, and the reader is made to share Marcher's horror—and at the same time to give a detached and penetrating analysis of the ravages of an obsession.

There is no need for further illustration of what is not, after

[1] "He was careful to remember that she had also a life of her own, with things that might happen to *her*, things that in friendship one should likewise take account of." And, "It was one of his proofs to himself, the present he made her on her birthday, that he hadn't sunk into real selfishness. It was mostly nothing more than a small trinket, but it was always fine of its kind, and he was regularly careful to pay more for it than he thought he could afford."

all, an uncommon Jamesian method. What this account of *The Beast in the Jungle* is intended to bring out is the sureness, the relevance and coherence of the minute particulars of the style—of James's art. For when I said that *In the Cage* and *The Beast in the Jungle,* in common with other stories of "trapped spectators," released "a sense of life," I hadn't in mind merely the explicit sense of opportunities missed, as when Marcher realizes that his "escape" would have been to love May Bartram—"then, then he would have lived"—or when Strether reviews his life in Gloriani's garden. The "life" that is in question is simply the extension and refinement of consciousness, of that intelligence which, in Santayana's words, is "the highest form of vitality." One would like to attempt a definition of "intelligence" and to relate it to James's style which, at its best, is a medium for projecting the immediate awareness if not of "opposite and discordant" qualities at all events of varied and (in most minds) contradictory impulses, so that the reader's consciousness is enlarged to admit a new relationship. But perhaps enough has been said to establish what should be an obvious truth: that "the amount of felt life" informing *any* work is in exact correspondence with the "art," that it depends entirely on the fullness and fineness with which the subject is presented.

This, in turn, suggests the dangers inherent in the attempt to find a simple "explanation" of an author's work in terms of his life. When we read those novels and stories of Henry James in which the preoccupation I have illustrated is present, it is impossible to avoid a reference to James himself, whose "almost distressfully uninvolved and unconnected state" is dwelt on in *Notes of a Son and Brother,* a state which was not to be a mere accident of the early years. But to the same measure that the art succeeds the personal reference becomes irrelevant. There is no means of comparing the success of a short story and that of a two-volume novel, but if we feel that *The Ambassadors* is less perfect in itself than *In the Cage* (for in Strether's "Paris" there is more statement than achieved representation) it may well be that Strether, "trapped" by the Genteel Tradition, is too close to his creator. *In the Cage* and *The Beast in the Jungle* are also personal in inspiration ("My attested predilection for poor sensitive gentlemen,"

HENRY JAMES AND THE TRAPPED SPECTATOR

James says when prefacing the latter, "almost embarrasses me as I march"), but here the personal motive serves only as the spring which releases the achieved work of art.

Of course James was isolated—and he knew it; but it is ridiculous to speak as if his plight were peculiar and unrelated to a more general predicament. It wasn't merely that he saw more clearly than anyone else, and recorded in his Prefaces, the increasing gulf between the artist and the public of common readers, he sensed also the forces that, in his time, were making for "the awful doom of general dishumanization." [1] And in his apprehension of the isolation of the individual

> —"I have heard the key
> Turn in the door once and turn once only"—

he showed himself the first of the "modern" novelists.

[1] Preface to *The Altar of the Dead*.

Chapter Ten

POETRY AND SOCIAL CRITICISM: THE WORK OF W. B. YEATS

IN THE SECTION of *Autobiographies* headed "Four Years: 1887-1891" Yeats has recorded the "monkish hate" that, as a young man, he felt for the world of thought corresponding to the world of nineteenth-century mechanical progress. His youthful objection to Huxley, Tyndall, Carolus Duran and Bastien-Lepage (he invested the quartet with a sort of symbolic significance) was never merely the aesthetic objection of the Nineties, but it rested on rather dimly grasped feelings, and in his poetry of that period simply prompted withdrawal and immersion in the pre-Raphaelite dream. When, in the first decade of this century, he began with such admirable vigour to work his way out of the Romantic manner a change in the subject-matter of his verse was no less apparent than the change in idiom. With the increasingly sinewy and "unpoetical" quality of his diction and rhythms went an increasing preoccupation with "public" themes, and at the same time his objections to the modern world took a more substantial form. What I wish to suggest in this essay is that Yeats's developed "social criticism"—scattered throughout his essays and autobiographical writings—illuminates the task that he set himself as a poet, and so helps to clarify the standards by which his poetry must be judged.

I

We can begin by noticing those features of "an age like this" that roused his most vigorous protests. From about the time of *The Green Helmet* (1912) onwards he protested emphatically and continuously against democratic vulgarity ("all things at one common level lie"), middle-class caution (". . . the merchant and the clerk breathed on the world with timid breath"), and ready-made newspaper notions and sentiments ("a mill of argument"); against violence of opinion ("an old bellows full of angry wind") issuing in physical violence and cruelty ("Nothing but grip of claw, and the eye's complacency"); against, in short, the related symptoms of a social, political and cultural disintegration summed up in the well-known lines from *The Second Coming* (1921):

> Things fall apart; the centre cannot hold;
> Mere anarchy is loosed upon the world,
> The blood-dimmed tide is loosed, and everywhere
> The ceremony of innocence is drowned;
> The best lack all conviction, while the worst
> Are full of passionate intensity.

To these features of a chaotic democratic world Yeats came to oppose the idea of an aristocratic *order*. His belief in an aristocracy contained a streak of snobbery, and occasionally it led him into absurdity, as when he declared that King George V should have abdicated as a protest against the dethronement of his cousin the Czar.[1] It was nourished by his preoccupation with the Irish past, particularly the eighteenth century, and it took small account of the actual conditions of an industrialized world in which aristocracy merges into plutocracy. Louis MacNeice, remarking that in his later years Yeats considered the possibility of a new aristocracy developing from the Irish bureaucrats of the present, says: "In pre-War years, however, before the Irish burnings, he was still pinning his faith to the Big House, and preferring to ignore the fact that in most cases these houses maintained no culture worth speaking of—nothing but an obsolete bravado, an insidious bonhomie and a way with horses."[2] An example of the distortion caused in Yeats's vision by his theories occurs in *Dramatis Personae* (p. 11), where he recalls, among other exploits, how the wildest of Lady Gregory's "Seven Brothers," "excluded by some misdemeanour from a Hunt Ball," had turned a hose on the guests." Not only is this silly prank recounted without criticism, it is plain that it is meant to take its place in a saga in which the brothers loom like legendary heroes. "These brothers," he says, "were figures from the eight-

---

[1] *Letters on Poetry from W. B. Yeats to Dorothy Wellesley*, p. 188.
[2] *The Poetry of W. B. Yeats*, p. 104. For a more favourable account of the Irish aristocracy at the end of the nineteenth century, see the essay by C. Day Lewis in *Scattering Branches: Tributes to the Memory of W. B. Yeats*, edited by Stephen Gwynn.

eenth century." Yeats's predilections for an aristocracy had decidedly their weak side, but it is only possible to speak of him as a "Fascist" or social reactionary by ignoring the reasons—or perhaps one should say, the intuitions—that led him to put such stress on the aristocratic life. It is these that are most relevant here.

At first sight it is easier to distinguish the negative aspects of Yeats's code than to grasp its positive implications. The aristocratic banner was his red flag—something with which he could make offensive gestures. "By aristocracy," says Dorothy Wellesley, "he meant the proud, the heroic mind. This included a furious attitude towards the cheap, the trashy, the ill-made. And he certainly deplored the passing of the stately houses, and the gradual effacement of the well or highly born." [1] To exalt the aristocracy was one way of expressing his "passion of hatred against the vulgarity and materialism whereon England has founded her worst life and the whole life that she sends us." [2] More positively, he valued the aristocratic life because it seemed to him to make possible the free play of instinctive energies which the mill of modern materialism ground into inert uniformity. Trying, for example, to account for the power of Lady Gregory's translations of the Irish heroic tales, he says: "I can see that they were made possible by her past; semi-feudal Roxborough, her inherited sense of caste, her knowledge of that top of the world where men and women are valued for their manhood and their charm, not for their opinions." [3] And in his Diary kept in 1909 he writes: "I see that between *Time*, suggestion, and *Crossroads*, logic, lies a difference of civilization. The literature of suggestion belongs to a social order when life conquered by being itself and the most living was the most powerful, and not to a social order founded upon argument. *Leisure, wealth, privilege were created to be a soil for the most living* [my italics]. The literature of logic, the most powerful and the most empty, conquering all in the service of one metallic premise, is for those who have forgotten everything but books and yet have only just learnt to read." [4] But

---

[1] *Letters on Poetry*, p. 196.
[2] *Dramatis Personae*, pp. 49-50.
[3] *Op. cit.*, p. 74.
[4] *Op. cit.*, p. 182.

it is a metaphor from his poetry that best expresses the essentially
humane longing that prompted him to indulge in his aristocratic
myth.

> Surely among a rich man's flowering lawns,
> Amid the rustle of his planted hills,
> Life overflows without ambitious pains;
> And rains down life until the basin spills,
> And mounts more dizzy high the more it rains
> As though to choose whatever shape it wills
> And never stoop to a mechanical
> Or servile shape, at others' beck and call.[1]

This comes from a distinguished poem in which desire is balanced by a keen sense of reality; the resulting irony—

> And maybe the great-grandson of that house,
> For all its bronze and marble, 's but a mouse

—acts as a purifying agent so that what is valid in Yeats's feelings
about aristocratic life is revealed with uncommon clarity.

> Mere dreams, mere dreams! Yet Homer had not sung
> Had he not found it certain beyond dreams
> That out of life's own self-delight had sprung
> The abounding glittering jet; though now it seems
> As if some marvellous empty sea-shell flung
> Out of the obscure dark of the rich streams,
> And not a fountain, were the symbol which
> Shadows the inherited glory of the rich.

The image of the fountain of life, "the abounding glittering
jet"—here explicitly associated with the "dream" inspired by Ancestral Houses—provides the criterion by which Yeats makes his
most significant judgments of human values. He held, with one
of the greatest of his masters, that "Everything that *lives* is holy,"
and those he condemns are those who refuse to live freely and
fully—the men of mere opinion, mere intellect or mere will. If,
then, Castiglione's Court of Urbino is a recurring symbol in his
verse and prose, it is because in his eyes it stood for a civilization
based on respect for the essential energies of the individual, for

[1] *Meditations in Time of Civil War, I, Ancestral Houses.*

"the natural impulses of the mind, its natural reverence, desire, hope, admiration, always half-unconscious, almost bodily," as opposed to the modern democratic substitute, "self-improvement."[1] Aristocracy, he thought, was the form in which natural vitality might combine with civilized ease, and if the development of his theories blinded him to some of the social realities of the present we can at least respect the intuitions that prompted his thinking. Before considering the relation of those intuitions to his literary criticism and his poetry we may remark that his idea of an aristocracy may perhaps be best regarded as a myth, complementary in some respects to the greater modern myth of a classless society. Its value lies in its assertion of those living energies without which equality will be worthless.

II

It was characteristic of Yeats that from one of Ben Jonson's few dull plays (*The Poetaster*) he remembered the fine tribute paid, it is believed, to Shakespeare's verse—

> so ramm'd with life
> That it shall gather strength of life, with being.[2]

"Life" is a key-word in Yeats's literary, as it is in his social, criticism, and for definition we cannot do better than turn to *Discoveries* (1906) and some other essays in which his own thought is beginning to emerge from the received ideas of his generation. Life is, in the first place, the instinctive life of the body. In a passage on "The Thinking of the Body" that deserves to be famous he wrote: "Art bids us touch and taste and hear and see the world, and shrinks from what Blake calls mathematic form, from every abstract thing, from all that is of the brain only, from all that is not a fountain jetting from the entire hopes, memories, and sensations of the body."[3] But it is "the personality as a whole," not merely "the tumult of the blood," that informs the greatest poetry.[4] He saw clearly that the divorce between "higher"

[1] See *Dramatis Personae*, p. 143.
[2] See *Dramatis Personae*, p. 98.
[3] *Essays*, p. 362.
[4] *Op. cit.*, pp. 331 and 337.

and "lower" faculties was a symptom of the disease which had afflicted the post-Renaissance world, so that by the beginning of the nineteenth century, "the highest faculties had faded, taking the sense of beauty with them, into some sort of vague heaven and left the lower to lumber where they best could." In literature, therefore (and Yeats touches here the now familiar contrast between the poetry of the seventeenth and the poetry of the nineteenth century), "partly from the lack of that spoken word which knits us to normal man, we have lost in personality, in our delight in the whole man—blood, imagination, intellect, running together." When, consciously and deliberately, he broke with his pre-Raphaelite past—abandoning "that conventional language of modern poetry" which, he said in 1905, "has begun to make us all weary"—it was in an attempt to develop "a technique sufficiently flexible for expression of the emotions of life as they arise," for the expression, that is, of energies which a decadent literary tradition had excluded from poetry.[1] The results were remarkable, and for many years now it has been a critical commonplace that the verse of Yeats's middle and later years has a vitality not found in that of his early manhood. Whether he actually achieved that highest kind of poetry which he set as his own standard—poetry expressing the life of "the personality as a whole"—is a question that the very greatness of his qualities forces us to ask. In some important ways, it seems to me, he remained a Romantic to the end.

Romanticism in literature, we may say, is the expression of a sensibility deliberately limited, both as regards its objects of interest and the modes of consciousness that it employs. In Yeats's early verse, for example, a narrow range of uncomplicated emotional attitudes is expressed in a technique incapable of variety, force or subtlety. What is less obvious is that even when in the interests of a fuller and more abounding life he had developed a technique of flexible and forceful speech, persistent habits of Romantic simplification remained. An example of what I mean can be found in his use of figures from heroic legend. Instead of impossible heroes and languishing queens with cloud-pale eye-

<hr>

[1] *Op. cit.*, pp. 330 and 370; *Autobiographies*, p. 392.

lids and dream-dimmed eyes, we now have "Helen and her boy,"
Solomon with Sheba "planted on his knees," and Leda, "that
sprightly girl was trodden by a bird." At first reading it seems
that the purpose served by these and similar phrases is the recre-
ation of the heroic world in modern idiom, the ironic application
—in Elizabethan fashion—of old fable to contemporary needs.
That perhaps was the intention, but the references also serve a
deeper need, a nostalgia for an imagined past in which painful
complexities are evaporated. Mr. MacNeice says rightly that
Yeats "was orientated . . . towards a simplified past"; and it is
significant that in the poem *Ancestral Houses* the irony relies on
an absolute acceptance of the past—"a haughtier age"—and is
directed solely against the present: there is no suggestion of the
two-way irony which in *The Waste Land* sets present *and* past in
a clearer light. To romanticize *any* element in a given situation
is to admit an inability to deal with it completely and with a full
awareness of all that is involved; and Yeats, even in his middle
and later periods, continued to use Romantic glamour as an
escape from difficult or painful problems. The poem, *No Second
Troy,* opens in the tones of straightforward speech:

> Why should I blame her that she filled my days
> With misery, or that she would of late
> Have taught to ignorant men most violent ways,
> Or hurled the little streets upon the great,
> Had they but courage equal to desire?

But from the sixth line the poem draws largely on romantic ideal-
ization:

> What could have made her peaceful with a mind
> That nobleness made simple as a fire,
> With beauty like a tightened bow, a kind
> That is not natural in an age like this,
> Being high and solitary and most stern?

And in the end a woman with whom only difficult relations were
possible is transformed into that Helen who exists only for the
imagination:

POETRY AND SOCIAL CRITICISM

> Why, what could she have done being what she is?
> Was there another Troy for her to burn?

In *Easter, 1916,* the refrain—

> All changed, changed utterly:
> A terrible beauty is born

—represents an escape from full realization. Sometimes, as in the instances just quoted, the nature of the transformation is indicated by a change in diction, a lapse into something like Yeats's earlier manner. At other times it is half concealed by the assured use of an idiom professedly non-Romantic. Yeats in fact uses his later colloquial technique with such self-confident swagger that often one gives him credit for doing all that he merely claims to do. The speech of "My Self" which ends *A Dialogue of Self and Soul* (*The Winding Stair*) has a sinewy vigour:

> I am content to live it all again
> And yet again, if it be life to pitch
> Into the frog-spawn of a blind man's ditch,
> A blind man battering blind men.

But when the poem ends,

> I am content to follow to its source
> Every event in action or in thought;
> Measure the lot; forgive myself the lot!

we have no warrant that "follow to its source," "measure" and "forgive myself" stand for explorations actually undertaken. And if the poems dealing explicitly with contemporary chaos are, in the long run, disappointing, it is for a similar reason. In *Meditations in Time of Civil War* and *Nineteen Hundred and Nineteen* (*The Tower*) there are memorable lines and striking images:

> Nothing but grip of claw, and the eye's complacency,
> The innumerable clanging wings that have put out the moon.

> Violence upon the roads: violence of horses. . . .
> Herodias' daughters have returned again
> A sudden blast of dusty wind and after
> Thunder of feet, tumult of images,
> Their purpose in the labyrinth of the wind;

but if the success of the poems seems partial and fragmentary it is because "the half-read wisdom of daemonic images" (which, we are told, "suffice the ageing man as once the growing boy") is made to take the place of a deeper understanding.

Perhaps the best way of defining the disappointment that one feels on returning to so many of Yeats's poems that had previously seemed deeply moving is to say that they fail to "gather strength of life, with being," to grow, that is, with one's own developing experience,—unlike so much of Eliot's poetry where each fresh reading brings fresh discovery. For not only does Yeats tend to simplify his problems, there is in much of his poetry a static quality which can be traced to the adoption of certain fixed attitudes in the face of experience. "There is a relation," he said, "between discipline and the theatrical sense. . . . Active virtue as distinguished from the passive acceptance of a current code is therefore theatrical, consciously dramatic, the wearing of a mask." [1] But his preoccupation with the mask was not merely a search for a discipline: sometimes it seems like the rationalization of a self-dramatizing egotism which made him feel happier if he could see himself ("Milton's Platonist") in an appropriate light. Consider, for example, his attitude of pride. One can relish his criticism of those who "long for popularity that they may believe in themselves" and of poets who "want marching feet," and at the same time recognize a danger to sincerity in a too persistent assertion of "something steel-like and cold within the will, something passionate and cold." [2] There is a smack of the Nineties here; and one remembers his fondness for Dowson's lines,

> Unto us they belong,
> Us the bitter and gay,
> Wine and women and song.

" 'Bitter and gay,' that is the heroic mood," he wrote in 1935. Like the aristocratic order that he imagined, pride is valued as an assertion of the living spirit confronted with democratic common-

---

[1] *Dramatis Personae*, p. 87. Compare p. 79 of the same volume ("Style, personality—deliberately adopted and therefore a mask—is the only escape from the hot-faced bargainers and the money-changers") and many passages in *Autobiographies*.

[2] The references are to *Dramatis Personae*, p. 84, and *Letters on Poetry*, p. 8.

ness; but there is something unliving in the use he makes of "cold" and "bitter" and "proud"—adjectives that tend to appear with the same regularity as the "emblems" which, in his later poetry, too often take the place of living metaphor. There is no doubt that the sap flows most freely when the conscious pride is forgotten, remaining only as a temper of mind that is sufficiently assured not to insist on its own firmness. The pose that results from over-insistence is most obvious in admittedly minor poems, like the short sequence *Upon a Dying Lady* and those verses that celebrate "the discipline of the looking-glass," which he seems to have continued to regard as the appropriate discipline for beautiful women; but it also betrays itself in work of greater power. In the third section of the title poem of *The Tower* he writes of "upstanding men,"

> I declare
> They shall inherit my pride,
> The pride of people that were
> Bound neither to Cause nor to State,
> Neither to slaves that were spat on,
> Nor to the tyrants that spat,
> The people of Burke and of Grattan
> That gave, though free to refuse—

The rhythm of these lines seems almost mechanical when compared with the vigorous protest against old age with which the same poem opens. The pride, in short, sometimes seems like another form of the escape from complexity. Referring, once more, to the mask, he wrote: "I think all happiness depends on the energy to assume the mask of some other self; that all joyous or creative life is a re-birth as something not oneself. . . . We put on a grotesque or solemn painted face to hide us from the terrors of judgment, invent an imaginative Saturnalia where one forgets reality, a game like that of a child, where one loses the infinite pain of self-realization." [1] Yeats knew as well as anyone that "the infinite pain of self-realization" is the price paid for "life"; and in the lines that he wrote for his epitaph there is a deep and unintended pathos:

[1] *Dramatis Personae*, pp. 121-122.

Cast a cold eye
On life, on death.
Horseman, pass by.

This account, I know, ignores many fine poems—poems on "that monstrous thing, returned yet unrequited love," and on the encroachment of age, some satiric pieces, and some others—and where much remains it must seem peculiarly ungrateful to insist on inadequacies and disappointments. But I hope I have made it plain that it is precisely because of his great qualities that one must judge Yeats's work, not simply in relation to the poetry of the late nineteenth century (his own included) but in the light of his own conception of the poet's function. That conception is not only defined in the prose criticism, it is embodied in two poems which, without any qualification, deserve the title of "great poetry." I refer to *Sailing to Byzantium* and *Among School Children*. These poems have been often and justly praised, and all I wish to do here is to suggest how magnificently they enforce the central doctrine of Yeats's criticism: that the higher forms of vitality (unlike gusto, swagger or self-assertion) are a function of the personality as a whole, "blood, imagination, intellect, running together." There is no doubt of their vitality, but the sense of "joyous energy" that they release is not purchased at the price of exclusion; there is, instead, a remarkably clear-eyed acceptance of things as they are. The opening of *Among School Children* has a cool, prose-like clarity:

> I walk through the long schoolroom questioning,
> A kind old nun in a white hood replies;
> The children learn to cipher and to sing,
> To study reading-books and history,
> To cut and sew, be neat in everything
> In the best modern way—the children's eyes
> In momentary wonder stare upon
> A sixty-year-old smiling public man.

The sight of the children calls to mind the childhood and youth of the woman he loved, and then, contrasting her youthful beauty with "her present image"—

POETRY AND SOCIAL CRITICISM

> Hollow of cheek as though it drank the wind
> And took a mess of shadows for its meat

—the poet is led to question the values which, men believe, give meaning to life:

> What youthful mother, a shape upon her lap
> Honey of generation had betrayed,
> And that must sleep, shriek, struggle to escape
> As recollection or the drug decide,
> Would think her son, did she but see that shape
> With sixty or more winters on its head,
> A compensation for the pang of his birth,
> Or the uncertainty of his setting forth?

Philosophy and poetry (verse vi)?—"Old clothes upon old sticks to scare a bird"; religion (verse vii) is born of man's need and can answer no questions; and the painful antinomy of desire and frustration is felt as rooted in experience. But this is to paraphrase too crudely; for just as elements which, in a lesser poem, might appear Romantic are balanced by a sober grasp of reality, as strong personal emotion ("my heart is driven wild") is blended with a play of mind, witty and ironic,[1] so in the consideration of the satisfactions that life has to offer there is a similar firm poise. The "honey" of verse v is not merely "the 'drug' that destroys the 'recollection' of pre-natal freedom" (see Yeats's note); it invokes a "positive" attitude to experience which is explicit in the wit and the lovely singing movement of the succeeding verse:

> Plato thought nature but a spume that plays
> Upon a ghostly paradigm of things;
> Solider Aristotle played the taws
> Upon the bottom of a king of kings;
> World-famed golden-thighed Pythagoras
> Fingered upon a fiddle stick or strings

[1] The irony modulates from a delicate intonation in verse i—

> To cut and sew, be neat in everything
> In the best modern way—

to the open self-mockery of verse iv:

> And I though never of Ledaean kind
> Had pretty plumage once—enough of that,
> Better to smile on all who smile, and show
> There is a comfortable kind of old scarecrow.

> What a star sang and careless Muses heard:
> Old clothes upon old sticks to scare a bird.

And in verse vii the "images" of religion may be "self-born mockers of man's enterprise," but they are also

> Presences
> That passion, piety or affection knows,
> And that all heavenly glory symbolize,

and the human emotions that inform them are real and valuable. It is this fine and complex balance of varied recognitions and energies that lies behind and justifies the final verse, which in one sense provides an answer to the questions and in another sense supersedes them.

> Labour is blossoming or dancing where
> The body is not bruised to pleasure soul,
> Nor beauty born out of its own despair,
> Nor blear-eyed wisdom out of midnight oil.
> O chestnut tree, great rooted blossomer,
> Are you the leaf, the blossom or the bole?
> O body swayed to music, O brightening glance,
> How can we know the dancer from the dance?

At the level of prose and logic the last four lines may be taken to imply the futility of dissecting life which is growth and movement in order to find its values; but the poetic force of the imagery conveys a triumphant affirmation of wholeness and spontaneity which is no less "real" for existing only in the form of a symbol of possibilities perpetually unfulfilled.[1]

Sailing to Byzantium reveals a similar "reconciliation of opposite or discordant qualities" as the source of its power. It opens with a richly concrete evocation of instinctive life:

> The young
> In one another's arms, birds in the trees,

[1] One may recall (without needing to insist on the differences) T. S. Eliot's lines from *Burnt Norton*:

> At the still point of the turning world . . .
> . . . Except for the point, the still point,
> There would be no dance, and there is only the dance.
> I can only say, *there* we have been: but I cannot say where.
> And I cannot say, how long, for that is to place it in time.

POETRY AND SOCIAL CRITICISM

> —Those dying generations—at their song,
> The salmon-falls, the mackerel-crowded seas. . . .

When the poet turns from "that sensual music" towards the un
changing world of art and contemplation, imagery and movement
—"as though mere speech had taken fire"—continue to express a
positive vitality.

> O sages standing in God's holy fire
> As in the gold mosaic of a wall,
> Come from the holy fire, perne in a gyre,
> And be the singing masters of my soul.
> Consume my heart away; sick with desire
> And fastened to a dying animal
> It knows not what it is; and gather me
> Into the artifice of eternity.[1]

There is a steady recognition of what is now, for the poet, un-
attainable, but not only is "Byzantium" itself alive (for images of
spontaneous movement and delight qualify the deliberately
chosen "monuments" and "mosaic"), the theme of its meditation
and its song is "what is past, or passing, or to come"; and the
function of the "artifice of eternity" is to celebrate that living
world of the first stanza in which the stress falls equally on dying
and generation.[2]

These two poems seem to me to represent the high peaks of
Yeats's poetic achievement. In them the "life" so ardently pursued is revealed as wholeness, integrity, with no surreptitious
finger on the balance; and they set a standard. Even that striking
poem, *Byzantium*, has a less rich and complex organization than
Sailing to Byzantium. As F. R. Leavis has said of it: [3] "There is,
on the one hand, no 'sensual music' . . . but instead:

> All mere complexities,
> The fury and the mire of human veins.

---

[1] Contrast the purely static suggestion of "beauty that is cast out of a mould in
bronze" in an earlier poem—*The Living Beauty*—on an apparently similar theme.
[2] In his *Diary Kept in 1909* Yeats wrote: "We artists suffer in our art if we do
not love most of all life at peace with itself and doing without forethought what its
humanity bids it and therefore happily. We are, as seen from life, an artifice, an
emphasis, an uncompleted arc perhaps. Those whom it is our business to cherish and
celebrate are complete arcs" (*Dramatis Personae*, p. 93).
[3] In a review of *Last Poems and Plays*, *Scrutiny*, March 1940.

On the other hand, instead of the 'monuments of unageing intellect,' which are felt as a positive presence in *Sailing to Byzantium,* we find the ironic potentialities implicit in 'artifice of eternity' developed into an intensity of bitterness and an agonized sense of frustrate impotence." In *Byzantium* "the unpurged images of day recede," but not into that "more powerful life" revealed in the earlier poem.[1] It is impotence and frustration that mark many of the latest poems, both in *The Winding Stair* and *Last Poems and Plays.* The pride tends more and more to narrowness and assertion ("A proud man's a lovely man"); poems such as *A Dialogue of Self and Soul* and *Vacillation* represent a recognition of the need for integration rather than achieved wholeness; talk about sex is, too often, offered as a substitute for vitality; and although the lechers and drunkards are *personae* deliberately adopted as a protest against "Whiggery"—

> A levelling, rancorous, rational sort of mind
> That never looked out of the eye of a saint
> Or out of drunkard's eye (*The Seven Sages*),

they are but fragmentary embodiments of a personality richer than any one of them can suggest. For a poet so gifted as Yeats, Crazy Jane—even at her haunting best—was an admission of failure.

> A strange thing surely that my heart when love had
>   come unsought. . . .
> Should find no burden but itself and yet should be
>   worn out.
> It could not bear that burden and therefore it went mad.
>   (*Owen Ahern and His Dancers*)

Measured by potentiality, by aspiration, and by the achievement of a few poems, it is as an heroic failure that one is forced to consider Yeats's poetic career as a whole. The causes were complex. Something, no doubt, must be attributed to defects of "char-

---

[1] Cf. *Essays*, p. 277 (of a Japanese dancer): "There, where no studied lighting, no stage-picture made an artificial world, he was able, as he rose from the floor, where he had been sitting cross-legged, or as he threw out an arm, to recede from us into some more powerful life. Because that separation was achieved by human means alone, he receded, but to inhabit as it were the deeps of the mind."—*Certain Noble Plays of Japan.*

acter"; and a very great deal must be attributed to the literary tradition of the nineteenth century which, as he came to see so clearly, offered the very opposite of an incitement to maturity. But, since "the death of language . . . is but a part of the tyranny of impersonal things," [1] that tradition itself appears as the symptom of a deeper disease. Yeats wrote of W. E. Henley: "He never understood how small a fragment of our nature can be brought to expression, nor that but with great toil, in a much divided civilization"; and of himself as a young man, already half-conscious that "nothing so much matters as Unity of Being"; "Nor did I understand as yet how little that Unity, however wisely sought, is possible without a Unity of Culture in class or people that is no longer possible at all." [2] These passages, representative of many others, are part of a diagnosis that is valuable not merely for the light that it throws on Yeats's poetry. For those who would understand our divided and distracted civilization, in which the "passionate intensity" of partial men offers itself as a substitute for the vitality than springs from the whole consciousness, few thing are more profitable than a study of Yeats's poetry and prose together. "The mischief," he said, "began at the end of the seventeenth century when man became passive before a mechanized nature." [3]

[1] *Essays*, pp. 373-374.
[2] *Autobiographies*, pp. 364, 435-436.
[3] Introduction to the *Oxford Book of Modern Verse*, p. xxvii.

Chapter Eleven

THE UNIVERSITY TEACHING OF
ENGLISH AND HISTORY:
A PLEA FOR CORRELATION

I

IT IS PROBABLY TRUE to say that there was never a time when the ordinary intelligent man felt so conscious of his ignorance as he does to-day. In order to reach a sound judgment on most of the important problems he is confronted with, he needs to have some knowledge of half a dozen highly developed specialisms which seem to have no common meeting-place; the multiplicity of knowledge is bewildering, and the intelligent direction of life—individual and communal—is daily becoming more difficult. Yet it is certainly true that there was never a time when it was so necessary for intelligence to assert itself, if only because machinery of such power has never before been at the disposal of the low. If intelligence is to play its part—if it is not to be inhibited by a sense of complexity to which the most intelligent are the most susceptible—it is plain that there are educational problems of the first order to be tackled. This article is concerned with only one of them: it is simply intended to suggest how university "History" and university "English" may be brought into profitable correlation and directed towards education for living in the twentieth century. But since a radical overhauling of present educational methods is involved I shall make no further apology for setting my small contribution to practical pedagogics in a context of more general discussion.

I suppose it will be agreed that an essential aim of education, as distinguished from vocational training, is to produce adult men and women who are equipped to deal intelligently and responsibly with the problems of contemporary civilization. Anyone familiar with the facts will know how far education is from being directed towards that end. In spite of what is, in the mass, a large amount of genuinely educative teaching by individuals, the *typical* product of the educational routine (from the elementary schools upwards) is the man or woman who, without asking awkward questions, will fit into the machinery of society as it exists at present. It may also be agreed that any attempt to give fresh direction to education as a whole must start from the universities. But the universities, instead of planning an education adequate to modern needs and educating the educators of society, continue to offer their abler students any one of a number of specialist courses; [1] and although some degree of specialization at the university level is both necessary and desirable the prevailing university honours system is based on the unthinking acceptance of certain assumptions which may, at some time, have been true, but which are certainly not true to-day. The first of these assumptions is that the sum of useful knowledge forms a stable, ordered and coherent whole: no individual can master it all, but all of it is theoretically capable of being known—or at all events discovered—and the individual can work happily within his special province, confident that what he doesn't know himself someone else will know or discover. The second assumption is that a specialist training offers a "discipline" that will fit the student to take a responsible position in society. The third is that the environment—the prevailing intellectual climate—will complement and complete the education that a specialist training has begun. It is only by postulating some such assumptions that one can explain the origin and development of university honours courses and the complacence with which they are accepted—and none of them has to-day anything but a remote connexion with reality. The field of possible knowledge relevant to human problems has not only increased enormously in extent during the last half century, it can no longer be thought of as a unity at all; in our happier moments we think of it as a complex multiplicity, but more commonly as a chaos. Physical science has entirely lost

---

[1] That the problems raised by modern specialization are now more widely recognized than they were when this was written has been shown by the discussion aroused by such different approaches to university education as F. R. Leavis's *Education and the University: a Sketch for an English School*, Bruce Truscot's *Redbrick University*, and Bonamy Dobrée's article in a recent number of the *Political Quarterly* devoted entirely to the universities.

its naïve nineteenth-century certainty; the disintegration of economic modes and social forms is reflected in the confusion of economic theory; and each of the newer sciences—psychology, sociology, anthropology—has added its quota of uncertainty and confusion. Nor can the student expect much help from the general milieu. At the older residential universities there is still a certain amount of give and take between people with different interests and different ignorances, but at most of the newer universities the opportunities for a fruitful exchange are so small as to be almost negligible; and after the university not one graduate in a hundred will find a society capable of acting as a clearing-house for the most important ideas of his time: for the majority there is no "current of fresh and true ideas" to give either stimulus or direction. (If anyone doubts this, let him question his friends in the teaching profession.) In these circumstances the "discipline" offered by a highly specialized training has little relevance outside the artificial limits of the university honours school. Everyone knows that a first-class honours man may be as ignorant of the world he has to live in as he is of any "subject" save his own. Proficiency in a given subject is no guarantee whatever of education in its fullest sense, but it is with this limited proficiency that the university graduate is left to make what headway he can in a society whose chief need is understanding and intelligent direction.

In a recent article in the *Sociological Review* (October, 1937) Professor Ginsberg showed how increasing specialization is sapping the educational vitality of university courses in the social sciences. Coming from a recognized academic authority, some extracts may be appropriately quoted here:

> An examination of the courses of study now followed in the universities shows that the teaching of the social sciences is almost completely divorced from the teaching of social philosophy. . . . While students are given careful instruction in marshalling and correlating factual data they have no parallel experience in weighing values or in disentangling the value elements in complex social situations. The result is that they hover between scepticism and dogmatism. They either conclude that moral judgments do not permit of rational analysis but are matters of taste or feeling about which there can be

no argument, or else they accept uncritically the now fashionable dogma that value judgments merely express the needs of the dominant sections within any given community. In moments of crisis, that is to say at times of profound conflict of loyalties, the moral assumptions underlying conduct are put to the test and the lack of systematic reflexion becomes painfully evident in the tangle of contradictions then brought to light.

After a short but convincing account of the kind of philosophical training necessary for a student of the social sciences (the examples used in illustration are all immediately connected with living issues and as such all the more impressive), Professor Ginsberg concludes that, as things are,

> the students of philosophy have seldom any detailed knowledge of social facts or even of the actual working of moral codes; while the students of social science are given no training in ethical analysis. It is clear that in these circumstances the synthesis of social studies which is so urgently needed is not likely to be attained, and that great changes will have to be made if the universities are to make the contribution they ought to make towards the rational ordering of society.[1]

I have quoted from this article at length because there is at present no university honours course of which a parallel account could not be given. Sooner or later every university teacher will have to take stock of his special subject and ask what educational value it has as an isolated specialism. "If the universities are to make the contribution they ought to make towards the rational ordering of society," if they are to produce, that is, not merely specialists but educated men, a number of artificial barriers which at present separate subject from subject will have to be broken down. An immediate task for all concerned with university teaching is to discover ways of correlating those kinds of study of which the full meaning, the full educational value, is brought out only when they are set in living relation to each other and to the problems of our time.

[1] Cf. "I agree that economics and sociology in general should be kept distinct from ethics, but would urge that they should also be brought into definite relation. Confusion is likely to arise if their distinctness is not recognized, but also if they never meet at all. The effective handling of social problems involves a synthesis, but not a fusion, of social science and social philosophy. If this be so, then the present organization of teaching in the universities is sadly out of balance."—*Ibid.* See also R. S. Lynd, *Knowledge for What?*

EXPLORATIONS

II

The problems which, to-day, everyone is most sharply aware of are, of course, problems of economics and the related problems of peace and war; their inescapable insistence needs no demonstration. But behind these problems there are others, for most people less obtrusive, but, in the long run, even more fundamental; and their importance is seen to increase in exact measure as we believe, or hope, that society may escape from the complete chaos with which it is threatened. To pay attention to them in the present crisis of civilization may seem absurd, but the two questions which the development of applied science has posed our generation—what to do with the immense mechanical forces which science has put at the disposal of society, and what to do with the human energy which mechanical force is capable of setting free—are more intimately connected than is commonly realized. They are, in fact, two aspects of the one question: towards what kind of society should we direct our efforts? Even the more immediate, the more "practical," questions can be adequately answered only by men who are at least aware of the more remote problems; for the means to escape from war and to abolish poverty are likely to be found only by those who know more positively what they would be at. The remoter problems will not automatically solve themselves.

The questions that I have in mind here are all what we vaguely call cultural questions—they have to do with the quality of living, with human ends as well as means. It is, for example, of decidedly more than academic importance to inquire into the relationship (in different periods) between "the methods of production in material life" and the "spiritual processes of life," between "social being" and "consciousness," [1] and, having done that, to ask if the relations of culture and economic processes in the future are likely (on the evidence of the present) to differ in any important respects from their relations in the past. Again, granted that the society of the future is bound to be mainly urban and industrial,

---

[1] "The methods of production in material life determine the general character of the social, political and spiritual processes of life. It is not the consciousness of men that determines their being, but, on the contrary, their social being determines their consciousness."—Marx, Preface to the *Critique of Political Economy*.

we should, even so, do well to consider the statement that, "No civilization, however advanced, can afford to neglect the ultimate foundations in the life of nature and the natural region on which its social welfare depends"; and its corollary that, "However far the process of degeneration has gone, there is always a possibility of regeneration, if society recovers its functional equilibrium and restores its lost contacts with the life of nature." [1] Essential questions are posed here; and connected with them there are others. What, to take some further examples, is the effect of mechanical power on "racial" or national characteristics? on social relations? on the use of leisure? What is the meaning of such concepts as "Progress" or "Tradition" or (in other than the obvious biological sense) "essential human needs"? What are the most important meanings of the word *culture*?

These questions—and many others related to them—are all necessarily involved in any long-range programme for human betterment. They are questions, one would have thought, to which some attention should be paid in any university course aiming higher than technical instruction; more particularly one might expect courses in "the humanities" to be consciously directed towards them. Yet both in history and in literary studies in the universities they are almost entirely ignored. Far from encouraging thought about such problems, the majority of university teachers deliberately avoid all "controversial questions" and retreat behind the ideal of "disinterested knowledge." There are history teachers, I know, whose teaching is consciously directed towards an understanding of the present,[2] but how many university lecturers in history are there, one wonders, who have read and pondered *The Education of Henry Adams*? ("Except in the abandoned sphere of the dead languages," Adams says in the Preface, "no one has discussed what part of education has, in his personal experience, turned out to be useful, and what not. This

---

[1] Christopher Dawson, *Progress and Religion*. The central thesis of this book— "A society which has lost its religion becomes sooner or later a society which has lost its culture"—also needs to be debated: it cannot be adequately answered by a mere assertion of the opium formula. Cf. T. S. Eliot, 'The Humanism of Irving Babbitt," *Selected Essays*, p. 427.

[2] The fertilizing effect of R. H. Tawney's books is plainly due to the fact that his interest in the present is as lively as his interest in the past. His books are also sufficient proof—if proof is needed—that the kind of contemporary interest here desiderated is not incompatible with the academic ideal of "sound scholarship."

volume attempts to discuss it. . . . [The writer's] object . . . is to fit young men, in universities or elsewhere, to be men of the world, equipped for any emergency.") How many, like Adams, have asked themselves what the essentials of a twentieth-century education may be and how the study of history can contribute towards essential education?[1] One feels similar doubts, though perhaps more strongly, when one contemplates university courses in literature—English or foreign. Here and there attempts are made to improve reading ability and to train taste; but at many places literature is still "taught" by means of cover-the-ground courses in which one bit of information seems as important as any other bit, deliberate personal choice (for teacher and student) is reduced to a minimum, and great books are treated as though they existed in some timeless sphere and had no roots in a life as real, as bewildering and exciting as our own. In English, at all events, there is rarely any attempt made to see the literature of a given period in relation to the economic, social, and cultural forms of that period—its whole complex pattern of living—and to relate the findings of such study to the needs of the present; though one would think it obvious that the condition of health for an "interest in literature" is that it should be an interest in very much more.

What I am contending is that an education adequate to modern needs involves a mastery of more than one kind of knowledge. I am not for one moment urging that the universities should abandon their attempts to turn out expert historians, or economists, or sociologists, or psychologists, or qualified critics and teachers of literature: the more expert knowledge there is available the better. But granted that the cultural questions I have indicated are important, that they lurk behind all the special and—as it were—departmental problems of our age, then it is not enough for anyone to be *simply* a historian, an econo-

[1] Cf. "The child born in 1900 would, then, be born into a new world which would not be a unity but a multiple. Adams tried to imagine it, and an education that would fit it." *The Education of Henry Adams* was written in 1905. I am not suggesting that Adams was the ideal historian (he himself seems not to have been satisfied with his "Dynamic Theory of History") or that his conception of education is completely adequate to our needs; but he asked the right questions—and he was capable of writing of himself at sixty-four: "Never had the proportions of his ignorance looked so appalling." He also remarked that "Nothing in education is so astonishing as the amount of ignorance it accumulates in the form of inert facts."

mist, a sociologist, etc. "History," properly taught, can show how the political-economic regime we live under came into being; it can trace the development of productive methods, of laws and constitutional forms, and relate them to each other. But as soon as cultural subjects are discussed—subjects, that is, bearing on the quality of living at any period—value judgments are involved, and the discipline of History needs to be complemented by the discipline of literary criticism.

Before attempting to suggest how this necessary union might be brought about I must speak briefly of the function of literary training in education as a whole. This is, to start with, a training in the use of words for any and every purpose, of words as "the tools of thought"—the means by which one mind can influence another; and training in the ways that words are used not only equips the individual for dealing with the modern environment (newspapers, propaganda, etc.), it is the necessary foundation for *all* education. It is, it seems necessary to add, the starting-point for the study of literature.[1] But even in elementary exercises in "practical criticism," analysis of what certain words are *doing* is— as I. A. Richards has made plain—inseparable from judgment concerning the *quality* of thought, feeling or perception that the words express. The reading of literature, in so far as it is anything more than a pastime, involves the continuous development of the power of intelligent discrimination. Literature, moreover, is simply the exact expression of realized values—and these values are never purely personal: even when they conflict with accepted modes they are conditioned by them, and it is part of the artist's function (whether he is a "representative man" or not) to give precise meaning to ideas and sentiments that are only obscurely perceived by his contemporaries. The discipline of strict literary

[1] Judging by the practice of the schools (encouraged, of course, by the School Certificate examination), this is not the hoary platitude it ought to be; elementary and secondary school English continues to hover uneasily between mechanical memory-work and vague "appreciation." Lest anyone should think I am exaggerating, I may say that in a recent university scholarship examination more than half the candidates in English fell for a blatant piece of pseudo-poetic jargon (a perfume advertisement), and very few indeed were capable of diagnosing a verbose and meaningless passage (by a Sunday newspaper pontiff) on the Jubilee celebrations of 1935. Until the schools can be relied on to provide the rudiments, the universities should make some attempt to provide first-year courses in elementary analysis and discrimination, not merely for English—and not merely for Arts— students.

criticism is the only means we have of apprehending those embodied values with sureness and subtlety. These assertions, I know, need further elucidation and argument, but if there is any truth in them it follows that in an attempt to understand the quality of living in a past period—to understand, that is, all those intangible modes of being which are only hinted at in the documents on which economic and political history is based—the study of that period's literature is central, and some degree of *critical* ability is indispensable to the historian of culture.[1]

III

It remains to suggest how, in the university curriculum, some attempt might be made to provide a finer and more relevant training than History or English, unrelated to each other, commonly do. Here, obviously, the practical problem is to make the proposed "course of study" manageable, and, at the same time, to prevent it from becoming an amorphous mixture of superficial knowledge flavoured with prejudice. A lesson may be learned from an existing specialism: in English teaching it is far better that undergraduates should get some genuine insight into the methods of literary criticism—that they should learn how to make a first-hand approach to a comparatively small number of authors and a few "periods"—than that they should scrape together an unassimilated body of knowledge about the whole course of English literature. Similarly, in the kind of co-ordinated study that I am urging, most could probably be achieved by the intensive investigation of a limited period: the Elizabethan period, the early seventeenth century, the Augustan age, or the mid-nineteenth century are possible examples. And just as the study of literature and the literary tradition is fruitful only when it is approached from the standpoint of the present, so the selected period would need to be studied with the questions of most importance for the present held steadily in view. (The mere attempt

[1] Historians frequently resort to literature for descriptions of the social scene, but in so doing they reduce literature to the level of documentation and ignore the qualities which, as literature, it embodies.

to decide what those questions are would be not the least valuable part of a university course!)

I am not of course proposing a straightforward informational survey in which the students would be told what was what in, say, a single series of lectures. (The tentative, the truly experimental nature of the work would always have to be insisted on.) In all the more valuable attempts to get understanding the investigator has to start from a number of apparently unrelated bases, working steadily from each until he finds the point of relation and interaction. In the proposed study the bases would be (a) the economic organization, and (b) the literature of the period—each considered at first simply in and for itself, and without any premature attempt to force a relationship. These, for a time—supposing such a course to have been instituted—would be studied separately, in lectures (a few), seminars, and private work, but there would be a constant attempt to discover the bearings—the causes, consequences and implications—of each finding. Thus a student would be required to know the main methods of production and exchange (including the more important aspects of applied science) and the prevailing forms of economic relationship within his period; but he would also be expected to trace the influence of these on the main social and political forms, on what is commonly called political history, and on the laws and statutes of the community; and—since the time available would be limited— he could at least be shown the more obvious effects of economic needs on education and current conceptions of morality.

Even within these limits there would be plenty of opportunity for stimulating comparisons with the present. It is a genuinely educative process, for example, to discover the genesis of the prudential morality of the nineteenth-century middle classes, or of the self-help conception of "Success," both of which linger on to-day; just as it is genuinely educative to discover the historical causes of social forms which most people think of as immutable. But all of this may be supposed (though the supposition is perhaps a generous one) to fall within the scope of ordinary History teaching. What part would "English" play in the investigation? How could a line stemming from the critical study of a period's literature be made to meet the line stemming from a study of its economic organization?

The difficulty of formulation is increased at this point since literature not only provides important evidence of the prevailing culture, it is itself a large part *of* that culture in its intellectual aspects, and it can only be used as "evidence" when it has been assessed critically as literature. The indispensable basis is, here, the first-hand apprehension of realized values; all further investigation presupposes, in teacher and student, the ability to discriminate between literature of lasting value and literature that is merely of historic interest, between the merely idiosyncratic and the genuinely individual statement, between the inert expression of convention and the vital embodiment of tradition, between, in short, different degrees of intelligence and intensity. But genuine criticism (as distinguished from the merely academic study of literature) can never remain purely "literary," or confine itself to investigating hypostatized "forms" and abstract "influences." In the cultural investigation of our selected period it would be part of the English teacher's task to show how it is possible to work back *through* literature—rooted, as it is bound to be, in a social milieu—to the life of the time. The connexions are rarely simple and straightforward, and dogmatic assertion must be avoided, but I suggest that there are three main paths along which exploration might be directed. There is, to start with, the evidence of style and language: the vivid, idiomatic raciness of Elizabethan English, the "polite reasonableness" of Augustan prose, the increasingly "literary" language of most nineteenth-century poetry, the debased idiom of the modern newspaper—none of these simply arose spontaneously, they were all conditioned by social factors which they can be made, in part, to reveal. In the second place, literature provides an opportunity for examining the tastes and intellectual ability of the audience for which it was intended; and the student can be encouraged to ask how the interests reflected in literature of different degrees of popularity were formed—by sermon-going, bear-baiting, skill in music, the cinema? at work or in religious ritual? through an interest in practical achievement, in the forms of social intercourse, or in theological controversy?—and so on. In the third place there is the question of the standards which every writer is bound, explicitly or implicitly, to assert. What is the relation, our investigators would have to ask, between these standards and current social codes? This is not, unfortunately, a simple question. There are writers, like Bunyan, who do little more than voice the accepted standards of the community to which they belong; there are writers, like Blake, who are in almost complete opposition to the ideals of their age; and between these extremes there is every variety of relationship. To determine with any exactness what that relationship is demands a cultivated literary sense as well as historical knowledge. Moreover, the "standards" of which one speaks so easily in the abstract cannot be simply extracted from the work in which they are embedded; they form part of a whole complex organization, and the greater the work the more intimately they are fused with it, so that their full meaning can be apprehended only in terms of the total statement. But to point to the difficulties is only to insist once more on the need for a flexible intelligence in the investigator, and my own experience leaves me in no doubt that Milton, Blake, Shelley, Yeats . . . , no less than Jonson, Bunyan, Pope, Burke . . . , can be made to yield highly important evidence of the standards current in their generation: evidence that cannot be obtained in any other way.[1]

It should be obvious by now that when the study of economic organization and the study of literature have, on the lines suggested, reached a certain point, each kind of study is indispensable to the other. The first would keep the student in touch with social realities, the second would give him a sense of the complexity of the issues involved and (one hopes) prevent him from finding in history merely a reflexion of his own prejudices. It is only when the two lines of work have been brought together that one can ask, with some hope of an intelligent response, such further questions as: What were the relations between "work" and "living," then and now? In what ways was the dominant moral code of the period *merely* "the product, in the last analysis, of the economic stage which society had reached at that particular

---

[1] The rough-and-ready division of authors in this sentence is not meant to imply any similarity between the writers grouped together, except that those of the first group were all more or less consciously in opposition to their age, and those of the second were all more or less consciously spokesmen of theirs.

epoch," and in what ways was it (to use another phrase from Engels) "a really human morality," i.e. a code which supported and enriched ways of thinking, feeling and behaving to which we can still respond?[1] How did various classes of people amuse themselves, and what is the qualitative difference, if any, between their amusements and modern leisure-time pursuits? What, in the given age, were the main lines of force as expressed in human thought and action? What were the underlying, conscious or unconscious motives and energies which shaped its art and philosophy, its social, moral and legal codes, no less than its scientific, industrial and political achievements? This last question is one in which all the others are subsumed; it is the central problem for the historian of any period,[2] and it would demand more knowledge than most university seminars can muster to give anything like a complete answer. But the student who had merely attempted to tackle it would, I think, be better equipped than the mere specialist to understand the forces that move his own age and to help guide them to a desirable end.

In any attempt to institute a university course of this kind there would be a number of practical difficulties which could be solved only by a process of trial and error. The essential condition for overcoming these, however, would be simply that the teachers themselves should be convinced of the value of the experiment. Given a small group of educated specialists, specialists, that is, who were aware both of the limitations and the correlations of their own specialism and who (however much they might differ in other respects) were agreed on the main needs of education at present, questions of curriculum, of the relations of lectures and seminar work, and so on, would appear of minor importance. But other, more radical, objections are likely to be

[1] Cf. "The Elizabethan morality was an important convention; important because it was not consciously of one social class alone, because it provided a framework for emotions to which all classes could respond, and it hindered no feeling" (T. S. Eliot, *Selected Essays*, p. 214). Engels, on the other hand, claimed that all *former* moral theories had ("in the last analysis") a limited class basis, and that, "A really human morality which transcends class antagonisms and their legacies in thought becomes possible only at a stage of society which has not only overcome class contradictions but has even forgotten them in practical life" (*Anti-Dühring* [translated by Emile Burns], pp. 107-108). A course on the lines suggested might provide an opportunity for examining both these statements.

[2] See the brilliant chapter, "The Dynamo and the Virgin," in *The Education of Henry Adams*.

brought. It will be urged, for example, that the kind of study I have proposed is far too complex to be pursued at the university level; that even so I have ignored—or virtually ignored—philosophy, the sciences, and all the arts except literature—all of which have a right to inclusion; that, therefore, the study would increase confusion instead of suggesting principles of order and direction, and that it had better be abandoned before it is tried. The objections are not so impressive as they at first appear. The suggestions put forward in this article are necessarily both tentative and general; defined in terms of a specific period of history their practicability would be more immediately apparent; so at least my own teaching experience leads me to believe. And in practice there would naturally be variations of stress according to the special interests of the students concerned. I am not claiming any magical efficacy for "cultural history"; all I am claiming is that the study of a limited period as a functionally interrelated whole would sharpen a student's perception of essential problems more effectively than any partial or specialist study can do. Since our present honours courses are not notably efficient in producing men who are equipped to think intelligently about present problems some university might at least find an experiment in correlation worth trying.[1]

[1] I can now (1944) refer the reader to F. R. Leavis's *Education and the University* for more specific suggestions. It is also possible to add that experiments in correlation have been made at some universities, even though at some places "Combined Honours" tend to be rather mechanically compounded of parts taken from different schools, without any informing principle of integration.